ECONOMICS HANDBOOK SERIES

SEYMOUR E. HARRIS, EDITOR

Monetary Theory and
Fiscal Policy

ECONOMICS HANDBOOK SERIES

SEYMOUR E. HARRIS, Editor

Advisory Committee: Edward H. Chamberlain, Gottfried Haberler, Alvin H. Hansen, Edward S. Mason, and John H. Williams. *All of Harvard University.*

Monetary Theory and Fiscal Policy

by *Alvin H. Hansen*

LUCIUS N. LITTAUER PROFESSOR OF POLITICAL ECONOMY

HARVARD UNIVERSITY

NEW YORK   TORONTO   LONDON

McGRAW-HILL BOOK COMPANY, INC.

1949

Preface

THE FIELD of monetary theory currently discloses a serious gap in economic literature. There is no comprehensive volume on modern monetary theory that one can place in the hands of a student. This handbook on *Monetary Theory and Fiscal Policy* is offered as a modest contribution designed to fill, in some measure, the current need.

This book is, moreover, designed to supplement the current standard textbooks on money and banking. These texts typically include comprehensive descriptive analyses of money and banking institutions but devote very limited attention to the theory of money and prices. It is hoped that the present volume may contribute something toward remedying this deficiency in money and banking courses in American colleges and universities.

In my *Business-Cycle Theory*, published in 1927, I stressed the role of *real* or *nonmonetary* factors—somewhat against the stream of Anglo-American thinking in the 1920's. This point of view also pervaded my *Economic Stabilization in an Unbalanced World* (1932), *Full Recovery or Stagnation?* (1938), *Fiscal Policy and Business Cycles* (1941), *America's Role in the World Economy* (1945), and *Economic Policy and Full Employment* (1947). All these books devoted only a limited space to money and monetary theory. The present work, however, is devoted *mainly* to the subject of money, and it gives a much fuller discussion of the role of money than I have presented in any of my earlier writings.

The point of view remains fundamentally the same, but I have come increasingly to feel that there may be some danger in current trends of thinking lest we take money, like the air we breathe, too much for granted.

Money does play (who will dispute it?) an enormously important role in economic life. We become painfully aware of this when something goes wrong. There *is* an optimum money supply, but the matter is not as simple as the quantity theory made it.

There is a lower zone in which a shortage of money begins to present difficulties both for private investment and fiscal policy, and there is an upper zone in which an excess of money begins to become apparent. The range between these lower and upper levels of the money supply is, however, rather wide in advanced and wealthy industrial countries such as the United States; in contrast, this range is comparatively narrow in the primary producing and relatively underdeveloped countries.

It is the job of monetary theory to elucidate the precise role of money in quite different situations and circumstances. This is no easy task. The subject matter is complex, but of great general interest and importance.

As on previous occasions I again wish to express appreciation for the facilities made available by the Graduate School of Public Administration of Harvard University, and for the unfailing stimulus of contact and discussion with graduate students and colleagues in the Department of Economics. I am, moreover, particularly indebted to Professor Seymour E. Harris, editor of the Economics Handbook Series, for very valuable suggestions and comments; to Dr. James Tobin of the Harvard Society of Junior Fellows, for a critical reading of several chapters; and to Mrs. Stephen Lax and Helen Poland for assistance in preparing the manuscript for the printer and for preparing the index.

ALVIN H. HANSEN

CAMBRIDGE, MASS.
January, 1949

Contents

Editor's Introduction

IN TRADITIONAL economics the theory of money and the theory of output have been treated separately with little or no tendency toward integration. First Wicksell and then Keynes gave impetus to the movement to combine the theory of money with that of output as a whole. Drawing on classical economics and the modern aggregate analysis of Keynes, Professor Hansen in this volume succeeds in writing a book which, unlike the classical studies, shows the importance of money in the theory of output as a whole; and which, unlike numerous modern writings (*e.g.*, of Hawtrey, Douglas, Hayek), avoids overemphasizing the importance of money. Here is a book that shows what monetary policy can and cannot achieve and why it has often failed in the past; the necessary supplementary role of monetary policy as an aid to fiscal policy; and the manner of integrating monetary and fiscal policy, in periods of both depression and inflation, as prerequisites for assuring a stable economy.

Professor Hansen has drawn on his rich experience over thirty-five years in the study of cycles, fiscal policy, and international economics, and on his many years as an economic practitioner to write a book that makes use of the riches of classical economics, as well as neo-classical and Keynesian economics. The book should, for many years to come, be the standard work on monetary theory and fiscal policy as determinants of output. The reader will find here not only the modern theory of money and fiscal policy, but also rich surveys covering the last 150 years, reinterpreted with the tools of modern economics. He will find also suggestions, based on theory and history, for a policy in the years to come that will yield the high levels of income and stability without which the survival of democratic institutions is most unlikely.

This book will be useful to teachers of courses in money and cycles, and many of the chapters will be helpful to the informed layman who wishes to obtain some insight into modern monetary economics.

SEYMOUR E. HARRIS

Chapter 1

The Historical Ratio of Money to Income

DURING THE PAST 150 years, the record discloses a marked long-run increase in the ratio of money to income.[1] As the community grew richer in terms of income and wealth, and as production more and more entered the market economy, the quantity of money which the public wished to hold has increased far more rapidly than income.

The Marshallian k

This historical relation may be subsumed in the equation $M = kY$, in which M is the quantity of money, Y the money income, and k the coefficient which brings the two sides of the equation into balance. k is that fraction of money income which from decade to decade the public wished to hold in the form of money.[2]

The equation given above stems from Alfred Marshall, though he was thinking of the short run and did not consider the matter in terms of the changes which have taken place *secularly* over time. Marshall's statement is as follows: "In every state of society there is some fraction of their income which people find it worth while to keep in the form of currency; it may be a fifth, or a tenth, or a twentieth."

Marshall quotes Petty's view that the money sufficient for a nation is equal to one-half a year's rent from all land, plus one-fourth of the annual rent from housing, plus one week's expenditures of all the

---

[1] David Hume in his essay "Of Money" (*Political Discourses*) noted that money, since the fifteenth century, had increased much more than prices. This was due, he thought, to the fact that "commodities have come much more to market." More money was thus needed for transactions.

[2] $Y = PO$, or price level times output. In the equation $M = kPO$, the k is defined as that fraction of *real* income which people wish *to hold command over* in the form of money.

people, plus one-fourth of the value of a year's exports. Locke estimated the desirable money supply to be equal to one-fiftieth of the
annual wage bill plus one-fourth of the yearly income of landowners
plus one-twentieth of the annual income of brokers. Cantillon concluded that the required amount of money was equal to one-ninth of
the net national product, or (what he regarded as roughly equivalent)
one-third of the annual rent from land. Adam Smith offered no
opinion himself, but mentioned that various authors had computed
the desired quantity of money at from one-fifth to one-thirtieth of the
total value of the annual produce. All the writers quoted by Marshall
meant "currency" when they used the term "money"; Marshall himself discussed the problem in terms of the quantity of currency.

In an earlier passage Marshall had put the matter on a broader
basis, including not only *income* but also *assets* among the relevant
factors. Thus he said:[1]

> "Let us suppose that the inhabitants of a country, taken one
> with another (and including therefore all varieties of character and
> of occupation) find it just worth their while to keep by them on
> the average ready purchasing power to the extent of a tenth part
> of their annual income, together with a fiftieth part of their prop-
> erty. . . ."

The phrase "ready purchasing power" might well be interpreted to
include not only currency but also demand and even time deposits.
Moreover, in this paragraph he takes account of "property" as well
as "income." This analysis could be summarized in terms of the following equation:

$$M = kY + k'A$$

in which M is money (currency plus deposits), Y is money income,
A is the aggregate value of assets, k is the fraction of *income* which
people desire to hold in the form of money, while k' is the fraction of
assets which people wish to hold in the form of money.

The asset part of Marshall's formula was quite forgotten by his
followers, and indeed by Marshall himself. We shall see later in this

---

[1] Alfred Marshall, *Money, Credit and Commerce*, The Macmillan Company, New York,
1923. Reprinted by permission of The Macmillan Company, New York and London.

volume that it deserves attention, especially with respect to recent events when liquid earning assets have become so important. In this chapter, however, we shall concentrate upon the ratio of money to income. We do so partly because throughout a large part of the last century assets and income apparently rose (though the statistical evidence is scanty) in something like the same proportion, and partly because the statistical materials relating to income are more accessible.

The Record: 1800–1950

In Table 1 are presented data covering nearly 150 years (1800–1947) on the following items: (1) national money income Y; (2) money supply—currency plus demand and time deposits M; and (3) the ratio of deposits and currency to national income $\dfrac{M}{Y}$.

The ratio $\dfrac{M}{Y}$ is the k in the Marshallian equation. The data reveal a marked upward trend of k. This means that as income rose the community was prepared to hold an ever increasing quantity of money per dollar of income. Throughout the period the value of money remained reasonably stable, and since income rose far more rapidly than population there was a marked rise in per capita real income.

But the upward trend of k (see Fig. 1) is by no means at a uniform rate throughout the period. In certain decades k rose rapidly; in others, slowly. The ratio of money to income did *not* rise at a constant compound rate per annum. There appears to be no dependable or fixed trend in the ratio of M to Y. It is therefore not possible to determine from historical experience what is the appropriate quantity of money, given the level of income. Conversely, given the quantity of money, we cannot determine what the level of income will be. The money supply holds no dependable constant relation to the national income.

The record does reveal a remarkably constant long-run upward trend in the total money supply—deposits and currency—increasing at the compound rate of around 5 to 6 per cent per annum for the entire period (the range being from 5 per cent to 5¾ in the first half, to 6½ per cent in the last half). Disregarding cyclical fluctuations (usually relatively moderate, though sharp declines occurred at times, as in 1929–1933) the money supply has increased at an amazingly stable rate. And this was true whether the secular trend of prices was upward or downward, and also whether the national income was rising rapidly or slowly.

Table 1 *

Year	National income, Y (in billions of dollars)	Deposits and currency, M (in billions of dollars)	Ratio of money to income, k
1800	0.73	0.038	0.05
1810	0.99	0.077	0.08
1820	0.95	0.094	0.10
1830	1.06	0.122	0.12
1840	1.77	0.262	0.15
1850	2.62	0.389	0.15
1860	4.67	0.689	0.15
1870	7.39	1.37	0.19
1880	7.83	2.93	0.37
1890	11.59	5.50	0.48
1900	17.5	8.8	0.51
1905	23.2	13.2	0.57
1910	30.4	16.9	0.56
1915	37.0	20.6	0.56
1920	69.5	39.6	0.57
1925	73.7	48.1	0.65
1930	75.0	54.1	0.72
1935	56.8	49.1	0.86
1940	81.3	66.1	0.82
1945	182.8	138.4	0.75
1947	203.0	164.1	0.81
1948†	216.3	164.1	0.76

* SOURCES: National income, 1800–1909, *The Economic Almanac*, National Industrial Conference Board; 1909–1947, Department of Commerce; Deposits and Currency, 1800–1830, J. P. Wernette, *Financing Full Employment;* 1840–1890, *Statistical Abstract;* 1895–1940, *Banking and Monetary Statistics*, Board of Governors, Federal Reserve System; 1945–1947, *Federal Reserve Bulletin*. See also Howard R. Bowen, *Money and Prices*, Irving Trust Company, New York.

† First half of year.

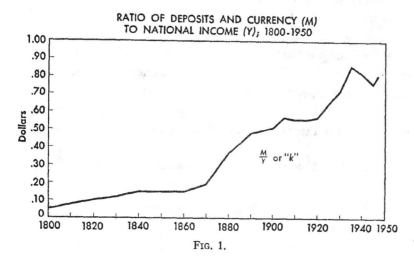

RATIO OF DEPOSITS AND CURRENCY (M)
TO NATIONAL INCOME (Y); 1800-1950

Fig. 1.

Four Subperiods

We may divide the century and a half covered in Table 1 into four subperiods: (1) 1800–1840, in which the *trend* of prices was downward; (2) 1840–1870, with a rising price trend; (3) 1870–1900, a falling price period; and (4) 1900–1947, in general a rising price trend.[1] The money supply trend rose at the compound rate of 5 per cent per annum in the first period, 5¾ per cent per annum in the second period, and 6½ per cent per annum in each of the two last periods. But the money national income rose slowly in the first and third periods when prices were falling, and rapidly in the second and fourth periods when the price trend was rising. These data are given in Table 2.

National income increased rapidly in the second and third periods, but the money supply increased rapidly and at a fairly uniform rate in each of the four periods. When the national income surged upward, the price level was rising; when the national income was sluggish, the price level declined. But whether prices were rising or falling the

[1] The period 1900–1947 was characterized by violent price fluctuations. But even at the low point in the 1930's the price level was 16 per cent above 1900, and the general average from 1917 to 1947 was about double the level of 1900. In 1947 the price index was 50 per cent above 1926 and nearly three times the level of 1900.

money supply kept on expanding at the fairly stable rates of 5 to 5¾ per cent in the first 70 years, and at 6½ per cent in the last 77 years.

These data suggest that there is no invariant relation of money income to the money supply. The quantity of money may indeed affect the level of income, but the connection is a tenuous one; and non-monetary factors affecting the flow of income at times cause marked divergencies in the rates of increase of money, on the one side, and of

Table 2. Compound Rates of Increase per Annum

Period	Deposits and currency, M (*per cent*)	National income, Y (*per cent*)	Ratio of money to income, k (*per cent*)	Price trend
1800–1840	5	2¼	2¾	Falling
1840–1870	5¾	5	¾	Rising
1870–1900	6½	3	3½	Falling
1900–1947	6½	5½	1	Rising

income, on the other. In some periods the flow of money income has outrun output; in other periods it has lagged behind output. In the former cases the price trend was upward; in the latter, downward. The nature and role of these nonmonetary factors, and their effect on income and prices will be discussed in subsequent chapters.

Looking at the whole 150 years, it is important not to lose sight of the generalization already made that the spectacular rise in the national income has been accompanied by a far more rapid increase in the money supply. Indeed, the money supply in 1947 was 60 per cent larger (relative to income) than in 1900, and 120 per cent larger than in 1880; eight times as large (relative to income) as in 1820, and sixteen times as large as in 1800. Evidently as the nation has grown in wealth and widened the market economy, the amount of money which people wished to hold, in relation to income, has grown decade by decade.

The Growth in Real Income

The growth in money income has been mainly a growth in real income. This is disclosed in Table 3. Wholesale prices are, to be sure, not a precise index of the changes in the value of money; and moreover, price indexes, when applied to a rapidly changing character of output over long periods of time, present at best only rough indications of the trend.

Table 3. Money Income, Real Income, and Prices

Year	National income in current dollars (in billions)	Wholesale prices (1926 = 100)	National income in 1926 prices (in billions of dollars)	National income per capita (in 1926 dollars)
1800	0.7	102	0.7	132
1840	1.8	71	2.5	146
1870	7.4	92	8.0	200
1900	17.5	56	31.3	412
1920	69.5	154	45.2	425
1930	75.0	86	87.4	710
1940	81.3	79	103.0	781
1947	203.0	152	133.6	940

Such as they are, the data disclose an upward drift in the purchasing power of money from 1800 to 1900, and a strong downward drift from 1900 to 1947. Thus it appears that the value of money rose in the nineteenth century and declined rather drastically in the twentieth. The nineteenth century was predominantly one of peace; the twentieth, a century of gigantic world wars. But this is by no means, as we shall see, the whole of the matter.

In column 3, Table 3, the national income is presented in terms of 1926 dollars as measured by wholesale prices.[1] It appears that real income approximately doubled every 20 years from 1800 to 1940.

[1] For the period since 1920 consumers' prices could also have been utilized, but for the purpose here in hand statistical refinement is not necessary. All we are interested in is the broad general tendency.

In the last column of Table 3 is presented the per capita income in constant (1926) dollars. These figures are of special significance in terms of the secular movement of k (the ratio of money to income). While there is certainly a considerable margin of error in the figures, it nevertheless appears plausible that the prodigious rise in real per capita income has played a significant role in the secular rise in k, as noted in Table 1. As the real income of people has increased, they have wished to hold a larger and larger amount of money in relation to income. The ever rising k is a reflection of growing per capita wealth and income. People have wished, as they became better off, to hold larger assets in highly liquid form; indeed, as real incomes have risen they have evidently wished to hold an increasing proportion of their income in the form of money. There are of course other factors, notably the increase in the proportion of goods entering the market economy.

Demand versus Time Deposits

The above data relate to currency and deposits, including time as well as demand deposits. It could of course be possible, therefore, that the growth of time deposits might largely account for the secular rise in k, defined as the ratio of all money (including time deposits) to income. Data are lacking to ascertain the growth in time deposits prior to 1892. Fortunately we can, however, trace these movements for more than half a century. The relevant data are given in Table 4, mostly by 5-year intervals from 1892 to 1947. The data for the *first half* of 1948 are also included.

From Table 4 it will be noted that demand deposits plus currency M_d rose slightly in relation to income from 1892 to 1905. From 1905 to 1930 the ratio remained fairly constant, then rose rapidly after 1930. The community, it appears, wished to hold—until 1930—currency and demand deposits equal to about one-third of the national income. After 1930 this ratio rose progressively to about one-half of the national income. With respect to time deposits M_t the community held one-sixth of the national income in this type of liquid assets in 1892–1900, and this proportion doubled or more by 1925–1940.

Marked differences appear in the relative increases from 1892 to 1930 in (1) time deposits, which we call M_t, and (2) demand deposits plus currency M_d. In these four decades M_d remained in approximately a constant ratio to national income, while M_t rose more than twice (indeed, 144 per cent) as rapidly as national income. By 1930 time deposits exceeded demand deposits plus currency by 4 billion

Table 4. Money in Relation to Income

Year	Demand deposits adjusted and currency (in billions of dollars)	Time deposits * (in billions of dollars)	$\dfrac{M_d}{Y}$, or k_1	$\dfrac{M_t}{Y}$, or k_2	$\dfrac{M}{Y}$, or k
1892	3.9	1.9	0.31	0.16	0.47
1895	3.9	2.1	0.28	0.16	0.46
1900	5.8	3.0	0.33	0.18	0.51
1905	8.7	4.5	0.37	0.20	0.57
1910	10.0	6.9	0.33	0.23	0.56
1915	11.4	9.2	0.31	0.25	0.56
1920	23.7	15.8	0.34	0.23	0.57
1925	25.0	23.2	0.34	0.31	0.65
1930	25.1	29.0	0.33	0.39	0.72
1935	25.2	23.9	0.44	0.42	0.86
1940	38.7	27.5	0.48	0.34	0.82
1945	94.2	44.3	0.52	0.25	0.77
1947	108.6	55.5	0.53	0.28	0.81
1948†	107.2	56.9	0.50	0.26	0.76

* Includes time deposits in commercial banks, mutual savings banks, and the postal savings system.

† First half of year.

dollars, while in 1892 time deposits were less than half the volume of demand deposits and currency.

A marked change occurred after 1930. In the period 1930–1947 demand deposits and currency more than quadrupled, while time deposits less than doubled.[1]

Thus by 1947 demand deposits plus currency were again about twice as large as time deposits, precisely as was the case in 1892. A full turn

[1] This decline in the ratio of time deposits to demand deposits and currency is probably connected with the sharp reduction in the rate of interest paid on time deposits.

in the cycle had been made; the two component parts of the money supply held about the same relation to each other in 1947 as a half-century before—demand deposits plus currency constituted about two-thirds of the total money supply, time deposits one-third.

Table 5. Velocity of Money, National Income, and the Rate of Interest

Year	$\dfrac{Y}{M_d}$ or V	National income Y (in billions of dollars)	Rate of interest i (Durand *—30-year maturity)	Rate of interest i (Moody's Aaa) †
1892	3.2	12.4		
1895	3.5	13.7		
1900	3.0	17.5	3.3	
1905	2.7	23.2	3.5	
1910	3.0	30.4	3.8	
1915	3.2	37.0	4.2	
1920	2.9	69.5	5.1	
1925	3.0	73.7	4.5	
1930	2.9	75.0	4.4	
1935	2.3	56.8	3.5	
1940	2.1	81.3	2.7	2.8
1945	1.7	182.8	. . .	2.6
1947	1.9	203.0	. . .	2.6
1948‡	2.0	216.3	. . .	2.8

* David Durand, *Basic Yields of Corporate Bonds, 1900–1942*, Technical Paper No. 3, National Bureau of Economic Research, June, 1942.

† *Federal Reserve Bulletin.*

‡ First half of year.

The Income Velocity

The income velocity V of money is usually defined as the ratio of income to demand deposits plus currency (here designated as M_d). These data are presented in Table 5. Also included are figures on national income and interest rates.

Income velocity fell from 3.5 in 1895 to 1.9 in 1947—a fall of nearly 50 per cent; or in other words, the amount of demand deposits plus currency held per dollar of income nearly doubled. In this interval income rose from 14 billion dollars to 200 billion dollars, while per capita *real* income rose by nearly 3 fold. As people became more affluent, they were in a position to hold more ready cash (demand deposits and currency) than formerly per dollar of income earned. This meant a fall in the income velocity of demand deposits and currency, V being the reciprocal of k_1. But there were many other factors, a full analysis of which would involve the whole theory of money—in other words, the general subject matter of this book.

The table also discloses an interrelationship between the velocity of money and the rate of interest. On the one hand, a large quantity of ready cash tempts some cash holders to shift into bonds, thus bidding up the price of securities and forcing down the yield on bonds. On the other hand, a low yield in securities makes it less costly to enjoy the luxury and convenience of holding large quantities of ready cash. Thus while there was no clear year-to-year correlation, the high-interest-rate years 1900–1930 correspond to the high-velocity years. The average velocity for these three decades was 3.0, while the interest rate was 4.1 per cent. After 1930 the velocity of money and the rate of interest fell together, rising again slightly in 1947 and 1948.

Gold and the Money Supply

In the context of this chapter—the relation of the money supply in the United States to the growth of the national income—it is not without interest to relate the historical changes in the monetary gold stock in this country to the secular rise in the quantity of money. The relevant data are presented in Table 6.

Formerly, gold or gold certificates constituted an important part of the currency in circulation. Later gold was largely concentrated in the Federal Reserve Banks and the government Treasury. In the Gold Act of 1934 title to all gold was transferred to the United States government, against the bulk of which gold certificates, or gold certificate credits, have been issued to the Federal Reserve Banks.

Evidently there has been no close relation between gold and the money supply (currency and deposits). Starting from a ratio of 30 per cent in 1860, gold fell in relation to money to around 10 per cent in 1910–1925, rose to 33 per cent in 1940, and fell again to 13 per cent in 1947.

The place occupied by gold in our monetary system has changed very much over the last hundred years in consequence of banking

Table 6. *Monetary Gold Stock and Money Supply in United States,*
1860–1947 *

(In billions of dollars)

Year	Gold	Money †
1860	0.2	0.7
1870	0.2	1.4
1880	0.4	2.9
1890	0.7	5.5
1900	1.0	8.8
1905	1.4	13.2
1910	1.6	16.9
1915	2.0	20.6
1920	2.6	39.6
1925	4.1	48.1
1930	4.3	54.1
1935	10.1	49.1
1940	22.0	66.1
1945	20.1	138.4
1947	21.3	164.1

* SOURCES: 1860–1910, *Statistical Abstract;* 1915–1940, *Banking and Monetary Statistics,* Board of Governors, Federal Reserve System; 1945–1947, *Federal Reserve Bulletin.*
† Currency, demand deposits, and time deposits.

legislation and developments. Important among these changes are (1) the spread of deposit banking after the Civil War, (2) the establishment of the Federal Reserve System, with the consequent introduction of Federal Reserve notes and the new reserve ratios applicable to member banks in the System, (3) the Gold Act of 1934, which took gold out of circulation, and (4) the new gold ratio (25 per cent) for the Federal Reserve Banks, enacted in 1945.

The huge gold inflows played a highly significant role in increasing the liquidity of banks and of the community generally after 1933 and served as a convenient basis for the vast wartime expansion of Federal Reserve credit. About these matters much will be said later in this volume. Gold continues today, as throughout our monetary history, to play a vital role. But the supply of money has never, since the development of deposit banking, been tied in any rigorous relation to gold. And today more than ever the connection between gold and the quantity of money is a tenuous one.

Chapter 2

The "Creation" of Money

Printing Money

Confronted with seemingly endless demands from local communities for state support, Governor Dewey is reported in *The New York Times*, Feb. 21, 1947, as saying jokingly: "It's unfortunate we can't print money in the State. That's a felony."

If every State in the union could print money, we should have monetary chaos. Hence the constitutional provision that forbids any State to coin money or emit bills of credit. Congress alone has the power to "coin Money" and "to regulate the Value thereof."

Nevertheless various States did, in a sense, circumvent the constitutional prohibition. They established and chartered banks which issued bank notes, and these circulated as money.

The public's money supply under modern conditions consists of (1) currency, or pocketbook money, and (2) deposits, or checkbook money.

Currency consists of (1) coins and paper money issued by the Federal Treasury, and (2) bank notes issued by banks chartered by the government and empowered to issue notes. Today this power is restricted in the United States to the Federal Reserve Banks. Thus, our currency now consists of Treasury currency and Federal Reserve notes.

In our early monetary history various States not only established State-owned banks through which they issued bank notes; they also chartered [1] privately owned banks and empowered them to issue bank notes.

---

[1] Nonchartered (or so-called private) banks also played an important role in the nineteenth century. Such banks accepted deposits and issued bills of exchange that in fact circulated as money.

15

In the National Banking Act of 1863 the Federal government chartered privately owned banks—national banks, so called—which could issue bank notes. In 1866 bank notes issued by State-chartered banks were driven out of existence by a tax of 10 per cent imposed by the Federal government.

The State banks, prohibited in effect from issuing bank notes, now turned to the issue of deposit or checkbook money. The national banks issued both currency (bank notes) and deposit money.

In 1860 the money supply in the United States consisted almost entirely of currency. This was divided about equally between Treasury currency (gold and silver coin or certificates) and State bank notes Of Treasury currency there was 228 million dollars, and of bank notes, 207 million dollars.

By 1875 Treasury currency had increased to 492 million dollars and bank notes to 342 million dollars. In addition, deposits were growing rapidly.

By 1895 Treasury currency amounted to 1,395 million dollars, bank notes to 207 million dollars, and demand deposits to 2,960 million dollars. Deposit money had relegated bank notes to a relatively small place (quantitatively) in the monetary system.

Thus both bank notes and deposit money were from time to time created and issued by privately owned banks. At times such issue was subject in many of the States to relatively little governmental regulation and control.[1] Moreover, banks could be organized relatively easily, so that it was not seriously difficult to "manufacture" money. Some banks maintained convertibility of their bank notes into Treasury currency, which was legal tender in payment of debts. But others frequently made no effort, or were unable, to convert their notes into legal-tender currency. Such notes could circulate only to the extent that the public was willing to accept them, and at such ratio (in relation to legal-tender currency) as the market established.[2]

---

[1] The Suffolk Bank System in New England and the Safety-Fund System in New York are leading illustrations of different methods of controlling and safeguarding the note issues.

[2] See Horace White, *Money and Banking*, 6th ed., Ginn & Company, Boston, 1936, for a good brief account of early banking methods.

The Monetization of Private Credit

The issue of money by privately owned banks was in large measure only an extension of the use of purely private credit. As wholesale trade developed over wider areas, stimulated by the building of turnpikes and canals, goods were sold on credit. By setting up a bank, business could arrange for the monetization of its own private credit. Privately issued bills of exchange were used to finance trade transactions; but only to a limited extent could these privately drawn bills circulate as media of exchange. When, however, such trade bills had been monetized at a bank—exchanged, in other words, for bank notes— then a generally acceptable medium of exchange had been created. Thus privately owned banks were established in part for the express purpose of monetizing private credit. They were created because trade and commerce required an adequate supply of money. Banks were set up to "manufacture" money.

It is no wonder that "free banking" was such a popular slogan in the first half of the nineteenth century. The country was expanding, and rich opportunities for investment in various enterprises were open on all sides—canals, railroads, wholesale and retail trade, manufacture, and construction. Credit provided access to productive resources, and it promoted technological developments. It was not enough that rich natural resources were available to be exploited by a rapidly growing and energetic population equipped with the necessary skills and techniques. New undertakings had to be established and new production had to be set going. And this required money. This money could not be drawn from the older and settled parts of the economy. *New* money was needed to set up a *new* circuit of production and to circulate the ever growing volume of trade.

Every enterprising frontiersman would have liked to set up his own "money factory" for the issue of money. In the "wild-cat" banking period of the 1830's free banking indeed went some considerable distance in this direction. Free banking was a natural development in an unrestrained frontier economy. Nevertheless, if everyone had in fact been permitted to "manufacture money" by setting up his own bank (in effect a private printing press) without such credit having any relation to productive effort, the newly created money would rapidly have depreciated toward zero. The problem was to permit such manufacture of money as was *needed* in order to promote enterprise and commerce without creating an excess supply.

The process of bidding resources *away* from others already using them efficiently is likely to result in price inflation, not in increased production and employment. If new money has this effect, the results are bad. But if new money facilitates an increase in employment and output, it serves a useful purpose.

This is the great "money conundrum." The issue of new money *may* create wealth. No wonder every age has its money cranks. Money is magic. What economist, at least in the United States and Canada, does not get almost a daily mail expounding "monetary cures" for all the ills of society! Money is still, in the eyes of many, the modern alchemy.

The Right Amount of Money

But extreme monetary conservatives are as mistaken as the monetary cranks. Afraid of monetary "tinkering," they become monetary "prohibitionists." Yet what is required is *temperance*—the pursuit of Aristotle's golden mean applied to monetary management.

This is no easy matter. Hence what seems on paper simple enough is in practice extraordinarily complex and difficult. Having discovered "fire"—the power of money for good and evil—the wonder is that it has not destroyed us. Money is an invaluable, but nonetheless dangerous, invention.

The trick was to permit enterprise (through privately owned banks) to manufacture its own money, yet to hold the privilege within bounds. Direct issue of money by the government had often been abused, and in the period of laissez-faire nineteenth-century liberalism, this method was not deemed to be trustworthy. Hence the search for an *automatic* formula which might regulate appropriately the private manufacture of money. The answer—and, in fact, it worked reasonably well—was commercial banking as practiced in the nineteenth century. Thus it was that while all sovereign governments retained the exclusive power to issue money, in fact they authorized private agents (for the most part) to do so. And this, of course, in no way involved any abrogation of the governmental prerogative: merely the delegation of power to institutions created by government itself and endowed with functions specifically authorized. In the case of a federal government such functions might be delegated to the constituent states in the absence of complete assumption by the federal government of powers ultimately residing exclusively in it.

Thus as the nineteenth century wore on it became increasingly bad form for governments to issue (print) money. That prerogative was delegated to privately owned banks. These issued (1) bank-note currency, and (2) deposit (or checkbook) money. Increasingly in England the note-issue privilege was restricted to the Bank of England, and in the United States (after the Civil War National Banking Act), to the so-called national banks and later to the Federal Reserve Banks. But checkbook money during the last half of the century became by far the more important; and this could be issued by all commercial banks, whether chartered by the States or by the national government.

The Federal government did, indeed, stand ready to coin any and all gold brought to the mint—and at times, under varying restrictions, also silver. Here the automatic formula was simple. Anyone was free to "manufacture" money by digging gold out of the ground. This being a difficult and costly process, there was no danger that everyone would turn to "manufacturing" money, thereby withdrawing resources from the production of goods and services. Only such resources would, under competition, be put to gold production as might earn a return equal to the normal reward that could be obtained in other lines of production.

But the business community was not content to rely on the laborious process of gold production as the sole method of manufacturing money. In this it was quite right. Modern industry needed more money than could be got by that procedure. The community was indeed wary of government-created paper money. But they wanted paper money nonetheless—bank notes and checkbook money. For this an automatic formula to ensure the right amount was urgently needed.

The Automatic Formula

Toward this end it was argued that banks should not just be permitted to issue money for any purpose whatever. This privilege was to be restricted to certain uses. Banks should issue money only to finance *current production*—goods-in-process. Fixed plant and equipment should be financed by the sale of shares (common and preferred stock), by bond issues, and by plowing back earnings.

The short-run financing of goods-in-process merely tided the business over until payment could be received from sales. Such loans were regarded as self-liquidating, since they could in a few months be repaid from sales. Fresh financing would again be needed as a new batch of materials was started on its way through the productive process. Thus as the old loans were paid off (and so deposits reduced), new loans and new deposits stepped in to take their places.

Always any such issue of money (notes or deposits) should set going, it was urged, a production process. Each circuit of production, from its inception to its completion, should be matched proportionally (though not necessarily on a one-to-one ratio) by the issue and retirement of money. If the productive process was expanding from year to year, the money supply would expand also; if contracting, the money would also contract. Thus, it was argued, the money supply would not outgrow production. Hence there would be no danger, it was thought, of an overissue of money. The money supply would rise and fall with production.

The quantity of money issued by banks to finance the needs of trade would normally be less than the final value of goods currently in process. Bank financing typically would cover only a part of the cost of financing the goods-in-process; a part would be financed from capital funds obtained from the sale of securities in the capital markets and from retained earnings. Every business is confronted with a certain fairly definite minimum requirement of working capital funds needed to finance current operations. Some substantial part of this minimum is likely to be financed from capital funds, leaving a margin (plus the fluctuating requirements as sales rise and fall) to be met from bank borrowing. Thus the bank issue of money to finance current production would very likely be substantially less than the value of the goods-in-process.

The long-run *growth* in the minimum requirements (growth due to a secular rise in production) could also be taken care of mainly by long-run capital financing. Thus only a portion of the *growth* of production need be financed from new money. Both money and production might rise in something like the same *proportion*, while the *ratio* of money to the value of goods-in-process might remain undisturbed. Accordingly, there need be no danger, so it was believed, that the quantity of money would outrun production in a growing economy and thereby upset the appropriate relation of money to trade volume.

If banks limited their issue of money to financing goods-in-process, according to commercial banking theory, there would be no danger of too much money, no danger of inflation. Business needs would provide the automatic regulator. It was not necessary to restrict your "monetary diet" to gold coin. You could safely partake of all the "food" you wanted. The economic organism would automatically indicate when you had had enough. But this was true (so it was argued) only if you limited yourself to appropriate "foods." Bank money—whether note issues or deposits—should be issued only to finance current production. No liquor on the tables! There was to be no wild drinking spree of monetary inflation.

The "liquor" which the commercial-loan "preachers of temperance" violently fought (as we have already indicated) was the issue of new money to finance fixed plant and equipment. Fixed investment was to be financed soberly from savings out of the "disposable" [1] income of individuals and corporations. But as more plant and equipment was built, production would rise, trade and transactions would grow, and more money would be needed to circulate the enlarged flow of goods and services. Bills of exchange drawn by manufacturers and traders, together with book credit, might indeed be employed to facilitate the exchange of the additional output of goods. But bills of exchange were not generally acceptable, nor could they be split up

---

[1] "Disposable" income is here used in the Robertsonian sense, meaning savings from income received "yesterday," not savings from current income—income which might in part have sprung from expenditures financed out of *new* money.

conveniently into the right denominations. Only the *monetization* of private credit could supply the efficient circulating media needed to effect the transactions arising from an expanding economy. It was appropriate and necessary that new money should be issued to satisfy the growing *transactions* requirements. But new money should not be issued to finance fixed plant and equipment; these should be financed out of savings from "disposable" income.

Thus the "commercial-loan" theorists were not afraid of the issue of new money. Following their rules there was no danger, so they believed, of an excess of money. Applying their principles money could not be independently created; it would spring from the "needs of business." The "banking" or "commercial-loan" principle was regarded as an automatic self-regulatory mechanism which would supply just the right amount of money.

The Principle of Convertibility

Still it was the antibullionist branch of the "banking-principle" school which alone was prepared to rely *exclusively* on the "needs of trade" as an adequate regulative device. Others believed that the "needs of business" could not *alone* be relied upon. Yet they wished to avoid authoritarian regulation. A further automatic device, so it was believed, was needed—the principle of convertibility.[1] If banks were required, upon penalty of being closed, to maintain convertibility of "bank-created" money into "standard" or legal-tender money, no overissue would (so it was believed) occur. So long as banks issued money in the form of bank notes, convertibility meant that bank notes could always be exchanged for gold [2] or other legal-tender currency. When later the power to issue bank notes had become exclusively a function of the central bank and the issue of commercial bank money took the form of deposits, convertibility meant that banks would always stand ready to pay out *currency* (central bank notes and Treasury currency) to any depositor.

---

[1] The currency school not only adhered to the principle of convertibility, but also maintained that an absolute limit should be placed on the paper issue.

[2] Under a bimetallic standard, gold or silver.

The principle of convertibility permitted great freedom in the issue of money, yet within automatic limits prescribed by experience. In general, it was found that banks could safely issue bank notes equal to some multiple of their gold or other legal-tender currency holdings and still meet the requirement of convertibility. Or later, when commercial banks turned to deposits, they similarly found they could issue deposit money equal to, say, ten times their holdings of cash.

Under a system of central banking it was not necessary for commercial banks to hold their cash in their own vaults in the form of actual currency. Cash could be carried as a deposit account with the central bank. The central bank always stood ready to redeem such deposits by the issue of central bank notes. Thus in the United States the member banks can always convert balances carried with the Federal Reserve Banks into Federal Reserve notes.

Reserve Ratios

As banking procedure and institutions developed in the United States the practice of convertibility, while required, was not in and of itself regarded as adequate. A legal ratio was established between deposits and the reserve of cash. Under the Federal Reserve Act member banks are required to hold all their legally required reserves in the form of deposits with the Federal Reserve Banks. Excess balances may always be drawn out in the form of Federal Reserve notes to meet the demands of bank customers for currency. But the legally required reserves cannot be drawn out. They do not, and are not intended to, serve the purpose of convertibility; they are intended simply to impose limits upon the member banks' power to expand loans and deposits. Convertibility of deposits held by the public is indeed provided, but not by reason of the *legal* reserves. Convertibility of the public's deposits into currency is provided, in the event of a run by depositors, through the power of member banks to rediscount or borrow from the Federal Reserve Banks. Under ordinary conditions convertibility of deposits is provided partly from some holdings of actual currency (relatively small) in the vaults of the member banks, and partly from excess reserve balances with the Federal Reserve Banks.

Thus the system of fractional reserves,[1] whether fixed by law (as in the United States) or roughly adhered to in practice (as in England), imposes a limit upon the expansion of bank credit and so upon the quantity of money which banks can issue.

But the limit (depending upon the reserve ratio) is several times larger than the member-bank reserve balances carried with the Federal Reserve Banks. In April, 1947 the Deposit money issued by member banks was 102 billion dollars (75 billion dollars of which was demand deposits), while the reserves were less than 16 billion dollars.

The 100 Per Cent Reserve versus Fractional Reserves

The 100 per cent money scheme is a proposal to prohibit the commercial banks from issuing money. This right, under the scheme proposed, would be centered exclusively in the Federal Reserve System.

Money would circulate in the community as now in the form of Federal Reserve notes or in the form of demand deposits. Demand

[1] "Whenever there is an increase in the total amount of cash money in the country, a certain proportion of it finds its way into the coffers of the banks. If the banks keep a reserve ratio of one-tenth (that is, if they keep their cash reserve at about one-tenth of their total deposits), it follows inescapably that for every additional cash dollar obtained by the banks they create ten dollars of bank money or deposits. The power of the banks to create money has frequently been condemned by reformers as a usurpation of the money-creating prerogatives of the state but until the 1920's the possession of this power was commonly denied by bankers.

"The banker would deny that anyone bringing an additional $1,000 of cash into his bank would enable him to increase his deposits by anything like the $10,000 that the theory called for. He would plead that he could increase deposits only by the $1,000 entered into the account of the individual who brought in the cash money. He could perhaps lend out the $900 of spare cash that would be available after putting aside $100 out of the $1,000 as the 10% reserve against the new $1,000 deposit, and such a loan of $900 would mean the creation of $900 of additional bank money. But the $900 of newly created bank money would disappear as soon as the borrower made use of the $900 he had borrowed, so that very soon the new credits would be back at $1,000 rather than $10,000.

"This apparent discrepancy arises because the theory refers to the whole banking system and not to any individual banker. When we look at the whole banking system we find that the creation of bank money does not come to an end with the $1,000 created by the first bank. This is because the first bank, lending the $900 of cash, keeps only one-tenth of the additional cash. The remaining cash can go from bank to bank, leaving one-tenth of its amount each time at every bank where it sojourns, so that when the whole $1,000 has been absorbed, the total amount of additional bank money created by all the banks together amounts to $10,000. As long as the sum of new loans, and so of the new deposits, amounts deposits would, however, always be balanced precisely by member-bank reserve balances plus a small amount of vault cash.

Time and savings deposits would lose their current easy convertibility into demand deposits and would become rigorously an investment of savings for a specified period, within which they could not be withdrawn. Thus time deposits would not be money.

Banking would be strictly divided into (1) deposit banking, and (2) savings institutions or departments. Deposit banking would become exclusively a checking service function for the convenience of individuals and corporations who prefer to pay their bills by check rather than by currency. Savings institutions or savings departments of banks alone could lend money—but only the money deposited with them by savers or subscribed by the bank's stockholders. Banks could not create new money. If the public wished to exchange money for a savings account, the savings institutions would stand ready to serve;

---

to less than $10,000 the additional cash needed for additional reserves is less than $1,000 and there is still some spare cash permitting some banks to make still more loans. The sum of new loans and of deposits therefore keeps on increasing. Only when they amount to $10,000 is the additional $1,000 of cash money entirely absorbed as additional cash reserves at the same ratio of 10%." A. P. Lerner, "Money," *Encyclopaedia Britannica*, 1946, p. 694.

Another excellent brief statement showing how "multiple expansion" of bank credit is dependent upon banks "keeping in step" is the following from Keynes: "It follows that the rate at which the bank can, with safety, *actively* create deposits by lending and investing has to be in a proper relation to the rate at which it is *passively* creating them against the receipt of liquid resources from its depositors. For the latter increase the bank's reserves even if only a part of them is ultimately retained by the bank, whereas the former diminish the reserves even if only a part of them is paid away to the customers of other banks; indeed we might express our conclusion more strongly than this, since the borrowing customers generally borrow with the intention of paying away at once the deposits thus created in their favour, whereas the depositing customers often have no such intention. . . . Every movement forward by an individual bank weakens it, but every such movement by one of its neighbour banks strengthens it; so that if all move forward together, no one is weakened on balance. Thus the behaviour of each bank, though it cannot afford to move more than a step in advance of the others, will be governed by the average behaviour of the banks as a whole—to which average, however, it is able to contribute its quota small or large. Each Bank Chairman sitting in his parlour may regard himself as the passive instrument of outside forces over which he has no control; yet the 'outside forces' may be nothing but himself and his fellow-chairmen, and certainly not his depositors." J. M. Keynes, *A Treatise on Money*, Harcourt, Brace & Company, Inc., New York, 1930, vol. I, pp. 25-27.

and similarly, if the public wished to shift its asset holdings from securities to savings accounts, this also could be done.[1]

The 100 per cent reserve scheme is simply a way of reverting to a pure currency monetary system. Under this plan commercial banks could not create money. The money supply would be created entirely by the Federal Reserve Banks. The money supply would consist wholly (except for minor coin) of Federal Reserve notes and demand deposits (backed 100 per cent by member-bank reserves), the proportion of each varying according to the desires of the public. Only the monetary authority (the Federal Reserve System) could create money.

If any individual (or corporation) wished to borrow or to float securities, he would have no recourse except to tap the savings of the public. He could not get bank credit; he could not be financed from the issue of new money created by commercial banks.

Yet this would not necessarily mean any shortage of funds for borrowers. New money could easily be created by the monetary authority. The Federal Reserve Banks could purchase outstanding United States government obligations in the open market. The sellers—individuals or corporations—would thus become possessed of new money. They would have obtained this new money from the sale of securities, not by borrowing.

The Federal Reserve System might, of course, not choose to purchase United States government securities privately held. Individuals and corporations would then have to dispose of their holdings or borrow funds in the private capital markets. But in this case no new money would be created. The monetary authority would reserve to itself the exclusive right to expand or contract the money supply.

---

[1] Let us assume that currency is deposited in a savings bank or department. This bank could then lend or invest a part of any cash so deposited, holding a part as required reserves. (Reserves are required currently against time deposits in the case of commercial banks, but not with respect to savings banks, the latter holding only such cash reserves as experience and prudence dictate.)

If, on the one hand, the savings bank made a loan with a part of the cash deposited with it, the cash loaned out would not likely remain in the savings bank system; it would quickly be returned to active circulation. Total savings deposits would in this case rise by only the initial deposit of cash. Similarly, if the savings bank purchased securities, the cash would likely be returned to active circulation.

New money could be created not only by monetizing government securities already outstanding, but also by authorizing the Federal Reserve Banks to finance a government deficit created either by reducing taxes or increasing expenditures. Such financing would in effect be interest-free. For even though the securities formally carried a rate of interest, the profits of the Reserve Banks ultimately belong to the government. The effect would therefore be much the same as if the Treasury had printed paper currency. The new deposits, created by the Federal Reserve Banks and credited to the account of the Treasury, would quickly be put into active circulation as soon as the government spent the funds.

Under a fractional reserve system, such as we now have, the money supply may be increased (1) by commercial banks lending to individuals or business, or by purchasing outstanding securities, and (2) by commercial banks taking new security issues to finance a government deficit. Under the prevailing system, in other words, the money supply is normally increased through an increase in the assets of the commercial banks. The monetary authorities can increase the money supply [1] by operating indirectly upon the commercial banks. The monetary authorities can affect the money supply by (1) open-market operations of the Federal Reserve Banks, thereby increasing the volume of bank reserves and stimulating the commercial banks to lend and to invest, and (2) by the Treasury financing a government deficit through the sale of securities to the commercial banks.

Under the 100 per cent plan individuals and business firms could not acquire new money by borrowing from commercial banks. But the monetary authorities (meaning both the Federal Reserve System and the Treasury) could put new money in their hands (1) by Federal Reserve purchases of United States securities in the open market, and (2) by creating a government deficit financed by the Federal Reserve Banks. New money would not be created through the commercial banks.

[1] Under American law the Treasury cannot finance itself directly by the sale of securities to the Federal Reserve Banks. For operational purposes, it may, however (under wartime legislation which has been extended for a limited period), sell up to 5 billion dollars of securities directly to the Federal Reserve Banks.

"Deposit Money" and "Reserve Money"

Concepts that I find particularly useful are (1) Deposit money (commercial bank money), and (2) Reserve (or Central Bank) money.[1]

Deposit money as here defined consists of (1) demand deposits, and (2) time deposits.[2] Reserve money (Central Bank money) consists of (1) Federal Reserve notes, and (2) member-bank reserve balances. Member-bank reserve balances are, of course, not a part of "money in circulation."

And member-bank reserve balances *alone* constitute the "legal reserves." The term "Reserve money" (Central Bank money), as here used, must therefore be sharply distinguished from the term "legal reserves."

Deposit money grows when the assets (cash, loans, and investments) of commercial banks increase; Reserve money grows when the assets (gold and securities) [3] of the Federal Reserve Banks increase.

Reserve money is a pool into which the public and member banks both dip. When the public draws out Federal Reserve notes, member-bank reserves go down; when the public returns notes from circulation, member-bank reserves rise. The two constituent parts of Reserve money are interchangeable; but the metamorphosis from one to the other is highly significant both for the public and for banks. Reserve money in the form of Federal Reserve notes is a part of the money in circulation; in the form of reserve balances it is legal reserves.[4]

Our modern system of Reserve (Central Bank) money—Federal Reserve notes and member-bank balances—is a modernized and flexible system of "basic" money which serves the two purposes of (1) supplying the community with hand-to-hand cash (currency), and

---

[1] The existence of nonmember banks complicates somewhat the concept of Reserve money; quantitively the matter is not very important, and the fundamentals are not altered by leaving these banks out of account.

[2] For certain purposes it is sometimes useful to exclude time deposits as a part of the "money" supply.

[3] I omit, for brevity, minor assets such as acceptances, rediscounts, and advances.

[4] Reserve money and Deposit money are likely to rise and fall together, but not necessarily in exact proportion. This is due to the fact that reserve ratios may change, and also the amount of Federal Reserve notes desired by the public.

(2) supplying the commercial banks with cash reserves. If there were no Federal Reserve System, the "basic" or standard money would consist exclusively of Treasury currency—paper money, minor coin, and gold. Whatever Treasury currency was issued would either be in circulation or held as cash reserves in the vaults of the commercial banks. As cash flowed in from hand-to-hand circulation, bank reserves would rise.

Now that is also precisely what happens with respect to Reserve money. If less currency is needed for circulation, Federal Reserve

Table 7. Reserve Money *

(*In billions of dollars*)

Year (Dec. 31)	Total Reserve money	Federal Reserve notes	Member-bank reserve balances
1929	4.3	1.9	2.4
1933	5.8	3.1	2.7
1940	18.9	5.9	14.0
1947	42.7	24.8	17.9

* SOURCE: *Banking and Monetary Statistics; Federal Reserve Bulletin.*

notes will be deposited in commercial banks and shipped back to the Federal Reserve Banks to swell the volume of member-bank reserve balances. Reserve money is the modern equivalent of standard money, used either for circulation or for bank reserves. Indeed, if the member banks had been required to hold their cash reserves in their own vaults, all Reserve money would necessarily assume the form of Federal Reserve notes. Under the prevailing system as soon as Reserve money becomes member-bank reserves the "note" liabilities of the Federal Reserve Banks are transformed into "deposit" liabilities.

Table 7 discloses the changes which have occurred in the volume of Reserve money, together with the constituent parts thereof, in the four years 1929, 1933, 1940, and 1947.

Bank Assets and the Quantity of Money

The rise and fall of Federal Reserve assets cause fluctuations in Reserve (Central Bank) money. These assets are (1) gold, (2) government securities, and (3) discounts, advances, acceptances, and industrial loans. These data are given in Table 8. The figures in the "Total" column may be compared with those in the "Total Reserve

Table 8. Gold and Reserve Bank Credit *

(In billions of dollars)

Year (Dec. 31)	Total †	Gold	Reserve Bank credit	
			U. S. government securities	Discounts, advances, acceptances, industrial loans
1929	4.3	2.8	0.5	1.0
1933	6.1	3.5	2.4	0.2
1940	21.9	19.7	2.2	0.01
1947	44.9	21.5	23.2	0.17

* SOURCE: *Banking and Monetary Statistics; Federal Reserve Bulletin.*

† This total, of course, does not exactly balance the volume of Reserve money (notes and reserve balances). Minor liabilities such as Treasury and foreign deposits, capital account, and surplus are omitted in Table 7, whereas minor assets such as "other cash," bank premises, etc., are omitted from Table 8.

money" column in Table 7. The former constitute the main *assets*, the latter the main *liabilities* of the Federal Reserve Banks.

The Reserve Banks can control the volume of Reserve money merely by increasing and decreasing their assets. The volume of gold held depends indeed upon our foreign balance of payments and upon Treasury policy with respect to monetizing or sterilizing the gold purchased. But the volume of Federal Reserve credit—government securities (and other Federal Reserve credit)—is rigorously subject to the "open market" and "discount policy" of the Federal Reserve

System. Thus the System can in the final analysis control the volume of Reserve money.[1] And this, as we shall see, is likely to affect more or less the volume of Deposit money.

And just as the Reserve Banks can raise or lower the volume of Reserve money merely by increasing or decreasing their holding of government securities (together with such acceptances, rediscounts, advances, and industrial loans as are available), so also can the commercial banks raise or lower the volume of Deposit money merely by increasing or decreasing their loans and investments. Reserve money is a function of the volume of assets of the Reserve Banks; Deposit money is a function of the volume of assets of commercial banks.[2]

The relation of the Reserve Banks to the commercial banks and of Reserve (Central Bank) money to Deposit (commercial bank) money may conveniently be shown in diagrammatic form as follows:

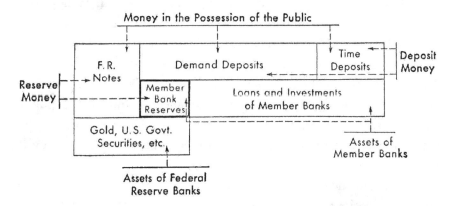

"Member-bank reserves" hold the key position in this diagram. On the one hand, they constitute "cash assets" of the member banks; on the other, they are a part of the Reserve (or Central Bank) money. "Member-bank reserves" are thus the link between the Federal Re-

---

[1] This is true at any rate within the limits of the gold reserve ratio. Currently the Reserve Banks must hold gold certificates equal to at least 25 per cent of their note and deposit liabilities.

[2] The power of commercial banks to create money is limited by their reserves. And what the volume of reserves will be is in the final analysis under the control of the Federal Reserve System.

serve Banks and the money supply held by the public. When the assets of the Federal Reserve Banks grow, Federal Reserve notes and/or member-bank reserves increase; when the assets of the member banks grow (which assets include member-bank reserves) the deposits held by the public increase.

The Role Played by the Public

Now while the volume of Reserve money is a function of the assets [1] of the Federal Reserve Banks, the manner in which the total is divided between Federal Reserve notes and member-bank reserves depends exclusively upon the wishes of the public. If the public wishes more currency, the member banks are compelled to exchange a part of their reserve balances at the Federal Reserve Banks for Federal Reserve notes. Accordingly, reserve balances go down (unless replenished) whenever Federal Reserve notes are drawn out into circulation.

Within the limits imposed by the reserve ratio Deposit money rises and falls with the rise and decline in bank assets—the increase or decrease in loans and investments of commercial banks. How the deposits are divided between demand and time deposits depends upon the wishes of the public. The banks can at will (at least so long as they are able by offering favorable terms designed to induce the public either to sell securities or to take loans) control the volume of Deposit money. But the public determines how much of that money it wishes to hold as *time*, and how much as *demand*, deposits.

To sum up, the public controls the division of Deposit money into demand deposits and time deposits, and also the division of Reserve money into Federal Reserve notes and member-bank reserves; the commercial banks control (within the limits imposed by the reserve ratio) the volume of Deposit money; and the Federal Reserve System controls the volume of Reserve money. Thus in the final analysis the monetary authorities, by raising or lowering the volume of assets held by the banking system, can influence the volume of money in the hands of the public.

---

[1] Other assets besides gold and government securities held by the Federal Reserve Banks include discounts and advances to banks, industrial loans, and acceptances. But these have in recent years been negligible in amount.

Yet some qualifications are necessary. In the absence of new government security issues, banks can only increase their assets by making loans to the public or by purchasing securities from the public, *i.e.*, by monetizing assets already held by individuals and corporations, together with new issues coming on the market. Thus, in a way, the public does have something to say about the volume of money. Individuals and corporations may not easily be induced (especially in depression periods) to borrow; and they can only be induced to sell securities by being offered attractive terms. The banks, to increase their assets, may be compelled to bid up the price of securities to a high figure. This means that the rate of interest goes down. Accordingly, if the banks insist on increasing (or decreasing) the quantity of money, the public can at any rate determine the *terms* on which this is done.

The government, through deficit financing (brought about either by a reduction in taxes or an increase in expenditures, or both) may supply the market with new issues. By combining fiscal and monetary policy, the monetary authorities *can* control both the money supply and the rate of interest. But it still remains to be seen what the public will do with the money at that rate of interest. Under certain circumstances the effect could be a price inflation; under other conditions, an expansion of output and employment; under still other conditions the effect may merely be to increase the volume of idle balances.

Thus, as we shall see at length later, the public enters the picture in three ways: (1) its willingness to hold money (liquidity preference), (2) its desire to spend (propensity to consume), and (3) its inclination to invest (investment-demand schedule). At each of these three points the public enters. But within the framework of these behavior patterns the fiscal and monetary authorities can play a powerful role in determining the quantity of money and the rate of interest, and so indirectly in controlling income, employment, and prices.

Wartime Financing and the Increase in Liquid Assets

The liquid assets of nonbank investors increased in 1940–1945 inclusive by 215 billion dollars.[1] By "nonbank" investors is meant all

---

[1] *Treasury Bulletin*, April, 1946, pp. A 11–20.

investors except the commercial banks and the Federal Reserve Banks. This increase in liquid assets comprised (1) increased holdings of currency, (2) increased holdings of deposits in commercial banks, and (3) increased holdings of United States government securities.

The *increase* in the nonbank holdings of currency and of deposits in commercial banks amounted together to 82 billion dollars; the *increase* in nonbank holdings of United States government securities was 133 billion dollars.

Individuals, corporations, and State and local governments are in the final analysis the nonbank investors. But they hold a considerable part of their liquid savings in the form of *claims* in mutual savings banks, savings and loan associations, credit unions, insurance companies, and government social-insurance trust funds. These institutions are in reality intermediaries which hold liquid assets for their beneficiaries—namely, the investors who initially account for the liquid savings—individuals, corporations, and State and local governments. Much of the increased volume of 133 billion dollars of United States government securities held by nonbank investors was in fact held by savings banks, insurance companies, and government trust funds. But for our purposes here this is not important. The significant point is that the *increase* in the public's liquid savings (whether held directly or indirectly through intermediary institutions) consisted of 82 billion dollars of currency and deposits in commercial banks and 133 billion dollars of United States government securities.

Of this vast expansion in liquid savings, totaling 215 billion dollars, 205 billion was due to the Federal budgetary deficit in the six years 1940–1945. The remaining 10 billion was due to a small increase in commercial bank loans and investments other than United States government securities. Thus the increase in liquid savings sprang almost entirely from the Federal deficit—in other words, from the increase in the public debt.

This fact constitutes for most people a great puzzle. They are very happy about the vast increase in liquid savings, but they are very unhappy about the public debt. Unfortunately, it is not possible to have your cake and eat it too. Currency, deposits, and securities are based on debt, public or private.

Only a part of the total increase in the Federal debt is held by the nonbank investors. The rest is held by the commercial banks and the Federal Reserve Banks. But for every increase in securities held by the banking system the nonbank investors hold an increased volume of currency and deposits.

The nonbank investors chose to hold 82 billion dollars of the total increase in liquid assets in the form of (1) currency, and (2) deposits in commercial banks. Against this increase in currency and deposits the commercial banks and the Federal Reserve Banks held mainly United States government securities. If the nonbank investors had preferred to hold the securities themselves, they could always have exchanged their holdings of currency and deposits for the United States government securities held by the commercial banks and the Federal Reserve Banks. If the public could be induced to make this exchange, the money supply—currency and deposits—would decline. This would not, however, result in any decline in total liquid savings. Nor would there be any decline in the public debt. All that would have happened is that nonbank investors would hold a larger part of their liquid assets in the form of United States government securities and a smaller part in the form of currency and deposits.

Clearly the rise in the public debt explains the growth of liquid savings. But now let us suppose that the war could have been financed without any Federal deficit. Various assumptions might be made. First, let us make the quite unlikely assumption that the money income could have increased as in fact it did from 1940 to 1946, even though there had been no deficit. On this assumption the money supply M—currency and checking deposits—would have increased in consequence of (1) bank loans to private business, and (2) bank purchases of privately issued securities. Alternatively, there might have been a large increase in velocity V, or some combination of the two involving an increase in MV equal to that which actually occurred. Assuming no Federal deficit, much of the increase in income would necessarily have been absorbed by the government in taxes. Liquid assets would have risen only by the increase in M—currency and deposits—plus some increase in new private security issues sold to nonbank investors. But, had there been no Federal deficit, taxes would have taken nearly half the total national income. Accordingly, the increase in liquid savings (other than money) would necessarily have been relatively small.

Second, if we could assume (as I think is even less realistic) the prodigious increase in production which the war expansion brought without any increase in total money income, we should then have experienced, as output rose, a drastic fall in prices. A heavy fall in prices would, according to this assumption, have permitted the government to tax away a sufficient part of the increased real income to finance the war output. Income after taxes would then have been just sufficient to purchase the limited output of consumers' goods together with a small volume of private-capital formation—but only on the assumption that every increase in output was accompanied by a corresponding fall in prices. Under these assumptions there could have occurred only a very slight increase in liquid savings. However, in view of the fall in prices the liquid savings already accumulated prior to the war would have risen in purchasing-power value.

No country has ever financed a war in this manner. The assumptions are absurdly unrealistic; they necessitate a fall in money wage rates with every increase in employment, and a fall in prices corresponding to every increase in total output.

As events actually unfolded, however, the liquid assets holdings of nonbank investors rose by 215 billion dollars, nearly all of which increase is to be explained by the wartime Federal deficit. The ensuing increase in the public debt was partly absorbed by the banking system —the commercial banks and the Federal Reserve Banks—and partly by the nonbank investors. That portion of new government issues purchased by the banking system was paid for by an expansion of bank credit—new issues of currency and deposits. And this increase in currency and deposits was held by the nonbank investors. Thus the entire increase in the public debt (whether held by banks or by nonbank investors) added to the liquid assets holdings of nonbank investors. That part of the debt which was not held by nonbank investors was monetized in the form of currency and deposits. Thus the nonbank investors' increased holdings of liquid savings consist of (1) monetized public debt, and (2) nonmonetized public debt.

Important consequences flow from this vast increase in liquid assets, as we shall see later in this book. Among other matters, the volume of liquid assets may affect commodity and security prices; and from the long-run standpoint the problem of sustained full employment.

That the increased liquid assets had their origin in the Federal deficit is simply a fact, but it is a fact that offends the sound finance instincts of many people. Unsophisticated people are likely to think that the vast increase in liquid savings was a product of thrift, and, indeed, in a sense it was. For while the total *aggregate* volume of liquid assets would of necessity have risen by the amount of the Federal deficit, the manner in which this total was distributed among the nonbank investors depended upon the action of individuals. The mere fact that total liquid assets holdings increased would not ensure an increase in the liquid holdings of any particular individual. Some managed to save much and others little out of the high war incomes. This was due partly to differences in individual thrift and partly to the unequal distribution of the enlarged wartime national income.

Moreover, without an increase in wartime thrift (whether voluntary or enforced) a price inflation would have destroyed much of the value of the liquid assets. An increase in thriftiness did in fact occur, in the sense that individuals and corporations saved a much higher per cent of a given income than they would have saved under peacetime conditions. This, to be sure, was in a large measure due to rationing, price control, and the unavailability of many kinds of durable consumers' goods, such as automobiles. Thus we conclude that the vast increase in liquid savings was mainly the result of certain specific policies; these involved on the one side a vast increase in the public debt, and on the other, various measures designed to curtail consumption expenditures.

It is an easy matter to make the community as a whole "rich" in terms of liquid assets. But it is not so easy to maintain a stable purchasing-power value of these assets. Indeed the events since June, 1946 reveal that we have already dissipated a considerable part of the real value of these assets in an inflationary rise in the consumer price index from around 130 to around 172 in June, 1948.

Clearly there is some optimum quantity of liquid assets. The criterion for judging this optimum is a major problem of monetary theory.

It is the job of monetary and fiscal policy to control the quantity of liquid assets; and it is the job of monetary theory to set up criteria for the guidance of policy.

It is no occasion for surprise to find that many citizens should not see clearly the connection between (1) the wartime increase in the Federal debt together with the expansion of Federal Reserve credit, on the one side, and (2) the rise of deposits and member-bank reserves, on the other. Practical men, looking directly at their own operations, are likely to argue that it was the growth of *sales* volume which accounted for the general growth in deposits. The hog farmer in Iowa, for example, received a big check for a carload of hogs sold in Chicago. This check was drawn on a Chicago bank. The farmer deposited the check in his local bank. The local bank cleared the check through the Chicago Federal Reserve Bank. Its cash reserves increased; and these reserves came to the bank via the farmer's deposit. What, it is asked, do the United States Treasury and the Federal Reserve Banks have to do with that?

It was through the process of a rising volume of business all over the country—the government purchases of farm products, minerals, munitions, airplanes, etc.—that the enlarged aggregate of bank reserves (initially built up by Federal Reserve open market operations in the great financial centers) was spread throughout the entire country. Federal Reserve credit to expand the reserve base and Treasury borrowing from the commercial banks—these are the sources of the deposits which flowed into the local banks in Iowa and elsewhere in the form of checks drawn on the great financial centers. Thus banks all over the country found themselves in possession of a growing volume of reserve funds which enabled them to participate in the purchase of new government issues. Accordingly, bank assets and deposits grew all around. But the basis of the whole expansion was (1) the increase in Federal Reserve credit, and (2) the sale of United States government securities to the banks.

Summary

The manufacture of money and the control of the value thereof are functions of the sovereign state. Historically, the government has performed this function, basically, in four ways: (1) by merely standing ready to coin the precious metals—gold or silver or both—into money, (2) by printing paper money, (3) by authorizing privately owned banking institutions to issue bank notes or create deposits, and (4) by authorizing central banks to issue notes and create deposits.

The first and the second methods have, at long last, become in large measure obsolete. Subsidiary silver coin is indeed issued in limited quantities for convenience in the small transactions of daily trade. But gold no longer circulates either as coin or as gold certificates. Gold is now reserved exclusively in some countries as an international monetary reserve—a means of balancing international accounts, filling the short-run gaps in the international exchange of goods and services. In other countries—notably the United States—gold serves two purposes: (1) as internal cover for Reserve money, and (2) as an international monetary reserve.

The second method—government paper money—remains, to a limited and restricted degree, an anachronistic feature of the American monetary system. In November, 1947 Treasury currency included 2.2 billion dollars of silver certificates and Treasury notes of 1890, 347 million dollars of United States notes (the greenbacks of Civil War time), and 492 million dollars of other remnants of bygone monetary episodes. But in most countries today, apart from subsidiary and minor coin, governments no longer issue currency directly. Paper money is issued through the banking system in the form of bank notes and Deposit money.[1] The printing of paper money—formerly widely resorted to by governments—is now outmoded.

Gold production remains a method of increasing the quantity of money. Any individual or corporation is free to mine gold and to sell any given quantity to the Treasury at the rate of $35 per ounce. Moreover, any firm or individual that acquires gold as a result of international transactions can similarly dispose of it to the Treasury. But the government no longer pays out gold coin or gold certificates in exchange for gold bullion. Instead the gold is "monetized" by

[1] The issue of Central Bank money is more or less the modern equivalent of printing government paper money.

issuing gold certificates (or gold certificate credits) to the Federal Reserve Banks, in exchange for which the Treasury is credited with a deposit against which it can draw checks. And the gold producer or importer is paid not in gold coin or gold certificates, but by a government check, which he may deposit at any commercial bank. Thus, even with respect to newly acquired gold, the new money comes into being in the form of a deposit created by the Federal Reserve Banks.

Leaving aside the anachronistic remnants from the past, money is created by banks—in the United States, by commercial banks (privately owned) and the Federal Reserve Banks. The commercial banks issue Deposit money; the Federal Reserve Banks, Reserve money. Deposit money, to repeat, consists of (1) demand deposits, and (2) time deposits. Reserve money consists of (1) Federal Reserve notes, and (2) member-bank reserve balances.

Deposit money is created by (1) the monetization of private credit (loans and discounts) as in the case of private individuals and corporations borrowing from banks, and (2) the monetization of securities, whether issued by private corporations or governments. These latter may be new issues taken directly by the banks, or they may be old outstanding issues held by individuals and corporations and purchased from them by the banks.

Deposit money can grow only to the extent that (1) businessmen and consumers borrow from the banks, (2) private corporations or the government dispose of *new* issues to the banks, and (3) the banks acquire by purchase securities (government and private) already outstanding and owned by individuals and corporations.

If indeed the entire banking system is "loaned up," if there are no excess reserves, then in fact banks cannot create additional new money. Thus in the final analysis the power of the commercial banks to issue new money must await the increase of Reserve money; and this, as we have seen, depends upon the growth of Federal Reserve assets— gold and government securities.[1]

Reserve money can grow only to the extent that the Federal Reserve Banks (1) monetize new gold by crediting new deposits to the

[1] As noted above, other forms of Federal Reserve credit—industrial loans, acceptances, rediscounts, etc.—are negligible in quantity.

Treasury account in exchange for gold certificates, and (2) extend Federal Reserve credit through the purchase of government securities, acceptances, and commercial paper in the open market; by making industrial loans; or by rediscounting for, or making advances to, member banks. In recent years Federal Reserve credit, except for insignificant amounts, has been used mainly to buy government securities. By and large, therefore, the growth of Reserve money depends upon (1) the monetization of gold, and (2) the monetization of government securities, whether new or outstanding issues.

The initiative in monetary expansion may be taken by individuals or by corporations who wish to have their credit (as in the case of loans) or their assets (as in the case of sale of securities) monetized. Or the initiative may be taken by banks when they undertake to expand their earning assets. Again, the initiative may be taken by the Federal Reserve System, as is the case when the Reserve Banks undertake, through open market purchases, to extend Federal Reserve credit. With respect to gold the initiative may come from the gold producer or the gold importer who sells his gold to the Treasury. Or finally, the initiative may come from the government when it undertakes to sell new issues to the banking system.

In brief, apart from the now obsolete method of printing government paper money, expansion of the quantity of money may be achieved (1) by monetizing gold, (2) by monetizing private credit, and (3) by monetizing government credit. Commercial banks by monetizing private and government credit create Deposit money; the Federal Reserve Banks by monetizing gold and government credit create Reserve money. Reserve money in part becomes reserve balances of member banks, on the basis of which they are able to undertake a multiple expansion of Deposit money.

Chapter 3

The Quantity Theory and the Marshallian Version

IT WILL, I believe, facilitate the exposition of the main lines of theory to place before the reader at once the relevant concepts with respect to (1) the uses to which any increase in the money supply may be put, and (2) the conditions which may occasion an increased supply of money. Under the first section we consider what the public may do with additional money created by the monetary authority; under the second section we consider the factors underlying an increased demand for funds leading to an increased volume of bank credit.

Let us assume that the monetary authority has decided to increase the quantity of money. The monetary authority has, let us say, purchased securities from the public. To pay for these securities new deposits have been created. The public now holds a larger quantity of cash; the banking system holds additional securities. A part of the earning assets of the community has been monetized.

Desired versus Actual Cash

At this point it is necessary to make a sharp distinction between (1) the volume of cash holdings *desired* by the public, and (2) the *actual* cash holdings. Prior to the creation of new money the public may have been quite content with its cash balances. The newly created cash will therefore, in the first instance, be extra, or spare, cash. Let *desired* cash holdings be L, and let *actual* cash holdings be M. Then $M - L$ will equal the extra or spare cash.

Prior to the creation of the new money we assume that *actual* cash holdings were equal to *desired* cash holdings. M and L were then in an equilibrium relation to each other; $M = L$. But now, after the new money has been created, $M > L$. This situation is an unstable one.

43

The public will wish to get rid of the extra or spare cash. What now may be done with the new money?

First, the extra money may be spent directly on goods and services. Accordingly, increased outlays would be made on consumption or investment goods. This would tend to cause an expansion in output, with or without (according to varying cost conditions) an increase in prices. The value of goods and services at market prices (National Product) would rise; the factors of production would receive more income from the process of production. Thus the monetary authority, by increasing the quantity of money, *might* bring about an increase in income, employment, output, and prices.

But then there is a second route. The individuals who had been induced to sell securities to the banking system on favorable terms (the inducement to substitute money for securities is of course made by offering higher prices for securities than those previously prevailing) might not themselves wish to spend the money for goods and services. In this event no increase would occur (at least in the first instance) in income, output, or commodity prices. Only the prices of securities would have risen. But an increase in bond prices would mean a fall in the rate of interest. And this might set in motion a chain of events which in the end might affect income and prices. A low rate of interest may stimulate the construction and purchase of new houses. Corporations may float new issues (in a capital market made favorable by a high degree of liquidity) in order to expand plant and equipment. Thus via the low interest rate the new money created by the monetization of outstanding securities might soon spill over into an increased demand for construction, equipment, and capital goods generally. Expansion in these lines would raise income and employment, and so before long consumption expenditures would also rise. Thus the second route—via the fall in the interest rate—may also lead to an increased purchase of goods and services and so to a rise in income and output—and probably more or less to some increase in prices.

These two developments are possible, but by no means inevitable. The monetization of outstanding securities might have the effect of placing money for the most part in the hands of the rich and well-to-do. A larger volume of cash holdings in the hands of these groups is not likely to increase consumption expenditures significantly. What then? The price of securities may already have been so high, prior to the new monetization, that a very small increase was sufficient to induce many holders to sell, preferring at so low a rate of interest to hold cash. Thus a considerable monetization of securities might be induced by a slight bidding up of security prices, or, in other words, a slight fall in the rate of interest. And this rate of interest may already have been so low that any further slight decline affords little inducement to investment in housing or in other forms of capital formation. Under these circumstances the increase in the money supply would have little or no effect on the commodity market, or even on the security markets. Income, output, and prices (whether commodity or security prices) would be little if at all affected. The new money would neither be spent directly on goods or services, nor would it indirectly (via a lower rate of interest) find an outlet in capital formation. The holders of the extra money would in these circumstances be content simply to keep it as a secure and safe liquid asset.

We have assumed in what was said above that deliberate action was taken by the monetary authority designed to increase the quantity of money. The community, having been splashed with cash, would then be forced to decide what to do with the extra money. Let us now look at the matter the other way round. Let us suppose that the public for various reasons should wish additional funds.

The Demand for Loanable Funds

There are two main reasons for an increased demand for funds. They are (1) the "trade" demand, and (2) the "finance" demand.

The first is well illustrated in the commercial-loan theory. Funds are wanted to satisfy the "needs of trade." This is the "trade" demand. The "trade" demand may rise owing to an increase in the physical volume or value of goods-in-process. In the absence of banking institutions business could indeed carry the goods through the productive process and transact a growing volume of trade by issuing its own bills of exchange. But it would greatly facilitate the production and exchange process if these bills were monetized by the banking system.

Money is far more efficacious as a means of payment than private bills. Being generally acceptable, it greatly facilitates the exchange of goods.

Second, there is the demand for funds to finance an expansion of fixed-capital facilities. Bank financing of such outlays was bitterly fought by the banking school. Nevertheless, in the nineteenth century, especially in the United States and Germany, no inconsiderable part of new fixed capital (contrary to the commercial-loan theory) was financed by a growth of bank credit. Schumpeter's theoretical analysis of credit expansion to finance innovations has a firm empirical basis in the industrial expansion of the nineteenth century.

Moreover, it may be noted that at the bottom of a depression the flow of planned savings[1] is likely to be quite inadequate to finance expansion. At low levels of income the current flow of planned savings will be small. There is need for bank financing.

Consider also the case of a governmental expansionist fiscal program. When incomes are low, large loan expenditures cannot be financed by the sale of securities to the public. Borrowing from the banks is necessary. Only after incomes have been raised to a higher level will it be possible to tap large sums by borrowing from the public. Thus from 1933 to 1936 the Federal government covered much of the deficit by sale of securities to banks; from 1936 to 1939, incomes having risen and the community having become more liquid, the deficit was financed mainly by borrowing from the public. The wartime expansion offers another illustration. Beginning in 1940 and extending into the early years of the war, the deficit was heavily financed by borrowing from the banks. The war program, thus financed, raised money incomes and increased the cash holdings of the public. As the national income rose to peak wartime levels and the cash holdings of the public increased, a larger per cent of the deficit could be financed by the sale of securities to the public.

Thus there may be need for bank financing of both private investment and governmental loan expenditures, especially in the early

---

[1] By "planned savings" I here mean savings in the Robertsonian sense, *i.e.*, savings from "disposable" or "yesterday's" income.

phase of recovery from low levels of income. This is the "finance" demand for monetary funds.

The Pure Quantity Theory

According to the pure quantity theory the monetary authority can control the level of income (and so indirectly the price level) merely by changing the quantity of money. As we have seen, under certain conditions an increase in the volume of cash balances may indeed directly stimulate the purchase of goods and services, or it may indirectly do so via the expansionist effect on private investment of a lower rate of interest. But the increased cash may also simply be held as an unearning asset.

Again, there may be some combination of all three. A part of the new cash may spill over directly into the commodity market, raising sales volume and (in part) prices; a part may take up new issues of securities, thereby providing funds for capital investment [1] at lower rates of interest than would otherwise have been possible; and finally, the lower rate of interest consequent upon the monetization of outstanding securities may merely induce the public to hold a larger part of their assets in the form of cash. Some combination of all three of these possibilities is not improbable.

From the standpoint of the simplified version of the quantity theory the matter is quite clear. All increases in cash balances lead to enlarged purchases of goods and services. Extra cash balances flowing into the hands of the public through credit expansion cause an increase in expenditures in excess of the current money income. Outlays exceed income because of the increase in cash. The new cash is unwanted cash. All around, there is an effort to get rid of the excess cash. In the process income and prices rise. As this occurs, more cash will be needed to effect payments. Thus as income and prices rise, the spare cash more and more becomes *needed* cash. Eventually a new level of transactions is reached at which all of the extra cash will be needed. At this point the increased *actual* cash will have become *desired* cash. L will again be equal to M in an equilibrium sense.

---

[1] By "investment" is meant the purchase of a capital good. *Real* investment must thus be distinguished from *financial* investment in a security or mortgage.

The pure version of the quantity theory was forcefully stated as early as 1752 by Hume. There are also many sophisticated versions, of which perhaps the most important one stems from Marshall.[1]

The Hume version, refined and elaborated, dominated economic thinking throughout most of the nineteenth century. The price level was thought to be a function of the quantity of money. $P = \phi(M)$. Hume's highly original and interesting analysis is discussed in Appendix A.

In its most naïve form the theory stated that prices varied in direct proportion to the money supply. But it was later seen that this would not do. Using equations of the type $P = \dfrac{MV}{O}$, it was pointed out that output O rises secularly in an expanding society with a growing population and an improving technology. Velocity might also change gradually and in a more or less dependable manner under the impact of changing monetary institutions, though such changes might be small compared with the rapid secular rise in output. Accordingly, it could not be true that P would vary *in direct proportion* to M. The price level P was, however, thought to vary secularly in relation to the money supply M in a fairly dependable and predictable manner.

The relationship might, however, be a somewhat complex one. Changes in M, after correcting for $\dfrac{V}{O}$, would produce changes in P varying according to different circumstances. Thus, for small-percentage increases in M within a given period, P might change relatively little in relation to changes in M; for large-percentage changes within a given period, P might change greatly in relation to M. In other words, P might vary not merely in response to *changes* in M, but also with respect to changes in the *rate of change* of M; velocity V might in special circumstances, such as hyperinflation, depart rather widely from its established secular trend. However, with qualifications like this and

---

[1] The pure quantity theory should be distinguished, on the one side from the quantity equation approach (which is not a *theory* but merely a way of posing the problem of money and prices); and on the other side from such variants of the quantity theory as the Marshallian theory which centers attention not primarily on the quantity of money as such but on the shifts in the desire to hold cash.

others of a similar character, P was regarded as varying in a fairly dependable relation to changes in M.[1] The price level was thought to be a function of the money supply.

This conclusion, if valid, would be highly important for policy decisions. If the relation of P to M was indeed firmly rooted in the behavior patterns of the community as determined by the customs, habits, and institutional arrangements of the society, then it would follow that the monetary authority could readily control the price level merely by changing the quantity of money. A control of the money supply alone would be a sufficient condition for the control of income and the level of prices.

The Marshallian Equation

The Marshallian version[2] of the quantity theory—$M = kY$—represents a fundamentally new approach to the problem of money and prices. It is not true, as is often alleged, that the "cash-balance" equation is merely the quantity theory in new algebraic dress. Substituting PO (price level times output) for Y, the Marshallian equation becomes $M = kPO$. *Arithmetically* k is therefore simply the reciprocal of V in the equation $MV = PO$.[3] But it does not follow from the mere fact that $V = \dfrac{1}{k}$, as an arithmetic identity, that therefore the Marshallian *analysis* is in fact the same thing as the Hume-Fisher analysis. To assert this is to miss entirely the significance of the k in the Marshallian equation.

The difference can be stated as follows: In the terms of the Marshallian approach, sudden and rapid *shifts* in the desire of the public to hold money may profoundly affect prices even though the monetary authority successfully maintains a high stability in the money

---

[1] For an excellent statement of a flexible version of the quantity theory, with many qualifications and refinements, see Irving Fisher, *The Purchasing Power of Money*, The Macmillan Company, New York, 1926.

[2] In Marshall's cash-balance equation, k represents that fraction of income which people desire to hold in the form of money. See Marshall's definition, pp. 1–2 in this book.

[3] In the equation $P = \dfrac{M}{kO}$, k becomes that fraction of *real* income which people wish to *hold command over* in the form of money.

supply. The desire of the public to hold cash balances—"liquidity preference"—enters as a powerful factor. Drastic and sudden shifts in the desire to hold money, reflected in a change in k, may produce large and quickly moving changes in the level of income and prices. Shifts in public psychology, in expectations, must be taken account of no less than changes in the money supply. In the Marshallian

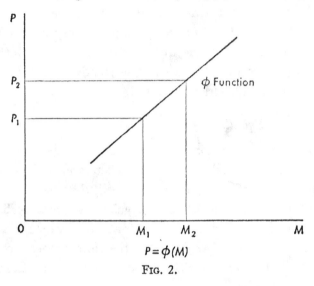

$$P = \phi(M)$$

Fig. 2.

analysis a shift in k may start an upward or downward movement. It is k, not M, that holds the stage.

The symbol k, it must be remembered, reflects the desire for liquidity—in other words, the desire to hold money, compared with the desire to spend it for goods. A shift in k, therefore, in the direction of an *increased* desire for liquidity represents a decreased demand for goods. There results then a movement away from goods to money. Persons holding stocks of goods begin to unload, and inventory holdings decline. Accordingly, production plans are revised downward, and output is curtailed. Thus the shift in k is likely to affect income through a reduction in both output and prices. As income falls, the increased desire for liquidity is satisfied, and so the downward movement comes eventually to an end.

In order to present a sharp contrast between the pure quantity theory and the Marshallian theory, the above diagrammatic presentation may be helpful to some readers. In Fig. 2 the schedule relation between P and M is represented by the ϕ function. This function is regarded as stable in the short run (any cyclical changes in O being offset by corresponding changes in V). Also the function is regarded as stable from the long-run standpoint, $\dfrac{V}{O}$ being thought to change over time according to some fixed pattern. Accordingly, P might be related to M in some such manner as indicated in the curve. If the money supply is M_1 (see Fig. 2), the price level will be P_1; if the money supply is M_2, the price will be P_2. This does not mean, however, that the changes in P are necessarily proportional to changes in M. The slope of the curve will indicate whether or not P varies *in direct proportion* to M. The crude quantity theory tended, however, to regard the relation as a proportional one.

In contrast with the pure quantity theory—which simply makes P a function of the actual quantity of M—the Marshallian analysis introduces the desires (or propensity) of the public to hold cash balances. In the Marshallian equation $M = kY$ the k is regarded as *controlling* the level of Y, if M is given by the monetary authority. If people's liquidity preference rises, there occurs a flight from goods to money, income falls, and so prices and output fall until Y holds the desired relation to M.

But now it may be useful to present the Marshallian analysis in a somewhat different algebraic dress. Let us write it as follows: $L = L(Y)$. By this we mean that the cash balances (which people *desire* to hold and which we call L) are a function of income Y. The L function is a schedule showing the size of the cash balances which people desire to hold at different levels of income. It represents the demand schedule for money at different income levels. For example, the schedule might be as follows·

Y	L
100	70
80	56
60	42

The L schedule tells us nothing about the *actual* quantity of money. It is a schedule showing the quantity of money which people *desire* to hold. It is not a supply schedule. If the supply of money is regarded as fixed by the monetary authority, we may regard the supply schedule of money—which we shall call the M schedule—as independent of the level of income; in other words, M remains fixed at all levels of income Y. We then have an elastic demand schedule for money (the L function) and an inelastic supply schedule (the M schedule). The level of income Y may then be regarded as determined by the intersection of these two schedules, as in Fig. 3.

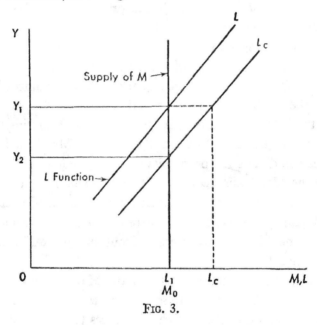

FIG. 3.

If the L function shifts from L to L_c, this means an increased demand for money (or conversely a decreased desire for goods in relation to money). This means a flight from goods to money, a fall in prices and output, and so a decline in income. Thus the shift in the L function toward greater liquidity, from L to L_c, will drive income down from Y_1 to Y_2, M remaining fixed at M_0.

Another way of stating the effect upon income of a shift in the L function is as follows: Assume (for a brief interval) no change in income after the L function has shifted from L to L_c. In this event the *desired* cash holdings would increase from L_1 to L_c. But this would mean that *actual* cash M_0 is less than the *desired* cash L_c. Everyone will therefore strive to increase his cash holdings. He will do so by unloading stocks of commodities in exchange for money. But this will result in a fall in prices and a curtailment of output, and so a fall in income. Eventually, as income falls from Y_1 to Y_2, the desired cash holdings will fall from L_c to L_1. But $L_1 = M_0$; accordingly, M and L are again in equilibrium, or in other words the actual cash holdings M are again equal to the desired cash holdings L.

Chapter 4

Liquidity Preference, Investment, and Consumption

Marshall and Keynes on Liquidity Preference

We have already translated Marshall's $M = kY$ into $L = L(Y)$. This is *one* of the components of Keynes's liquidity preference function—the transactions-demand function.[1]

Marshall also anticipated, in his $k'A$, the *second* liquidity function of Keynes—the speculative and precautionary demand for money, or what Haberler calls "liquidity preference proper." We shall often refer to this function as the "asset" demand for money. But Marshall made in fact very little out of his $k'A$, and it was wholly forgotten by his followers. The Marshallian version which came into general use was $M = kY$, not $M = kY + k'A$.

The proportion of one's assets k' which one wishes to hold in the form of money is determined by the relative advantages of holding (1) money, and (2) earning assets. Now this is a step *toward* the Keynesian concept, but it is not the same thing. Nor is it the "bearishness" function in Keynes's *Treatise*. The schedule showing the volume of cash balances which the public desires to hold at various security *prices* (including equities, from whose prices it is possible to determine yields when earnings are given) is the "bearishness" schedule of Keynes's *Treatise*. This function may be written $L_a = L_a(A_a)$. This schedule should be distinguished not only from the Marshallian $k'A$, but also from that showing the volume of cash balances which the public wishes

---

[1] Keynes writes his transactions-demand function: $M_1 = L_1(Y)$. The author prefers, as indicated above, to reserve the symbol M for the supply of money, autonomously determined by the monetary authority. The author will write the demand function for transactions cash balances as $L_T = L_T(Y)$, and will use such subscripts as L_{T_1}, L_{T_2}, etc., to indicate specific *points* in the L_T schedule.

to hold at various interest rates—interest rates being inversely proportional to the prices of fixed-interest securities.[1] This latter is the second liquidity preference function of *The General Theory of Employment, Interest and Money*. In our system of notation it is $L_L = L_L(i)$.[2]

Keynes split up his liquidity preference function $M = L(Y, r)$ into two functions: $M_1 = L_1(Y)$, and $M_2 = L_2(r)$. In our system of notations these become $L = L(Y, i)$; $L_T = L_T(Y)$; and $L_L = L_L(i)$.

As a pedagogical device this separation of the function is helpful, and for analytical purposes useful at times. But it is impossible (unless one adopts rather arbitrary assumptions) to separate, statistically, active cash from idle cash. Moreover, under certain conditions the transactions demand for money L_T is a function not only of the level of income Y but also of the interest rate i; and similarly under certain conditions the "asset" demand for money L_L is a function not only of the rate of interest i but also of the level of income Y. Thus it is often better to consider desired cash balances as a whole, whether intended for transactions purposes or intended to be held as an asset. The total demand for money L is then regarded as a function of both income Y and the rate of interest i.

But now we have again lost sight of Marshall's $k'A$. True, in the L_L function we have taken account of the *price* of bonds, since the rate of interest is inversely proportional to the price of bonds. But Marshall's A is the aggregate *value* of bonds and other earning assets. Now the total value of earning assets is one of the determinants of the volume of cash balances which the public desires to hold. Thus, the demand for money L is a function of (1) income Y, (2) the rate of interest i, and (3) total assets A. Put in the form of an equation, $L = L(Y, i, A)$.

The crude quantity theory recognized that the L function was income-elastic, but it denied that it was interest-elastic. Any increase

---

[1] The Marshallian A is the *aggregate value* of assets; the "bearishness" function of the *Treatise* relates the demand for money to the *prices* of assets; and the liquidity preference function of *The General Theory of Employment, Interest and Money* relates the demand for money to the *prices* of *securities* (equities omitted).

[2] Keynes wrote it $M_2 = L_2(r)$ using r for the rate of interest. We shall use r to mean marginal efficiency of capital.

in the quantity of money would, therefore, be spent on goods and so raise income; none of the increased cash would be held as an idle asset. And the crude quantity theory had nothing to say about the effect of the aggregate value of assets on the desire to hold money. Moreover, Marshall did not specifically recognize the interest-elasticity of the demand for cash—the L_L function. Yet a partial recognition of the influence of the rate of interest is necessarily present when the aggregate value of assets is included (as Marshall had it) as a determinant of the demand for money. This is so because the rate of interest affects the value of whatever bonds are held. But it is only one factor. The *A* determinant of the demand for money is the total value of assets (largely securities). Now the total value of securities depends upon (1) the net *earnings* of securities (including equities), and (2) the rate of interest.

The demand for money (liquidity preference) is, particularly in the short run, mainly a function of income and the rate of interest. We shall therefore concentrate on the equation $L = L(Y, i)$. In short-run analysis, A may be neglected on the ground that it can be changed only by a small amount compared to the total stock.

Two other functions must be considered—the investment-demand schedule or the I function; and the consumption function $C(Y)$.

The Investment Function

The volume of investment is determined by the rate of interest in relation to the investment-demand schedule. The investment-demand schedule (the investment function) relates the *marginal efficiency* of capital—which we shall call *r*—to the *volume* of investment: thus $r = f(I)$. Now, since the volume of investment will be pushed to the point on the investment-demand schedule [1] where the marginal efficiency of capital *r* is equal to the rate of interest *i*, we can say that *r* tends to equal *i*. The volume of investment in any period of time is therefore a function of the rate of interest, given the investment-

---

[1] See Keynes, *The General Theory of Employment, Interest and Money*, Harcourt, Brace & Company, Inc., New York, 1936, pp. 136–137. See also Lerner, *The Economics of Control*, The Macmillan Company, New York, 1944, Chaps. 21 and 25.

demand schedule. The I function (the investment-demand schedule) may then be written, for short, as follows: $I = I(i)$.

The marginal efficiency of capital r is the expected rate of return on the investment in a specific new capital good, a machine for example. If the expected rate of return is in excess of the rate of interest, it will be profitable to invest in the machine.

If the *value* of a new capital good is in excess of its *cost*, it will pay to make an investment in it. Now the *value* of a new capital good is determined by its expected future yields, discounted (at the prevailing rate of interest) back to the present. If this *value* exceeds the *cost* of the capital good, investment in such good will be profitable.

If the expected future yields on the new capital good are high, the value of the capital good may far exceed the cost. How far the value will exceed the cost can neatly be stated by ascertaining the rate of discount which will equate the expected yields with the cost; this rate of discount is the marginal efficiency of capital. Thus, if the *value* of a new capital good exceeds the *cost* of the capital good, the marginal efficiency of capital r will exceed the rate of interest i.

Let the future yields over the life of the machine, say 3 years, be Q_1, Q_2, Q_3. Let r equal the rate of discount that will equate the present value of these future yields with the cost C of the machine. Then

$$C = \frac{Q_1}{1 + r} + \frac{Q_2}{(1 + r)^2} + \frac{Q_3}{(1 + r)^3} \, .$$

If C and the Q's are known, the r can be calculated. This r is the rate of return that it is expected can be earned on the cost of the machine—the marginal efficiency of capital.

The investment-demand schedule for the economy as a whole shows the amount of investment which can profitably be made in a given period at different rates of interest. This schedule is the I function, $I(i)$.[1] Thus in Fig. 4, if the rate of interest is i_0, the volume of investment will be OA; if the rate of interest is i_1, the volume of investment will be OB.

---

[1] In this book I use alternatively any one of the following three phrases as meaning the same thing: (1) investment-demand schedule, (2) the schedule of the marginal efficiency of investment, (3) the investment function. Sometimes the phrase "the schedule of the marginal efficiency of investment" is abbreviated to "marginal efficiency schedule."

Investment is also a function of income $\dot{Y}$ in the sense that the volume of investment is influenced by *changes* from one level of income to another—the acceleration principle. Moreover, investment may to some extent be a function of aggregate assets A. Thus $I = I(i, \dot{Y}, A)$.

The interest-elasticity of the investment function plays no part in the naïve form of the quantity theory which holds that *extra* cash

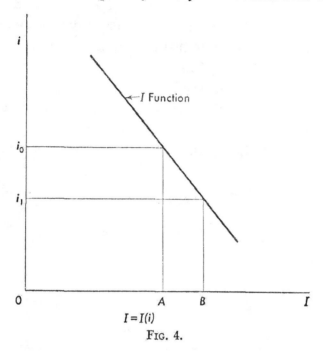

$I = I(i)$

FIG. 4.

balances (over and above those required for current transactions purposes) will quickly be spent in the commodity markets, whether for consumption or investment goods. The more sophisticated view [1] recognized that the relation between an increase in cash balances and the purchase of capital goods (investment) may be less direct. The flow of extra cash into increased investment may occur only as a result of a decline in the rate of interest. In this analysis, therefore, the interest-elasticity of the investment function *is* taken into account.

[1] See James Tobin, "Liquidity Preference and Monetary Policy," *Review of Economic Statistics*, May, 1947.

The Consumption Function

But it is also possible that increases in spending incident to increases in the quantity of money may be directed toward consumption goods. Accordingly, a third function must be taken account of—the C function. An increase in the quantity of money may cause an upward shift in the consumption function.

The consumption function is the schedule showing the various amounts that will be spent on consumption at different levels of income. Empirical data indicate that as income rises consumption rises also, but at a slower rate. At low income levels all of the income is consumed; at high income levels a considerable proportion is saved. Thus (using the time series concept of the consumption function [1]) the following figures drawn from the income data of the Department of Commerce illustrate the relation of consumption to income.[2]

Table 9

Year	National income (in billions of dollars)	Consumption expenditures (in billions of dollars)
1940	81.3	72.1
1937	73.6	67.1
1935	56.8	56.2

Consumption outlays are mainly a function of income; $C = C(Y)$. But consumption may also be a function of assets A, and perhaps also

[1] For a fuller discussion of the consumption function (both the time series concept and the family budget concept) see Alvin H. Hansen, *Economic Policy and Full Employment*, McGraw-Hill Book Company, Inc., New York, 1947, Chap. XIV. For a discussion of the *average* propensity to consume and the *marginal* propensity to consume, see Hansen, *Fiscal Policy and Business Cycles*, W. W. Norton & Company, New York, 1941, Chap. 11.

[2] Strictly speaking, these figures should be corrected for price changes. In this period, however, there were no large changes in the price level, and so the data given are substantially in *real terms*. Also population remained relatively constant. For a discussion of the importance of making corrections for price and population changes, see Alvin H. Hansen, *Fiscal Policy and Business Cycles*, p. 252.

of the rate of interest i. Accordingly, $C = C(Y, A, i)$, the variables involved being listed in the order of probable importance.[1]

The Three Functions: Summary

Putting the L, I, and C functions all together, we then have the following:

$$L = L(Y, i, A)$$
$$I = I(i, \dot{Y}, A)$$
$$C = C(Y, A, i)$$

If we concentrate upon what appear to be the more important factors[2] in each case we have:

$$L = L(Y, i)$$
$$I = I(i)$$
$$C = C(Y)$$

The role played by these three functions, together with the quantity of money in the theory of income determination, will be considered in detail in Chap. 5. The remainder of this chapter is devoted mainly to an analysis of the L function, together with its component parts, the L_T function and the L_L function.

The L_T Function

In Fig. 5 we show graphically the L_T function. This function is a schedule (or curve) showing the *desired* volume of active or "transactions" cash balances at various levels of income Y. If the level of income is Y_0, the desired volume of "transactions" cash will be L_{T_0}; if the income rises to Y_1, the cash balances desired will rise to L_{T_1}. In the event that the *actual* volume of "transactions" cash M_T can readily be increased whenever the desired volume rises, we may then assume that at each income level $M_T = L_T$, or *actual* cash balances equal *desired* cash balances. Thus at income Y_0 actual cash will be M_{T_0},

[1] For other complicating factors (notably a former high level of income) see James S. Duesenberry, "Income-Consumption Relations and Their Implications" in *Essays in Honor of Alvin H. Hansen*, W. W. Norton & Company, 1948, Chap. III.

[2] Note what is said on p. 57 about dropping A in short-run analysis.

and $M_{T_0} = L_{T_0}$; at income level Y_1 actual cash will be M_{T_1} and $M_{T_1} = L_{T_1}$.

Thus if the L_T function is a linear function of the form $L_T = kY$ and $L_T = M_T$, as represented in Fig. 5, then it follows that the velocity V of M_T is constant. As we shall see later, this need not necessarily be the case.

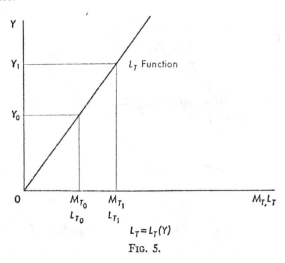

$$L_T = L_T(Y)$$

FIG. 5.

The L_L Function

In Fig. 6 the L_L function is shown graphically. It is a schedule of the *desired* volume of idle balances ("asset" money) at different levels of the rate of interest i.[1]

At a high rate of interest (i_0) only a small volume of idle balances L_{L_0} will be desired; at lower rates of interest, i_2 for example, the *desired* cash balances will rise to L_{L_2}. Put the other way round, the public cannot be induced willingly to hold large idle cash balances unless the rate of interest is pushed down to low levels.

The rate of interest is inversely proportional to the price of bonds. If the *actual* supply of money were increased, as was the case in the

---

[1] A *change* in expectations with respect to what is regarded as a *safe* level of i will produce a *shift* in the L_L function. See Keynes, *General Theory*, pp. 201–202. An interesting formulation of the role of the normal or *safe* level of i appears in Jørgen Pedersen, *Pengeteori Og Pengepolitik*, Copenhagen, 1944.

1930's owing to the gold inflows, the public (and in this case also the banks) found itself in possession of extra cash—more than it wished to hold at the existing level of interest rates. This means that the public was prepared to get rid of the extra cash in exchange for securities. Individuals and business firms bid against each other for bonds; and this process raised the prices of securities, causing a fall in the yield, *i.e.*, in the rate of interest. Eventually a price was reached at which the public was prepared to hold the extra cash; in other words, actual

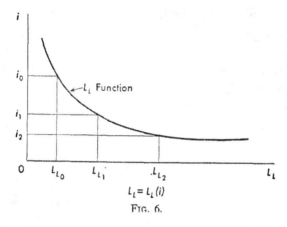

$$L_L = L_L(i)$$

FIG. 6.

cash balances were now no longer in excess of *desired* cash. An equilibrium point was again reached at which $L_L = M_L$.

In the case of the gold inflows, not only did deposits rise *pari passu* with the gold inflows; in addition, there occurred a corresponding increase in member-bank reserves. Thus banks also were flooded with excess cash. Naturally there would be a tendency for banks to convert this unearning cash asset into an earning asset. If commercial loans could not readily be made, at least the banks could buy outstanding bonds from the public. In so far as this was done the prices of bonds were bid up, and so interest rates declined.[1] The bonds were purchased from the public in exchange for newly created deposits—the public being induced to exchange the bonds for money by reason of the

[1] *Cf.* Walter S. Salant, "The Demand for Money and the Concept of Income Velocity," *Journal of Political Economy*, June, 1941.

favorable price offered for the bonds. Accordingly, the public was flooded with still more cash. This in turn would necessarily lead to still further competitive bidding for the outstanding bond issues held by individuals and business firms. This competitive bidding raised the price (lowered the rate of interest) until eventually a point was reached at which everyone was satisfied. The increased cash was now willingly held, in view of the new low rate of interest. The desired cash balances would thus again be brought into equilibrium with the enlarged volume of actual cash.

It will be noticed that the L_L function (as shown in Fig. 6) becomes highly elastic with respect to the rate of interest, the lower the rate of interest. This means that at a very slight fall in the rate of interest the public is willing to hold very large increased quantities of cash. In other words bond prices will rise very little (interest rates will virtually cease to fall) even though the money supply continues to grow.

The reason for this is the fear (or hope) that the price of bonds may fall. Many prospective investors may *fear* a loss, should they exchange the additional cash for very high priced bonds. A point, in other words, has been reached at which it seems safer to hold on to the cash. This is so because there is a danger that the price of the bond that is being considered for purchase might fall a point or two. If the bond is already so high priced that the yield amounts to only 2 per cent or less, a slight market decline within a 12-month period could easily wipe out all the interest yield, or even more. The higher the market price of bonds, the more dangerous it is to hold them. Thus any increase in cash may willingly be retained as idle balances rather than venture into the market. At this point the bond market can be pushed little or no further. Thus the fear of *loss* may induce the public to refrain from further security purchases; the alternative is simply to hold the additional cash as an idle asset.

Some heavy holders of cash may *hope* that the market will soon fall. If the bond market is likely to fall, it will be wiser to hold cash preparatory to entering the market later on more favorable terms. Those who confidently believe that the market will fall are likely to hold most of their assets in cash. The cash is held in the expectation that a profit can be made by waiting for a more favorable turn of the market. As is well known, conservative investment services advise clients in periods of uncertainty to hold a large part of their assets— often up to 50 per cent—in cash.

The holding of some part of one's total assets in cash may be regarded as prudent in order to ensure that much at least against loss of principal. Some part may be risked in earning assets, but not all. Holding cash means the foregoing of any return on that part of one's assets.[1] The foregoing of any yield is the price paid for the convenience and security of holding cash compared with holding earning assets. The rate of interest equates the relative advantages of holding securities with the advantages of holding cash. If the yield on securities is low, one foregoes little income by holding cash. The advantages of holding cash may in those circumstances outweigh the loss of yield. The lower the rate of interest, the less one pays (opportunity cost) for the privilege of holding one's assets in cash.

When the yield on securities is high, the risk of loss of principal is amply covered by the high rate of return. Accordingly, one may afford to risk *all* one's assets in income-yielding securities. But when the yield is low, the margin above the risk of loss is narrowed to a point at which one cannot afford to risk all one's assets in securities or other noncash assets; it then becomes prudent to hold a part in cash. The lower the yield, the greater will be the ratio of cash to earning assets that the investing public will deem it prudent to hold.

Thus the lower the rate of interest, the more difficult it becomes to push it down still further by monetary policy. If under these circumstances the monetary authorities increase the money supply, the public will be content simply to hold the extra cash. At the low yield there will be no tendency for individuals to bid securities away from each other, since in this case the premium paid for the advantages of liquidity and safety is slight. These advantages are (1) the prospective profits which may be made by having ready cash on hand should the market fall to a point believed favorable for investment, (2) the pros-

---

[1] If cash is held in the form of time deposits some interest may be earned. Time deposits are not quite equivalent to cash since they presumably involve a commitment not to withdraw the funds for a specified period. If withdrawn before this period, no interest is paid. They then become in effect demand deposits.

pective losses (when the market appears uncertain) which may be avoided by holding some part of one's assets in cash, and (3) the convenience of holding cash for unforeseen contingencies. Taken together, these reasons for holding cash illustrate the speculative and precautionary motives.

The Transactions versus the Asset Demand for Money

The quantity theorists believed that the demand for money was interest-inelastic. Even Keynes made the L_T function (our notation) interest-inelastic. But this is not necessarily the case. Let us suppose that income has risen so high that *all* the money supply has been drawn from idle cash balances into active balances, and that with further increases in income the monetary authorities refuse to add to the money supply. The crude quantity theorists would argue that this could simply not be possible, since no increase in income could in fact occur unless accompanied by increases in the transactions volume of money. But this is not so. If the money supply has been entirely absorbed for transactions purposes, further increases in income, in the absence of an increase in the quantity of money, would result in an increase in velocity. This the crude quantity theorists denied as a possibility. Income, in their view, could not increase if the money supply remained fixed. But this rigid position is not tenable. A higher rate of interest would indeed have to be offered in order to induce *a more intensive utilization* of the limited money supply. An entrepreneur who formerly held on the average $10,000 of cash for transactions purposes at a rather leisurely velocity may be induced at an attractive rate of interest to loan $2,000 to other businessmen whose sales have sharply increased and who desperately need larger cash balances. He can effect his own volume of transactions with average cash holdings of $8,000 if he uses his cash balance more intensively—in other words, increases the velocity or turnover of his balances. Thus at this point, even in the transactions sphere the demand function for money L_T becomes interest-elastic. This may be illustrated by the following diagram.

In Fig. 7 it is assumed that in the transactions sphere the L_T function is elastic with respect to interest at high interest rates, but wholly inelastic at a fairly wide range of low to medium rates of interest. The income effect on desired cash holdings L_T is here represented by shifts in the $L_T(i)$ function. As income rises from low levels to high levels, the $L_T(i)$ function shifts to the right. As this occurs money is drawn from the "assets" sphere to the "transactions" sphere. But eventually no idle money remains—the total money supply has been drawn into the transactions sphere. A higher volume of transactions must now

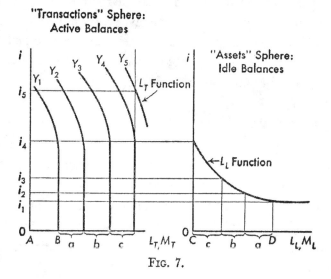

FIG. 7.

be circulated at a higher velocity of the constant transactions money supply. And this higher velocity can be squeezed out of the system, since many individuals and business firms can be induced to use their cash holdings more intensively (thereby setting funds free for the most needy users) by offering them a high rate of interest for the spare cash which they can loan out.

Starting (Fig. 7) with income Y_1, the *actual* cash is divided AB for transactions and CD for assets, and the interest rate is i_1. As income rises to Y_2, money equal to the volume designated by a is drawn from the assets sphere and added to the transactions sphere. Accordingly, interest rises to i_2. As income rises still higher to Y_3, more money b is drawn from the assets sphere (idle money) and added to the transactions sphere; interest rises to i_3. When income rises to Y_4, the last supply of idle cash balances c is drawn from the assets sphere and added to the transactions sphere; interest now rises to i_4. When income rises still higher to Y_5, no idle balances are available, and so the payments required to effect the exchange of goods at the higher volume of transactions can only be made by utilizing the fixed money supply more intensively, *i.e.*, at a higher velocity. And this more intensive use of the available money supply can only be induced by offering a higher rate of interest. Some individuals and businesses, especially those that are not expanding, can lend some part of their cash balances, using their remaining balances more intensively, *i.e.*, at a higher transactions velocity. Thus when no more idle money can be pumped into the transactions area, the interest rate is pushed up into an area in which the L_T function becomes interest-elastic. At income Y_5 the interest rate becomes i_5.

So long as money can be drawn from the assets (idle-balance) sphere into the transactions sphere, the velocity of transactions money M_T may remain nearly constant. But of course any transfer of money from idle balances to active balances means an increase in the velocity of the *total* money supply M. The idle money is drawn into the active sphere through the "pull" of the higher rate of interest. Thus the velocity of the *total* money supply tends to correlate directly with the rate of interest.

The Consolidated L Schedule

All this can conveniently be presented by means of a diagram consolidating the M_T and M_L into M, and the L_T and L_L functions into the L function. When this is done, as in Fig. 8, every increase in income induces an upward shift in the L function. If now the *actual* money supply is fixed, an upward shift in the L function will produce an increase in the rate of interest. And at this higher rate of interest it is possible to effect the larger transactions volume, incident to the rise in income, by means of a higher velocity of the total money stock M.

In Fig. 8 we have five L functions for each of five levels of income—Y_1, Y_2, Y_3, Y_4, Y_5. Every rise in income increases the transactions demand for money. Accordingly, the demand schedule for money as a whole is likely to rise.[1] In this event, if the actual money supply is fixed, the increased demand for money as a whole (active and idle) will raise the rate of interest. This increase in the rate of interest is the necessary compensation required to induce a more intensive utilization of money. The result is a rise in velocity.

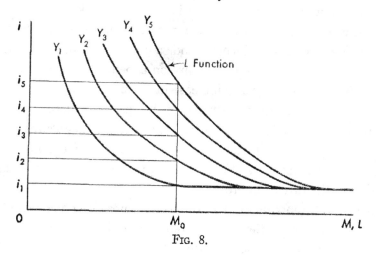

FIG. 8.

The Interest-elasticities of the Three Functions

We have considered the interest-elasticity of the L_T, L_L, and L functions. We turn now to the investment function. Whether or not, and to what degree, it is interest-elastic is highly significant for monetary theory and policy.

For the naïve quantity theorist, indeed, it makes no difference. The reason for this is that if the L function is regarded as wholly inelastic with respect to the rate of interest, any increase in the money supply would spill over *directly* into the commodity markets. Increased

---

[1] It is of course always possible that an increase in income might induce a fall in the demand for money to hold as an idle asset. When incomes are high and profits are promising, idle money may be drawn into active use. Thus it is possible that the rise in the L_T function may be exactly offset by a fall in the L_L function, so that the total L function remains where it was. In this event the increased demand for transaction cash will raise the velocity of the total money supply (M) without raising the rate of interest. But it could also be true that the initial increase in income may induce speculators to desire large idle cash preparatory to making *real* investment in inventories or equipment at the most favorable moment. In this event, both the L_T function and the L_L function would simultaneously rise.

purchases of consumption and investment goods would follow without any stimulation from a lower rate of interest. It is enough that the money supply is increased. The assumption is that no one would wish to hold any extra cash. If people temporarily should hold extra cash, they would want to get rid of it.

If this were necessarily the case, any changes in cash balances would at once affect the level of income (and so prices), regardless of the rate of interest. Investment and consumption expenditures are thought to be *directly* stimulated by any increase in the money supply.

In the more sophisticated version of the quantity theory, increased cash balances are indeed expected to raise total expenditures (and so income and prices), but via the interest-elasticity of the investment function. And in some versions consumption is also regarded as responsive to the rate of interest.

But if the L function at low levels of interest becomes completely elastic with respect to the rate of interest, then increases in the money supply will not be able to stimulate either investment or consumption. Thus the only effect of an increase in the money supply would be an increase in idle balances. If the L function is, in a part of the schedule, highly elastic (but not perfectly so) with respect to the rate of interest (as represented in the charts in this chapter), a reduction in the rate of interest consequent upon an increase in the quantity of money can have but little influence upon either investment or consumption expenditures.

Thus the interest-elasticities of the L function and the I function, together with the responsiveness of consumption to changes in the rate of interest, are fundamental in determining whether or not, and in what degree, an increase in the quantity of money can affect income, and through income the price level.

Four factors are needed to determine the relation of the rate of interest to income: (1) the investment-demand schedule, (2) the consumption function, (3) the liquidity preference schedule, and (4) the quantity of money created by the monetary authority. It is to a consideration of these factors that we shall turn in the next chapter.

Chapter 5

Income and the Rate of Interest

AN INCREASED QUANTITY of money may be spent in the commodity markets, thereby raising income to a point at which the excess cash becomes desired cash needed for transactions; or the extra cash may be applied to the purchase of securities, thereby reducing the rate of interest until the excess cash is willingly held as an idle balance. Accordingly, changes in the quantity of money may affect, more or less, both income and the rate of interest.

Determinants of Income and the Rate of Interest

But the quantity of money is only one determinant of income and the rate of interest. Other determinants are (1) the investment-demand schedule, (2) the consumption function, and (3) the liquidity preference schedule. These three, together with the quantity of money as fixed by the monetary authority, determine together the level of income and the rate of interest.[1] Put in the older terminology, we may restate the proposition as follows: There are four determinants of income and the rate of interest: (1) productivity, (2) thrift, (3) desire for cash, and (4) the quantity of money.

An equilibrium condition is reached when the desired volume of cash balances equals the quantity of money, when the marginal efficiency of capital is equal to the rate of interest, and finally, when the volume of investment is equal to the normal or desired volume of saving. And these factors are interrelated. Thus when the marginal efficiency of capital is high enough to promote a volume of investment adequate to balance the normal savings as determined by the thrift

---

[1] The analysis given in this chapter is based on Keynes's *General Theory;* but heavy reliance is placed upon the brilliant work of J. R. Hicks in his "Mr. Keynes and the Classics: A Suggested Interpretation," *Econometrica*, 1937.

habits of the community (*i.e.*, $I = S$ in the equilibrium sense), then it will be seen that the quantity of money will necessarily prove just sufficient to satisfy the public's desires to hold cash.[1]

We are thus launched upon a difficult and complicated course with many ramifications and interrelations. The relevant equations are: $I = I(i); C = C(Y); L = L(i, Y); M = L;$ and $Y = I + C(Y).$[2] The last equation means that the level of income, given the consumption function $C(Y)$, is determined by the volume of investment. And investment, in turn, is determined by the schedule of the marginal efficiency of investment in relation to the rate of interest. Finally, the liquidity preference function and monetary policy play important roles, as we shall see, in determining both the level of income and the rate of interest.

We begin with an analysis of the schedule of the marginal efficiency of investment. This is the "productivity" plank in the "four-piece" platform. The investment function $I = I(i)$, in conjunction with the investment multiplier, serves to establish a relation between the rate of interest and the level of real income.

In Fig. 9 the rate of interest is measured on the vertical axis and income on the horizontal axis. Given a certain marginal efficiency schedule, we know what the volume of investment will be at various rates of interest. From the equation $Y = I + C(Y)$ we can then determine the various levels of income.

In other words, given the investment function $I(i)$ and the consumption function $C(Y)$, we can determine the level of income for each rate of interest. The schedules showing the relation of income to the rate of interest, so determined, are shown in Fig. 9 in the *IS* curves.

The *IS* curves are drawn so as to show the relation of income and the rate of interest when the multiplier process has fully worked itself out; investment and savings are then in equilibrium. Savings and investment are always *equal*; but only when the full multiplier effect has been reached are savings and investment in *equilibrium*. At this

[1] This means that $M = L$ in the equilibrium sense.
[2] It is assumed that the various functions are stated in *real terms*.

point actual savings equal normal savings as determined by the normal marginal propensity to save.[1]

The IS Schedule

Given a certain marginal efficiency of investment schedule, a high rate of interest will permit only a little investment. This means a low

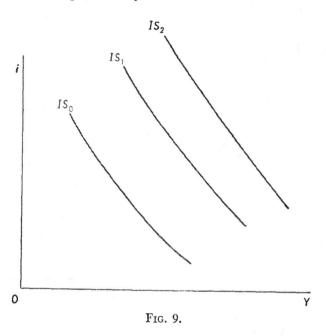

FIG. 9.

level of income, even where account is taken of the multiplier. At a low rate of interest, however, investment will be larger, and so the level of income (account being taken of the multiplier) will be relatively high. Accordingly, the *IS* curves slope downward to the right. Given the investment function and the consumption function (from which latter the multiplier is derived), income [2] is high at low rates of interest, and low at high rates of interest. The *IS* curves show the relation.

We begin with the IS_0 curve. Assume now an upward shift in the marginal efficiency schedule with no change in the rate of interest.

---

[1] See Appendix B, "A Note on Savings and Investment."

[2] It should be noted that the variables are measured in *real* terms. To translate money values into real terms various units of measurement might be used such as the wage-unit (Keynes), a weighted factor-cost-unit, or constant-value dollars.

This will cause the IS_0 curve to shift upward. Consumption may, however, lag behind for a time and only after several months reach a
normal relation to income. During the interval of this time lag income
will not rise by the full, or normal, multiplier. Eventually consumption
will have risen to normal, *i.e.*, by the full amount indicated by the
consumption function. Thus we finally reach the IS_1 curve. At this

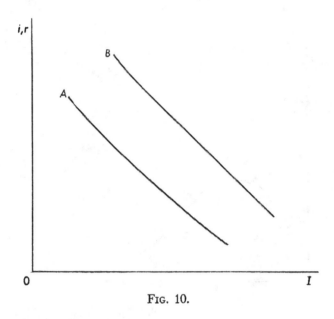

FIG. 10.

point investment and savings are again in equilibrium, and income
will have risen not only because of the increase in investment, but also
because of the induced rise in consumption. The full multiplier process,
in other words, will have worked itself out.

The curve IS_0 is based on the specific marginal efficiency schedule A,
the IS_1 curve, on the higher marginal efficiency schedule B, as shown
in Fig. 10. Thus the marginal efficiency schedule is the first determinant of the IS curves. The second determinant is the consumption
function. This is shown in Fig. 11.

Assume now an upward shift in the consumption function from C_1
to C_2 as shown in Fig. 11. With no change in the marginal efficiency
schedule (this schedule remaining as shown in curve B, Fig. 10) the
IS_1 curve (Fig. 9) would now shift upward to IS_2.

To repeat, the *IS* curves depend upon the level (and slope) of the marginal efficiency of investment schedule and equally upon the level (and slope) of the consumption function. An upward movement in the marginal efficiency schedule or in the consumption function, or both, will raise the level of income corresponding to each rate of interest. Thus in Fig. 9, IS_0 is shown shifting upward to IS_1 when the marginal

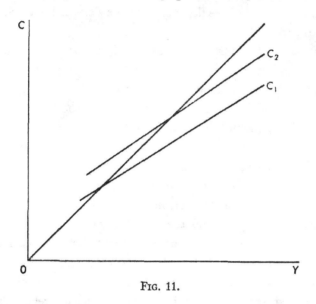

FIG. 11.

efficiency schedule is lifted (for example, through a surge of inventions and innovations) from A to B (Fig. 10); and finally it shifts to IS_2 if the consumption function is raised from C_1 to C_2 (Fig. 11).

A rise in the consumption function means a decline in thrift. The effect of changes in consumption (or thrift) upon income and the rate of interest can, as will be seen from the chart, be simply stated as follows: An increase in the propensity to consume, if the interest rate is given, will increase the level of income; a decrease in thrift (corresponding to a rise in the consumption function), the level of income being given, will raise the rate of interest. These relationships are disclosed in Fig. 9.

We have shown how shifts in (1) the marginal efficiency schedule, and (2) the consumption function will cause shifts in the *IS* schedules.

Now the *slope* of the consumption function, taken in conjunction with an upward *shift* in the marginal efficiency schedule, determines how far the *IS* schedule will shift. If the consumption function is steep, the multiplier will be high. This means that any increase in investment incident to an upward shift in the marginal efficiency of investment schedule will raise income (the interest rate remaining, we assume, unchanged) by some multiple depending on the slope of the consumption function.[1]

The slope of the marginal efficiency of investment curve—the *I* function—at different levels of the interest rate, together with the slope of the consumption function at different levels of income, determine together the slope of the *IS* curve. Assume that the investment function $I(i)$ is fairly elastic with respect to the interest rate at high rates, and fairly inelastic at low rates. Assume also that the consumption function is fairly steep (consumption being highly elastic with respect to income) at low income levels and flattens out (*i.e.*, becomes inelastic with respect to income) at high income levels. If the slopes of the investment function $I(i)$ and the consumption function $C(Y)$ are as described above, the effect is to make the *IS* curve elastic at high rates of interest and inelastic at low rates. In other words, given a marginal efficiency schedule and a consumption function of the character indicated above, income will rise rapidly with relatively small decreases in the rate of interest in the high-interest-rate range, but will increase very little even with large decreases in the rate of interest in the low-interest-rate range. Accordingly, under the conditions assumed the *IS* curve, which shows the relation of income and the interest rate, will be elastic with respect to interest rates in the upper range and inelastic at the lower range. But other assumptions could equally well be made, at any rate with respect to the interest-elasticity of the investment function. This is likely to change from one phase of the cycle to another, and from decade to decade in response to changing tech-

---

[1] The multiplier $= \dfrac{1}{1 - \dfrac{\Delta C}{\Delta Y}}$. See Keynes, *General Theory*, Chap. 10; and Hansen, *Fiscal Policy and Business Cycles*. Chaps. 11 and 12.

nological conditions. In the depression phase of the cycle, however, the I function is likely to be interest-inelastic.

The LM Schedule

Now the liquidity preference function L and the money supply M also establish a relation between income and the rate of interest.

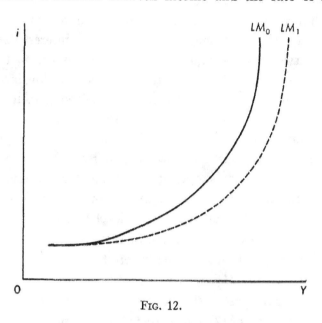

FIG. 12.

Given a certain liquidity preference (demand schedule for money) and a certain supply of money fixed by the monetary authority, the rate of interest will be low when income is low and high when income is high. The curve showing this relation we shall call the LM curve. It is the curve showing the relation between income and interest (given the L function and the supply of M) when the *desired* cash equals the *actual* cash, or when $L = M$. The LM curve presupposes equilibrium between L and M, just as the IS curve presupposes equilibrium between I and S. The LM curve is shown in Fig. 12.

From the liquidity preference schedule shown in Fig. 8 in Chap. 4, it is evident that the rate of interest tends to vary inversely (though not proportionally) with the quantity of money. An increase in the money supply will tend to lower the rate of interest. But the money supply must be regarded as large or small according to the size of the national income. If now we assume a money supply rigidly fixed by the monetary authority, a low level of income will mean a *relatively* abundant money supply and so a low rate of interest; a high income will mean a *relatively* small money supply and so a high rate of interest. This is what the curve *LM* shows.

At high levels of income there is a large "transactions" demand for the limited quantity of money, and so the rate of interest rises steeply; the *LM* curve becomes highly inelastic with respect to the rate of interest at high income levels. On the other hand, at low income levels there is a small "transactions" demand for the fixed quantity of money, and so a large part of the money may be held as an idle balance; the effect is to lower the rate of interest. But since the liquidity preference function *L* is highly elastic at low interest rates, the relative super-abundance of the money supply at low income levels cannot drive the rate of interest much below a certain minimum. Therefore no matter how low (beyond a certain point) the level of income may fall, the rate of interest will cease to decline further. In other words, the *LM* curve at low income levels becomes interest-elastic. .

The dotted curve LM_1 represents a shift in the *LM* schedule caused by either (1) an increase in the quantity of money *M* controlled by the monetary authority, or (2) a decrease in liquidity preference. Assuming no change in liquidity preference, any increase in the quantity of money will shift the *LM* curve to the right; and similarly, assuming no change in the quantity of money, any decrease in the demand for money (the *L* function) will ease the situation and so tend to lower the rate of interest at any given income level, or conversely raise the level of income consistent with any given rate of interest. Thus either a decrease in the liquidity preference or an increase in the quantity of money will shift the *LM* curve to the right, as shown in LM_1.

The Intersection of the IS and LM Curves

Let us now combine the *LM* curve and the *IS* in one single diagram. The *LM* curve is interest-inelastic at high income levels [1] and interest-

---

[1] Income levels are expressed in real terms.

elastic at low income levels; the IS curve may be interest-elastic at high levels of income and interest-inelastic at low income levels. At least in the depression phase (low income levels) the IS curve is likely to be interest-inelastic owing to the interest-inelasticity of the I function in this phase of the cycle. This is shown in Fig. 13.

In this diagram (Fig. 13) three IS curves are drawn. The IS_0 curve intersects the LM_0 curve at a point at which the IS_0 curve is rela-

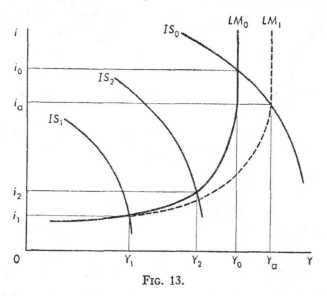

FIG. 13.

tively interest-elastic while the LM_0 curve is interest-inelastic. At this point of intersection of the two curves the interest rate i_0 and the income Y_0 are mutually determined.

Assume that Y_0 is less than a full employment income. If now the monetary authority should increase the money supply so that LM_0 is shifted to LM_1, the rate of interest would fall to i_a and income would rise to Y_a. This would mean boom conditions, since Y_0 already represents high employment. Thus if the IS curve is interest-elastic while the LM curve is interest-inelastic, an increase in the quantity of money will have an expansionist effect.

Consider, on the other hand, the intersection of the IS_1 curve with the LM_0 curve. The IS_1 curve at the point of intersection is relatively interest-inelastic, while the LM_0 curve is highly interest-elastic. This situation represents a condition which may under certain circumstances be found in advanced industrial countries, rich in the accumulated volume of capital formation.[1] In such countries the marginal efficiency of capital may have been pushed to a relatively low point, and it may be difficult to open investment outlets of any considerable magnitude by merely lowering the rate of interest. The investment function $I(i)$ being interest-inelastic, the IS curve would also tend to be interest-inelastic. In this circumstance investment outlets would have to await an upward shift in the marginal efficiency schedule, caused for example by technological innovations, the invention of new processes and new products, public development of regional resources, public investment in urban redevelopment, public lending and guaranteeing operations stimulating private investment in housing and rural electrification, etc. Technology and public investment (wisely chosen) can push the marginal efficiency schedule far to the right, thereby opening large investment outlets even though the I function is interest-inelastic.

At the point of intersection (Fig. 13) of the IS_1 and LM_0 curves, the LM_0 curve is highly interest-elastic. Obviously in this case income and employment cannot be raised by increasing the quantity of money; monetary policy is ineffective. In order to raise income from Y_1 to Y_2 it is necessary to shift the IS_1 curve to IS_2. And this can be achieved only by either raising the marginal efficiency schedule or shifting upward the consumption function. Either or both of these actions would shift the IS_1 curve to the right toward IS_2.

At the point of intersection of the IS_2 and LM_0 curves the IS_2 schedule is interest-inelastic. Monetary policy designed to increase the quantity of money would shift the LM curve to LM_1. This would have the effect of lowering the rate of interest a little, but it would have very little effect on income. Such action would not be noticeably expansionist. The main effect would be that at a lower rate of interest more money would be held as idle balances.

---

[1] Of course a devastating war, such as the Second World War, will for a time make even rich countries capital-poor. A destructive war opens up for many years vast investment outlets. It is easy to overcome any tendency toward secular stagnation if we fight a great war every 10 or 15 years; but this is not a tolerable method of solving the savings-investment problem.

Price Inflation

If the investment function is interest-elastic *when full employment is reached*, the quantity theory may give a fairly accurate account of the relation of money to prices. In these conditions an increase in the money supply will raise the aggregate money demand *without increasing real income*. Thus prices will rise.

This inflationary process can readily be represented in a diagram similar to Fig. 13 *but stated in money terms*. On this basis the *IS* curve and the *LM* curve would *both* move to the right simultaneously, leaving the rate of interest about the same or possibly higher. Thus in an inflationary situation the rate of interest and the money income may *both* rise together. This is the Wicksellian inflationary process in which the *IS* curve (in money terms) is shifting to the right more rapidly than the *LM* curve; the "natural" rate tends to outrun the "money" rate.

Summary

In this chapter we have considered the role of productivity, thrift, the *L* function, and the money supply as determinants of both income and the rate of interest. The analysis shows that income and the rate of interest are mutually determined by (1) the marginal efficiency schedule (productivity), (2) the consumption function (the level of the curve varies with the degree of thriftiness), (3) the liquidity preference schedule, and (4) the quantity of money.

It is clear that productivity and thrift have very much to do with the rate of interest.[1] A change in thrift will affect the consumption function and in this way influence the level of income; and the level of income will in turn affect liquidity preference and so the rate of interest. It is not true that an increase in the marginal efficiency of capital (caused, for example, by a higher level of technique) will have no effect on the rate of interest. An upward shift in the marginal efficiency schedule will affect the rate of interest through its effect on

[1] See D. H. Robertson, *Essays in Monetary Theory*, P. S. King & Staples, Ltd., London, 1940, Chap. I. Considering the Keynesian system as a whole without concentrating too narrowly on certain passages in the *General Theory*, there is much more agreement between Robertson and Keynes than appears on the surface.

income, which in turn will affect the liquidity preference schedule and so the rate of interest. Thus when Keynes says that the rate of interest is determined by liquidity preference and the money supply, he is concentrating on the immediate determinants, and for the moment taking for granted the influence of changes in the marginal efficiency schedule and the consumption function on liquidity preference. Taking a broad view of the Keynesian theory of the determination of income and the rate of interest, it is evident that account must be taken of the combined roles of the marginal efficiency schedule, the consumption function, liquidity preference, and the money supply. Indeed, all these factors are heavily drawn upon in the analysis which emerges, looked at as a whole, in *The General Theory of Employment, Interest and Money*.[1]

[1] It is quite true, as many critics have pointed out, that Keynes was prone to emphasize unduly new features of his analysis, and in so doing often made striking but incomplete statements which, taken by themselves, give the impression that he neglected the role of (1) the consumption function (and so thrift), and (2) the marginal efficiency schedule (productivity) in his interest theory.

Chapter 6

The Income Theory:
Tooke, Wicksell, Aftalion, Keynes

Volume of Expenditures versus Quantity of Money

Keynes's theory of money and prices, while it has some novel features and adds considerably to our analytical equipment, runs nonetheless in a stream of thinking that has its sources far back in the history of monetary ideas. His approach is the income approach. It is the volume of expenditures, not the quantity of money, to which primary attention must be given. Monetary policy is nonetheless important. But the quantity of money is relegated to a secondary, though still significant, place.

Leading attention has increasingly been given to total expenditures and income. The rise and fall of expenditures represents a broader field of inquiry; and the factors determining aggregate outlays (income) are more complex than those traditionally considered by the quantity theory of money.[1]

The quantity theory concerned itself with prices, not with income. This indeed could be expected, in view of the traditional economic theory—according to which real income, or output, was determined by the quantity and efficiency of the factors of production and by the prevailing level of technique. On this basis the volume of money expenditures, or money income, had no significance in terms of em-

[1] "The quantity of money is a secondary factor compared with the volume of expenditures. The notion that the quantity of money is a causative factor in the state of business has given way to regarding it as a consequence. Changes in the level of prices are not the most important phenomenon of the economic system, and we hold today that it is a lack of spending, a lack of income rather than a lack of money, that produces a depression. The quantity of money, in short, is not a dominant cause of the fluctuations of prices and is a very imperfect guide to the causes of the trade cycle." G. Findlay Shirras, reviewing the work of Irving Fisher in the *Economic Journal*, September, 1947, p. 398.

ployment, output, or real income. The volume of money outlays only affected *prices*. If indeed it were true that output and employment were exclusively determined by *real* factors such as those enumerated above, then the volume of money expenditures could have no significance except in terms of prices.

The volume of total expenditures may, however, affect employment and output no less than prices. Total expenditures are outlays made in the process of production, and these outlays are received by the factors of production; they thus become, in the period in question, income at factor cost. Thus the income theory of prices and output can be stated in the form of an equation as follows: $P = \dfrac{Y}{O}$, in which P means the price level, Y the level of money income, and O the level of output or real income.

Wicksell, in his *Lectures on Political Economy*, stated the income theory in the following manner:

"A general rise in prices is therefore only conceivable on the supposition that the general demand has for some reason become, or is expected to become, greater than the supply. . . . Any theory of money worthy of the name must be able to show how and why the monetary or pecuniary demand for goods exceeds or falls short of the supply of goods in given conditions." [1]

The Velocity of Money

Money transfers involve the turnover of money in a round of transactions. The total transactions volume represents the total purchases and sales of all goods and services in a given period. But this represents a vast amount of double counting. Raw materials are partly fabricated by one firm and sold to another firm for further fabrication. Eventually in finished form they are sold to a wholesaler, who in turn sells them to a retailer, and he to a final consumer. These materials, in various stages of fabrication, are thus sold over and over again.

---

[1] Knut Wicksell, *Lectures on Political Economy*, The Macmillan Company, New York. 1935, vol. II, "Money," pp. 159–160. Reprinted by permission of The Macmillan Company, New York and London, and George Routledge & Sons, Ltd., and Kegan Paul, Trench, Trubner & Co., Ltd., London.

Total transactions, therefore, are many times larger than the value of the goods and services flowing to the final purchaser. Thus the total value of transactions may be ten to twelve times larger than the value of the final goods and services which constitutes the net national income. The turnover of money for transactions payments is therefore many times greater than the turnover of money for income payments. The transactions velocity of money we shall call V', and the income velocity V. Thus MV' equals the money value of transactions, and MV equals income Y. Accordingly $Y = MV = PO$; in other words, *money income* equals *money* times *income velocity*, and this in turn equals the money value of output PO.

A fundamental difference between the quantity theory and the income theory can be stated in terms of two opposing interpretations of the equation $MV = Y$. According to the quantity theory it is the quantity of money and its "behavior" (velocity) which explains the level of income. According to the income theory it is the flow of expenditures which explains the quantity of money and its velocity.

The Money Supply: Active or Passive Role

An increase in the flow of total expenditures on final goods and services (which becomes income to the factors) will indeed necessitate an increase either in M or V or both; so also, if a man grows corpulent he will be compelled to wear a larger belt. But according to the quantity theory, if you first "let out your belt" you will in *consequence* of this action necessarily grow fat![1]

Let us assume that businessmen decide to expand operations and so to make outlays on additional fixed and working capital. Partly they may invest their own funds, partly they may borrow from the capital market, and partly they may borrow from banks. Thus the quantity of money may be increased *because* they see opportunities for profitable investment. The increase in the money supply is a consequence of investment activity. The same analysis applies to an expansion of consumer credit. In these cases it is the decision to spend, whether for investment or consumption, that causes the money supply to grow.

[1] This analogy has been used somewhere by Keynes, and perhaps by others.

So also with the government war outlays. It was the rapid increase in governmental expenditures which caused income to rise. It is true that the money income would have risen less rapidly if a smaller proportion of the outlays had been financed by borrowing from the banks (monetary expansion). As a practical matter, however, all the funds could not be raised by borrowing from the capital market and by taxation. As often in the case of large private investment, bank credit was used. The war outlays were not made because the money supply increased; the money supply was increased because the expenditures had to be made.

The banking system, in what is said above, is regarded as playing a passive role, increasing and decreasing the money supply in accordance with the requirements of private outlays and governmental expenditures. This was the position taken by Tooke and the banking school.[1]

But of course the monetary authority *could* increase [2] the money supply in the first instance—say, by monetizing existing assets. The banking system could purchase securities held by the public, thus increasing deposits; and the increase in the quantity of money *could* cause an increase in spending. All this the income theory does not deny. The income theory, however, refuses to take short cuts. It holds that there is not any direct route from quantity of money to level of expenditures or income. Increased outlays *may*, according to circumstances, follow from an increase in money. That all depends. And the answer runs in terms of the theory of income determination.

In particular we need to know (1) the interest-elasticity of the investment function, (2) the sensitiveness of the consumption function to shifts in the rate of interest, and (3) the interest-elasticity of the liquidity preference function. The income theory does not deny an

---

[1] Wicksell states Tooke's position as follows: Apart from loans to government, "the banks are entirely dependent on the requirements of the business world for means of payment and have no means of affecting these requirements or of influencing prices." *Interest and Prices*, The Macmillan Company, New York, 1936, p. 82. Reprinted by permission of The Macmillan Company, New York and London.

[2] According to the quantity theory, not only could the banks control the *quantity* of money, but also its *value*. "The above question, as to whether it is in the power of banks to regulate at will the exchange value of money and conversely prices, was answered by Ricardo with a decided affirmative." *Ibid.*, p. 81.

important role to the money supply. Money is one of the variables in the equations. Its impact on prices is, however, not taken for granted. The question is: what part does money play in income determination? In short, to paraphrase the statement quoted above from Wicksell: Any theory of money worthy of the name must show how and why the level of money income rises or falls in relation to aggregate output.

Tooke on the Income Theory

Tooke argued that it was income that determined prices. In his *An Inquiry into the Currency Principle*, his twelfth proposition was: "That the prices of commodities do not depend upon the quantity of money . . . but that, on the contrary, the amount of circulating medium is a consequence of prices."[1] The famous thirteenth proposition stated:

> "That it is the quantity of money, constituting the revenues of the different orders of the State, under the head of rents, profits, salaries, and wages, destined for current expenditure, that alone forms the limiting principle of the aggregate of money prices, the only prices that can properly come under the designation of general prices. As the cost of production is the limiting principle of supply, so the aggregate of money incomes devoted to expenditure for consumption is the determining and limiting principle of demand."[2]

Here we have one of the earliest and perhaps the first clear statement of the income theory of prices. It is the level of income that determines the effective demand for consumers' goods. By reading a little between the lines, we have here, moreover, in general terms a statement of the consumption function. The "power of purchase by the consumers depends upon their incomes; and the measure of the extent and of the exercise of such power is . . . in that portion of their revenues which is destined for expenditures on objects of immediate consumption."[3] Thus consumption expenditures are a function of income, and this

[1] Thomas Tooke, *An Inquiry into the Currency Principle*, London, 1844, pp. 123–124.
[2] *Ibid.*, p. 124.
[3] *Ibid.*, p. 71.

relation "forms the limiting principle of the aggregate of money prices."
On the other side, "the cost of production is the limiting principle of
supply." Thus the level of prices is determined by the relation of
aggregate demand to aggregate supply. In equation form we may
state this as follows: $P_c = \dfrac{D_c}{O_c}$, in which P_c is the price level of consumers' goods, D_c is the aggregate demand for consumers' goods, and
O_c is the aggregate supply of consumers' goods.

Tooke's emphasis on income and aggregate demand led him to
stress the effect of high wages on demand. But he also recognized that
wages cut both ways—they affect both demand and costs. If wage
increases are not offset by increased efficiency, then higher wages will
raise aggregate demand without increasing the aggregate supply, and
so prices will rise.

> "Of the revenues or incomes of the community devoted to
> immediate expenditures, by far the largest proportion consists of
> wages. . . . Any increase, accordingly, of incomes, of which wages
> constitute the largest part, will raise general prices, and a fall in
> wages will depress them, supposing no alteration in the cost of
> production, or in the actual and contingent supply." [1]

Aggregate demand is a function of private and public spending.
Thus it was that the

> "enormous amount of the government expenditure caused the
> great and increasing demand for all the leading articles of con-
> sumption. . . . But the theory of war-demand, as having raised
> prices, and of the peace as having, by the consequent cessation of
> that demand, been necessarily followed by a fall of prices, is now
> rarely advanced. The preponderant, and almost exclusive theory,
> is that which refers all the phenomena of high prices from 1793
> until 1819, and of the comparative low prices since 1819, to
> alterations in the system of our currency. . . ." [2]

[1] *Ibid.*, pp. 71–72.

[2] Tooke and Newmarch, *A History of Prices*, Adelphi Company, New York (6 vols.),
vol. I, p. 2.

Wicksell's Analysis

Wicksell found Tooke's analysis of income, aggregate demand, and prices highly suggestive and makes it the starting point for his theory of money and prices. But he disagreed with Tooke's version of the role of interest in the dynamic process of income determination. Accepting Tooke's analysis of the relation of income to prices, he set himself the task of explaining how and why income (aggregate demand) rises and falls. His analysis of the relation of the loan rate of interest to the natural rate is an outstanding contribution to the theory of income determination. By concentrating upon the rate of interest, he swept away the narrow foundations of the quantity theory. But his influence on the English-speaking world was negligible for more than a quarter of a century after he published his *Geldzins und Güterpreise* in 1898.[1] Moreover, his work falls short of an adequate theory of income determination. It related mainly to one determinant of income—the investment function.

Investment was, in his view, determined by the rate of interest in relation to the natural or real rate. A decline in the loan rate below the real rate must "provide a stimulus to trade and production, and alter the relation between supply and demand of goods and productive services. . . ."[2]

An expansion of investment in durable capital "will take place when their earnings increase or when the rate of interest falls, so that their capital value now exceeds their cost of reproduction."[3] This statement corresponds very nearly not only with Keynes's definition of the marginal efficiency schedule, but also with his formulation of the determinants of investment. For both Wicksell and Keynes, investment will expand when the present capitalized value of the prospective earnings of new capital goods exceeds their cost. In other words, investment will be made when there is a spread between the marginal efficiency of capital (Wicksell's natural rate) and the rate of interest.

According to Wicksell, an increase in investment would raise aggre-

---

[1] This work was translated into English and published under the title *Interest and Prices*, The Macmillan Company, New York, 1936.

[2] Wicksell, *Interest and Prices*, p. 89.

[3] *Ibid.*, p. 134.

gate demand, and this in turn (at full or nearly full employment) will raise prices. A fall in the rate of interest below "normal" will cause the general level of prices to rise, and in the same way a rise in the rate of interest above "normal" will result in a continuous fall in the prices of goods and services.

"These statements sound extremely bold and indeed paradoxical. But it has to be remembered that the rate of interest referred to . . . as the 'normal' rate, away from which our deviations are imagined to originate, does not always remain the same and cannot be thought of as so much per cent. It merely means that rate which, having regard to the situation in the market, would be necessary for the maintenance of a constant level of prices. . . . That there must always be such a rate was the implicit assumption underlying our whole argument.[1] [The rate which is] neutral with respect to commodity prices comes to much the same thing [as] the current value of the *natural rate of interest on capital.* . . .[2] The natural rate is not fixed or unalterable in magnitude. . . . In general, we may say, it depends on the efficiency of production; on the available amount of fixed and liquid capital. . . ." [3]

Wicksell made it clear that he had "purposely avoided the statement that for the maintenance of stable prices it is necessary that the money rate and the natural rate should be *equal*. In practice they are both rather vague conceptions." It might be a question simply of the

"constancy of the excess of the natural rate over the money rate, corresponding to the unavoidable risks of enterprise and the like. The essential point is that the maintenance of a constant level of prices depends, other things remaining equal, on the maintenance of a certain rate of interest on loans, and that a permanent discrepancy between the actual rate and this rate exerts a *progressive and cumulative* influence on prices.[4]

[1] *Ibid.*, p. 100.
[2] *Ibid.*, p. 102.
[3] *Ibid.*, p. 106.
[4] *Ibid.*, pp. 120–121.

"But the explanation suggested by the Quantity Theory—that rising prices are due to an excess of money, falling prices to a scarcity—does not accord with actually observed movements of the rate of interest. . . . Observation teaches us, however, that when prices are rising there is a continual *rise* in rates of interest, and that when prices are falling there is a continual *fall* in rates of interest.[1]

"All these difficulties and complications at once disappear when it is changes, brought about by independent factors, in the *natural rate of interest on capital* that are regarded as the essential cause of such movements. These changes can be regarded as the cause, not only of the movement of prices, but indirectly of the analogous but somewhat later alterations in the money rate of interest. Abundance or scarcity of money, and in particular the quantity of cash held by the banks, is now imbued with a merely secondary importance. Such factors are to be regarded as consequences of changes in the demand for instruments of exchange brought about by changes in the level of prices. It still remains true, however, that they *may* take their origin in independent causes (the production of precious metals, issue of paper money, development of the credit system, etc.), and that they then have an independent significance in regard to movements of prices, in so far as they accelerate or retard the movement of the money rate of interest to the new position of the natural rate. . . .[2]

"A rise in industrial productivity raises in the first instance the natural rate of interest, so that prices rise if the money rate is for the moment kept unaltered.[3]

With respect to the long period of peace after 1815, Wicksell said: "While the development of industry continued unceasingly, it gave rise at the same time to a tremendous accumulation of capital. . . . There must have been a rapid fall in the natural rate of interest."[4]

"The period 1851–73 was distinguished, not only by a general progressive movement in industry, but in particular by the

[1] *Ibid.*, p. 167.   [3] *Ibid.*, p. 171.
[2] *Ibid.*   [4] *Ibid.*, p. 172.

freezing of enormous quantities of liquid capital as a result of the completion of the west European railway system. For both of these reasons, the natural rate of interest is generally admitted to have stood abnormally high. [It seems very doubtful that the money rate of interest] rose as much as the natural rate, partly because the large increase in the production of gold and the issue of paper money in America, in Austria, and finally in France, were working in the opposite direction.[1]

"Since 1871 [to 1898] western Europe and the United States have enjoyed uninterrupted peace. [Many milliards have indeed been swallowed up in the] frightful growth of armies and armaments; [still there can be] no comparison in point of capital wastage with an actual war. Railway building, though it was continued on an enormous scale, took place mainly in countries outside Europe, or in its more remote regions. In short, there was a considerable lack of really profitable openings for the additions to liquid capital which arose out of the savings of almost all classes of the community. . . . The natural rate of interest consequently fell everywhere. . . .[2]

"The money rate of interest also fell, but whether it fell to *a corresponding degree* must be regarded as doubtful. . . . The production of gold was slackening . . . cash payments were resumed in several countries (France, the United States), and finally silver was extensively demonetized. . . . But the extent of the banks' reserves . . . warns us against . . . attaching undue importance to these influences. It has rather to be supposed that the banks, as a result either of discretion or of routine, have often been reluctant to allow their rates of interest to accommodate themselves immediately to the situation on the market, and have preferred to allow an ever increasing amount of their cash reserves to lie idle, earning no interest." [3]

All proposals for stabilizing the value of money can "attain their objective only in so far as they exert an indirect influence on the *money*

---

[1] *Ibid.*, p. 174.
[2] *Ibid.*, pp. 174–175.
[3] *Ibid.*, p. 175.

rate of interest, and bring it into line with the natural rate, or below it, more rapidly than would otherwise be the case." [1]

These quotations disclose the gulf between Wicksell and the quantity theory. Fluctuations in the marginal productivity of capital, together with a lagging adjustment of the rate of interest, cause expansion or contraction of the aggregate demand for goods and services. But the multiplier analysis, based on the consumption function, was missing. There is, moreover, implicit in much of Wicksell's work an excessively optimistic view with respect to the interest-elasticity of investment. And he saw very dimly the relation of the demand for cash holdings to the rate of interest.[2] He failed to see that in certain situations the investment function may be interest-inelastic while the liquidity preference function may be highly interest-elastic.[3] Wicksell did not clearly understand the conditions under which interest-rate policy becomes futile. Accordingly, he enormously exaggerated the power of the banking system to control, by means of interest-rate manipulations, the flow of aggregate demand and the level of prices.

Aftalion

Aftalion,[4] in 1925, made an effective statement of the income theory of money and prices, putting it for the first time in the form of an

---

[1] *Ibid.*, p. 188.

[2] Wicksell did indeed point out that in periods when the natural rate is low, banks "have preferred to allow an ever increasing amount of their cash reserves to be idle, earning no interest." (*Interest and Prices*, p. 175.) But he means by this only that the banks tend in such situations to hold their rate of interest too high in relation to the natural rate. In his *Lectures on Political Economy* (The Macmillan Company, New York, 1935), vol. II, "Money," p. 23, there is a limited recognition of the precautionary motive for holding cash, at least for short periods. Also he says (citing Mangoldt) that at "low rates of interest, especially in primitive conditions, a number of people, for reasons of convenience or fear of taking risks, prefer to have large sums of money idle. . . ." (*Ibid.*, p. 197.)

[3] Ricardo rightly insists, says Wicksell, "that a fall in money interest can only take place so long as the surfeit of money has not led to a corresponding increase in prices. As soon as this occurs there no longer exists any surfeit of money, relatively to the requirements of turnover. . . ." (*Ibid.*, p. 179.) Ricardo's statement, it should be remembered, was intended to apply to conditions of full employment.

[4] See *Revue d'économie politique*, May-June and July-August, 1925. Aftalion's thinking was stimulated by Wieser's article "Der Geldwert und seine Veränderungen," *Schriften des Vereins für Sozialpolitik*, 1909. Another important steppingstone in the development of the theory was Schumpeter's "Das Sozialprodukt und die Rechenpfennige," *Archiv für Sozialwissenschaft und Sozialpolitik*, 1917.

equation, $R = PQ$ (R being the money income, P the price level, and Q the total production). Price fluctuations, Aftalion explained, depend upon the respective movements of the *money* income in relation to the *real* income. If the first increases while the second is stationary or lags behind, prices will rise.

Aftalion pointed out that the income theory has the advantage that it squares with the modern theory of value with its supply and demand schedules. Instead of a truistic, identity equation, as the quantity theory has it, the income theory introduces concepts of schedules of economic behavior. As the money income changes, shifts occur in the demand and supply schedules for goods and services. Instead of viewing the problem mechanistically, as the quantity theory does, the income theory is able to formulate the problem in terms which explain why buyers and sellers act as they do. The income theory substitutes an explanation in terms of *men* for the explanation of the quantity theory which runs in terms of *things*. The income theory takes account of the incomes of individuals and the psychological effect of variations in income on demand and price. It does not forget that economic movements are imputable to human desires, aspirations, and wants; that economic laws cannot be explained except in terms of the behavior of human beings. It substitutes economic motives for mechanical and external necessities.

The effect of an increase of incomes upon price will be different, depending on who the individuals are who are benefited. What kind of people have had their incomes raised—rich or poor, savers or spenders, consumers of luxuries or consumers of necessities? The increase of income does not affect price mechanistically or automatically. It operates through the desires of those whose incomes are raised.[1]

But Aftalion, like Tooke, did not undertake any systematic analysis of income determination. Aftalion was indeed concerned, in his work in business cycles,[2] with *oscillations* of the economy. These he thought were to be explained mainly in terms of the difficulties of entrepreneurs to adjust production, in a society using the roundabout or capitalistic process, to consumer demand. These oscillations are intensified by

[1] See Alvin H. Hansen, *Business-Cycle Theory*, Ginn & Company, Boston, 1927, pp. 145–146.

[2] Albert Aftalion, *Les Crises périodiques de surproduction*, M. Rivière et Cie, Paris, 1913.

reason of the acceleration principle under which the derived demand for producers' goods fluctuates more violently than the relatively stable movements of consumer demand.[1]

Keynes

Neither Wicksell nor Aftalion offered any satisfactory theory of income determination, but only a theory of an upward or downward cumulative process. It remained for Lord Keynes to construct a theory which set forth the determinants of income—not simply a theory of oscillation or of upward and downward movements. This more general theory can indeed be used to explain (or at least help explain) the oscillations about any equilibrium norm. But more than that, it seeks to explain the level of income toward which the economy tends. The Keynesian theory, discussed very briefly here, is developed in greater detail in Chap. 9 of this book.

Aggregate expenditures or outlays consist of (1) private investment outlays on capital goods such as houses, factories, and machines, (2) private consumption expenditures, and (3) government outlays on public services, public works, and other public investment projects. If we designate the aggregate outlays (which constitute the income flow) by Y, investment outlays by I, consumer outlays by C, and government outlays by G, we get the following equation: $Y = I + C + G$.

Private investment outlays and governmental outlays are in large measure autonomously determined, independent of the level of income. Hence these outlays are peculiarly important in the generation of income.[2] For when private investment and governmental outlays increase, consumption expenditures will also rise. This follows from the fact that an increase in private investment and in governmental outlays will bring about an increase in the Net National Product (or the market value of the flow of all final goods and services produced in the period in question), and this will cause an increase in the disposable income of individuals (personal income after taxes). Now consumer expenditures are determined primarily by the level of dis-

[1] See Hansen, *op. cit.*, pp. 104–120.

[2] Both Tooke and Wicksell emphasized in varying degree the role of governmental outlays and private investment in income formation.

posable income; and disposable income, taking account of the existing tax structure, transfer payments, and the undistributed profits of corporations, depends on the Net National Product. Accordingly, increases in private capital outlays and governmental outlays on goods and services, taking account of the relationships indicated above, will raise disposable income, and so consumer expenditures, by a fairly determinable amount, unless exceptional disturbances interfere with the more or less stable pattern of behavior affecting the variables involved.

If the aggregate outlay expended on goods and services by business units, consumers, and government rises, we should expect employment to increase until most of the labor force is employed. This would normally result in an increase in the physical volume of goods and services. If the output of goods and services should increase as rapidly as money outlays, it would be reasonable to expect that prices would not rise. A rising aggregate demand (outlays) would then be matched by a rising aggregate supply (output). If this were true, we should expect that the larger volume of goods and services would sell at about the same prices. If, however, total outlays continue to increase to a point at which output can no longer be increased (owing to shortages of labor or of capital facilities, and to special bottleneck situations) then prices will rise.

The Income Theory: Demand and Supply

The income theory of prices involves on the one side an analysis of income and aggregate demand, and on the other an analysis of costs and aggregate supply. Prices are determined by (1) money income and (2) real income; $P = \dfrac{Y}{O}$, in which P is the general level of prices, Y is money outlays (which produce a flow of income), and O is the physical volume of goods and services produced. When money outlays rise more rapidly than output, prices will tend to rise. If, on the other hand, O increases more rapidly than Y, P may be expected to fall.

Very roughly we may divide the physical volume of output into two categories: (1) industrial output, including all kinds of manufactured products, and (2) agricultural output. Now it is a matter of general knowledge and experience that the physical volume of manufactured or industrial products can readily be increased so long as additional labor can be employed. In a period of recovery from a serious depression employment typically rises and industrial output is greatly increased. Thus from 1932 to 1941 industrial production increased 180 per cent. This enlarged output came about in response to a rising volume of expenditures (money outlays) on industrial products. However, the great increase in physical output substantially matched the increased money expenditures on these goods, so that the prices of finished manufactured goods rose relatively little, in fact only about 27 per cent.

The experience with respect to agricultural products was very different. Agricultural output from 1932 to 1941 increased only 18 per cent while the prices of agricultural products rose 71 per cent.[1]

Agricultural output, being in large part dependent upon the available amount of fertile land, cannot easily be increased in the short run when the aggregate demand for these products rises. It is true that the use of increased fertilizer, machinery, and labor can raise output to some extent. But this possibility is relatively limited in the short run.

Accordingly, as total money outlays for goods and services are increased, the effect is to raise agricultural production a little, but mainly to raise the prices of these commodities. In contrast, as aggregate money expenditures for industrial products increase, the output can usually be raised rapidly until all the labor supply has been absorbed. In consequence, the prices of industrial products in a period of recovery from depression and unemployment typically rise relatively little in comparison with the rise in agricultural prices.

In terms of our equation, if we consider the market for *agricultural* products alone, we may designate demand (outlays), output, and prices with the subscript a, as follows:

$$P_a = \frac{D_a}{O_a}$$

---

[1] Some part of this increase in agricultural prices was due to the governmental policy of restricting the output of certain agricultural commodities.

Increased *demand* for agricultural products D_a has mainly the effect of raising prices P_a, since it is difficult to increase agricultural production O_a. With respect to *industrial* products, using the subscript i we get the equation $P_i = \dfrac{D_i}{O_i}$. But in this case an increase in money expenditures D_i has the effect of greatly stimulating output O_i, and so prices P_i are held in check.

Combining both categories into one general whole comprising both agricultural and industrial products, then $D_a + D_i = Y$, or total money income. As total outlays increase, aggregate output as a whole O rises substantially, but not as rapidly as income Y; and so there is a substantial increase in the *general* price level P; $P = \dfrac{Y}{O}$. Thus if aggregate income Y doubled, we might expect aggregate output (including agricultural and industrial products combined) to increase perhaps by about two-thirds. The general effect would be to raise prices substantially, but not nearly so much as would be the case if output did not greatly increase.[1]

Thus the income theory of money and prices involves not only an analysis of aggregate demand and income, but also of costs and aggregate output. What is said in the preceding paragraphs about the conditions of supply is intended merely to suggest the nature of the problem. It is necessary now to examine more closely the nature of cost functions and their relation to prices. To this we shall turn our attention in the following two chapters.

[1] See Garver and Hansen, *Principles of Economics*, 3d ed., Chap. IV.

Chapter 7

Cost Functions, Employment, and Prices

ECONOMISTS ARE INCREASINGLY concerned, and rightly so, with the problem of rising costs and inflationary pressures under conditions of high employment.[1] Sometimes it is indeed alleged that inherent in the cost situation are deep-seated conditions that render high employment precarious and unstable—that a private-enterprise and price system, in the nature of the case, is compelled to stop short of full employment by a very considerable margin in order to prevent inflation.

Postwar Demand and Supply Conditions

It is necessary first to clear away certain matters which are in fact irrelevant to the issue at hand. The problems involved in reconversion from a gigantic war to peacetime conditions are of a special character. On the one side there are pent-up accumulations of demand; on the other side are temporary shortages (pipelines not yet filled) growing out of the difficulties of reconversion.

These temporary, war-created excesses of demand and short supplies cannot fail, in a free-price market, to produce abnormally high prices. About this very little can be done, if rationing and price control are ruled out. The 42 per cent increase in consumer food prices in the United States from May, 1946 to November, 1947 was a case in point. It was suggested that these high prices placed foods out of the reach of the mass of consumers and that money incomes should therefore be raised to match this increase. Yet such a procedure would

[1] Adapted from Alvin H. Hansen, "Cost Functions and Full Employment," *American Economic Review*, September, 1947.

achieve nothing. Raising incomes to match the increase in food prices would, under the conditions cited, only raise prices again. Rationing and price control being ruled out, inflationary processes are set in motion, though appropriate fiscal and monetary policy could in a measure hold them in check.

Abnormally high prices eventually come down if *"scarcity* (or temporary) price inflation" is not followed by a corresponding "income (or general) inflation." A downward adjustment of prices which are out of line with the general structure of prices is not, properly speaking, "deflation." A true deflation of prices means the crumbling of the whole cost structure—a structure based fundamentally on labor cost or "efficiency-wages."

Any fall in the prices of commodities which are temporarily in short supply—prices which are far out of line with the normal longer run cost structure—represents a movement toward a balanced price structure and is a healthy development for the economy. A deflation of the whole cost-price structure has, however, disastrous consequences for the economy. The price decline which began in 1920 was, at least in some measure, of the corrective type; that beginning in 1929 was basically of the deflationary type.

Now it is not merely the special problem of scarcities here and there in the economy that worries the economist when he considers the economics of full employment. More important is the danger of wage inflation, *i.e.*, wage rates outrunning advances in productivity.

Cost Functions and Full Employment

But the matter to which I wish to direct attention here is something different: a third alleged danger of inflation due to general under-capacity of fixed plant and equipment. Granted that wages are held in line and that there are no unmanageable temporary scarcities, we still have to consider the structure of costs, prices, and profits as they unfold when a peacetime economy reaches high levels of income approaching full employment.

Is there something inherent in the cost-price structure under full-employment conditions which produces abnormally high profits? If this were so, such profits could not be tapped by trade-union demands. For such wage demands, if granted, could only raise both the cost curves and the demand curves, leaving profits largely unaffected. But a condition of abnormally high profits under continuing full employment would be a highly unstable one. It would create social unrest. It would also render the task of *maintaining* full employment difficult, since abnormally high business savings cannot for any considerable period continue to find adequate investment outlets.

The thesis I wish to examine, then, is that under the price system continuing full employment is in the nature of the case not feasible, and that to secure stable prices it is necessary to have several million unemployed. Demand curves high enough so that the marginal revenue curves will cross steeply rising marginal costs at points corresponding to full employment will, so the thesis runs, produce enormous profits. Prices will be far above total unit costs. This, be it noted, is not due to wage inflation. The steeply rising marginal cost curves are due to inadequate fixed-capital capacity. This is the alleged dilemma. Nor is this situation easily curable, since the distortion is said to be inherent in the nature of the cost structure. If labor unions tried to capture the high profits by pressing for higher wages, the effect would be to raise both the marginal revenue curves and the marginal cost curves together, leaving the spread between total unit costs and prices, by and large, as high as before, but at an inflated price level. A way out, it is suggested, is to reduce employment and output, thereby moving down (and back) on the cost curves sufficiently far to restore a balance in the cost-price structure. But this means perhaps six to eight million unemployed.

Profit Variations over the Cycle

We may distinguish three types of conditions affecting the average revenue curves confronting entrepreneurs: (1) perfect competition, (2) monopolistic competition, and (3) administered prices rigidly maintained regardless of volume of sales. In Fig. 14, the marginal revenue curves are horizontal and coincide with the demand or average revenue curves; but every *increase* in aggregate demand causes an *upward shift* in these curves. In Fig. 15, the marginal revenue curves slope downward, but they shift to the right (or up) with each increase in aggregate demand.[1] In Fig. 16, the marginal revenue curve is represented by a horizontal line indicating the administered price that is rigidly held throughout the cycle regardless of sales volume.

Consider each of these situations in the typical business cycle of an unstable economy, yet one experiencing approximately full employment in each boom period. We assume also, as economists usually have done, that marginal cost curves rise fairly sharply before full

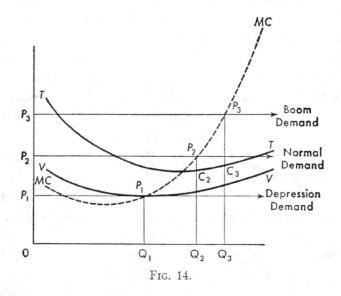

FIG. 14.

employment is reached. What are the implications with respect to profits in each of the three cases: (1) in boom, (2) in depression, and (3) at some intermediate "normal" level of business activity such as Schumpeter's "neighborhood of equilibrium?"

In Fig. 14, at "depression demand" variable costs VV are barely covered by the price Q_1P_1, making it just worth while to produce OQ_1 amount; at "normal demand" moderate profits are made, the price being Q_2P_2; at "boom demand" very large profits are made, the margin between total unit cost TT and price being C_3P_3 while the sales volume is OQ_3.

---

[1] It may be, as suggested by Harrod, that the demand curves become less elastic in prosperity years as compared with depression years. If this were so, profits would rise still more in boom years.

In Fig. 15, at "depression demand" the optimum output OQ_1 (marginal cost equals marginal revenue) will be sold at price Q_1P_1 slightly above variable unit cost VV but below total unit cost TT; losses are sustained. At "normal demand," optimum output OQ_2 can be sold at price Q_2P_2 somewhat above total unit cost TT; moderate profits are realized. At "boom demand" optimum output OQ_3 can be sold at

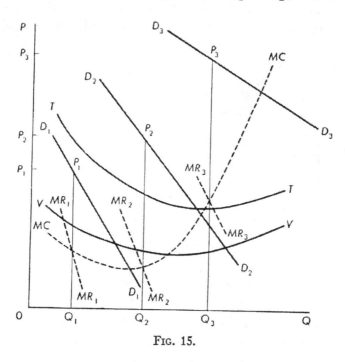

FIG. 15.

Q_3P_3, far above total unit cost TT, and very large profits are earned.

In Fig. 16, at "depression sales" OQ_1, variable unit costs VV are just covered, but total unit costs TT are far above the administered price. At "normal sales" OQ_2, there is a considerable margin between price Q_2P_2 and total unit costs Q_2C_2, yielding moderately good profits. At "optimum sales" OQ_3, the margin between the administered price Q_3P_3 and total unit cost Q_3C_3 is about the same as in the case of OQ_2 sales, but profits are much higher in view of the larger sales volume. At "boom sales" OQ_4, profits are lower than in the case of OQ_3 sales, since marginal cost has now risen above the selling price. This decline in profits is presumably tolerated only because the heavy volume of

sales is regarded as temporary and it is believed good long-run policy
to satisfy the extra boom demand. The policy of holding a fixed price
throughout the various phases of the cycle is for various reasons regarded as being in the long-run interest of the firm.

Without committing ourselves at this point to any conclusion with
respect to the shape of the cost curves, we assume for the moment
that something of the sort indicated does occur in the swings of the
cycle. Our models are, however, overly simplified. For one thing the

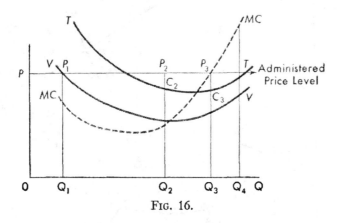

FIG. 16.

cost curves may in fact *shift* to lower levels as depression deepens,
owing perhaps to falling money wage rates, to falling prices of raw
materials, and to gains in efficiency (improvements in methods of
production whether in terms of technology or organization). Conversely, as one moves from depression to boom, the cost curves may
shift upward due to money wage rates rising faster than productivity
and to rising raw material prices. In this case, however (contrary to
the downward movement) the upward shift in the cost curves would
be slowed up by continued gains in technological or organizational
efficiency.

Definition of "Capacity" in Long and Short Run

The term "capacity," as the literature reveals, is not easy to define
in a satisfactory manner, since there is no one "capacity" output
which could not be exceeded more or less if the fixed plant were more
intensively utilized. "Capacity" may perhaps best be defined in terms

of the total unit cost at varying degrees of intensive use of the fixed factor. Thus in a highly fluctuating economy, it might be true that a firm would tend to adjust its fixed factor so as to produce the "normal" (Schumpeter) amount at lowest total unit cost. But as boom conditions of demand develop, marginal cost would rise more or less steeply. Thus one could say that the economy was operating at "optimum capacity" at the "normal" phase in the cycle. Accordingly, if demand rises sufficiently under boom conditions so that marginal revenue will equal the rising marginal cost, then very high profits would inevitably be earned in the high prosperity phase of the cycle.

In a highly fluctuating society such high profits might indeed not be eaten into by new investment coming into the industry, because the boom profits are regarded as temporary and highly precarious. Neither the old firms, nor any new entrant to the business, are likely (so it may be argued) to extend fixed investment to a point at which "low-unit-cost" capacity will correspond with full-employment output.[1] The boom being temporary and often short-lived, there is neither time nor adequate incentive to bring capacity up to a level which would yield low total unit cost at full employment. Under continuing full employment, however, there would be both time as well as the incentive to enlarge capacity, thereby pushing the cost curves to the right so that the horizontal, or nearly horizontal, portions of the curves will encompass full employment. Accordingly, even though convincing evidence were presented to the effect that short-run marginal cost curves do rise steeply in a highly fluctuating society, that would prove nothing with respect to a *continuing* full-employment society.

If full-employment output were continuously maintained at a marginal cost high up on the steeply rising curve, this situation would indicate a high return (or "quasi rent") to the limited fixed factor, or in other words, a high marginal efficiency of capital. This situation is one calculated to induce an expansion of investment in fixed capital.

---

[1] In opposition to the above statement it might be suggested that the leading characteristic of the boom is a high level of investment, and that this would therefore tend to raise "capacity" output toward lowest total unit cost. It is perhaps sufficient to say in reply that the new plant and equipment installed during a boom is largely completed late in the boom phase and often even after the upper turning point.

Larger fixed capacity would mean that the total unit cost curve is pushed out to the right so that the lowest point on the curve is at or near full-employment output. Momentarily (demand and price being at first unchanged) this would mean higher profits. But all the old firms, having increased their capacity, will now expand output, and moreover, new firms will enter the industry. Thus the margin between price and total unit cost would be narrowed and the abnormally high profits or quasi rents would be whittled away. Continuing full employment would accordingly tend toward an equilibrium profit rate

The period of transition during which fixed-capital capacity was being built up to the requirements of a sustained full-employment society would, under the conditions discussed above, exhibit all the characteristics of unbalance and distortion of the typical boom. Profits would remain abnormally high; marginal costs would be up; and prices would be far out of line with total unit costs. These inherently unstable conditions might indeed cause no great difficulty during the short period of a transitory boom, but are they tolerable for a longer, sustained period such as would be needed to build up capacity to the new required level of full employment? The social strain might possibly be too great. In these circumstances a wage inflation might break loose, and with it a cumulative price inflation.

The alternatives, it might be suggested, would be either price control or excess profits taxation. Price control (if feasible over a prolonged period, as in fact is not probable) might indeed close the gap between prices and total unit costs, but it could not compel an enterprise to extend output beyond the intersection of marginal cost and marginal revenue (the latter under price control being a horizontal line). It is conceivable that, short of complete monopoly, a firm might wish to sell all the market could take at the controlled price merely to hold its place in the market and prevent its competitors from gaining an undue proportion of the total business. But while an administered price may momentarily in a fluctuating society be held below marginal cost when boom sales run high, there is less reason to expect entrepreneurs to refrain from maximizing their profits when there is prospect (in a sustained full-employment society) for continued future high volume of sales.

Empirical Analysis of Cost Functions

Thus, if the conditions were as stated, serious difficulties would present themselves in a full-employment program. It now becomes necessary, however, to inquire more fully into the assumptions made above with respect to the shape of the cost curves in a society characterized by industrial fluctuations such as we have had in the past. Until relatively recently economists have usually assumed, it is perhaps fair to say, that marginal cost curves do rise steeply as boom conditions are approached. Keynes took this for granted in his *General Theory*. Accordingly, he concluded that as aggregate demand was increased, prices would necessarily rise, and so real wages (in the absence over the short run of gains in productivity due to changes in technique and organization) would necessarily fall. Part of the increase in aggregate demand would thus spill over in higher prices, and only a part in larger output and employment. Had money wages risen to offset the higher prices, this would have meant an upward *shift* in the cost curves, and so output and employment would rise less than might otherwise have been the case. But the increase in wages would cause a further shift in the demand curves, with inflationary consequences. In his later article in the *Economic Journal*, March, 1939, on "Relative Movements of Real Wages and Output" Keynes reexamined this thesis and concluded that possibly the cost curves were flatter than he had formerly supposed. But he ended the article on an uncertain note, and suggested that the matter required further examination.

Keynes's rigorous assumptions—no changes in productivity or technique—are often overlooked. Increased productivity, together with lower unit fixed cost in a period of expansion, may permit increases in real wages when aggregate demand raises employment.

Since the appearance of Keynes's article we have the very illuminating theoretical discussion, together with the comprehensive survey of empirical data, contained in Chap. V of *Cost Behavior and Price Policy*, prepared by the Committee on Price Determination under the chairmanship of Professor Edward S. Mason.[1] The committee

---

[1] National Bureau of Economic Research, 1943. See the bibliography of the various empirical studies cited on pp. 81–82, 84, 89–92, 96, 100, 105, 108, and 112; also the bibliography of empirical data cited by R. A. Lester, *American Economic Review*, vol. XXXVI, No. 1 (March, 1946), pp. 67, 68, and 71.

concludes that empirical studies indicate with few exceptions a linear cost-output relationship. "These results are of particular interest, since economic theory has usually presumed an inverted ogive for total costs and marginal costs that are markedly U-shaped." [1] The belief that marginal costs "describe a smooth U-shaped curve reflects a bias in economic theory." The suggestion that marginal costs approach the "horizontal over large ranges of output" is of the utmost significance since, if this is so, small changes in demand will tend to permit large changes in output without significant price increases. If the economic system has linear cost functions, this is a highly favorable fact for full-employment policy.

As one element in the explanation of linear cost functions the committee offered the suggestion that fixed factors are more or less divisible. The more divisible the plant and equipment, the more likely that variable costs will be linear. Parts of a plant and groups of machines may be shut down or put back into use as output varies. "Within wide limits the fixed factors may be compared to small units whose combined costs are simply proportional." [2] Moreover, a plant may be operated at optimum output a few hours per week, or with one or more shifts. In addition, as output expands, identical machines may be added within wide limits, as in a shoe factory. A machine may run at two or three different speeds, or make several widths and thicknesses or lengths of material. Or there may be flexibility with respect to types of products. Flexibility means less specialized fixed factors [3] and hence relatively more nearly linear cost functions. If "empirical studies should show that conditions of divisibility and flexibility were typical, only a linear function could be both pertinent and useful for the interpretation of economic phenomena." [4]

The data accumulated by Professor R. A. Lester [5] from discussions

[1] P. 109.   [3] Pp. 112–113.
[2] P. 111.   [4] P. 113.

[5] *American Economic Review*, vol. XXXVI, No. 1 (March, 1946). Prof. Fritz Machlup's interesting criticism [*American Economic Review*, vol. XXXVI, No. 4, pt. 1 (September, 1946), pp. 519–554] is excellent with respect to his defense of the theoretical apparatus of marginalism, but I am not able to see that he has successfully attacked Lester's empirical findings.

with numerous business executives and from written replies by some fifty concerns are in general agreement with the findings of the researches examined by the Committee on Price Determination. These empirical findings, while not conclusive, at any rate challenge the assumptions usually made with respect to sharply rising marginal cost curves long before full employment is reached.[1]

If the view tentatively expressed by the Committee on Price Determination should prove to be correct, one may take (fortunately for capitalism) a more optimistic view with respect to the possibility that full employment may be reached without serious distortion in the cost-price relationship. There remains, to be sure, the danger of wage inflation. But this is a problem of labor-management relations and collective bargaining and not a question of an inherent "flaw," so to speak, in the capitalist or price mechanism whereby full employment cannot be reached except under conditions of grave cost-price unbalance, profit inflation, and a distortion of income distribution. If the structure of the cost curves is such as to permit full employment without the economy being perched high up on steeply rising marginal cost curves, then there is at least no inherent reason why full employment could not be achieved without creating violent distortions of a character which would render economic stability improbable.

An examination of price movements in past periods of high peacetime employment could (but not necessarily) be interpreted as lending support to the conclusions of empirical studies with respect to linearity of the cost functions. Some boom periods which have nearly reached full employment have not been characterized by serious price in-

---

[1] The view that capacity may have been adequate, and even more than adequate, over past cycles even in terms of the requirements of boom-time ouput has often been advanced in business cycle literature. Thus it has often been alleged that there is an inherent tendency toward "over-capacity" throughout the economy stemming from: (1) the nature of the competitive system of industry and its quasi-monopolistic variants, and (2) errors of judgment growing out of the "round about" nature of the capitalistic system of production.

"In cases of 'building ahead of demand' and with imperfect competition, in particular in the presence of oligopolistic struggles, the latter situation [i.e., falling total unit cost] will be much in evidence—firms may possibly even move within the descending interval of their marginal cost curves—and account for many instances of 'over-production' and 'over-capacity.'" J. Schumpeter, *Business Cycles*, McGraw-Hill Book Company, Inc., New York, 1939, p. 91.

flation. In the high employment years culminating in 1907, average annual prices did indeed range from 58.9 to 61.8 from 1902 to 1906 and rose to 65.2 for the year 1907. But this was a period of secular rise in prices when special factors were operating on the price level—factors which have no relevance to the shape of the cost curves. In the high 1920's, full employment was reached, yet prices declined from 103.5 in 1925 to 100.0 in 1926, 95.4 in 1927, 96.7 in 1928 and 95.4 in 1929.

But price stability alone does not prove that the cost functions are linear. The behavior of finished goods prices in boom years could not in the nature of the case offer convincing evidence either way with respect to the steepness of marginal cost curves as boom employment conditions are reached. This is true because, even though cost curves did rise steeply, prices might be fixed on an administered basis, with no attempt at short-run maximization of profits. On the other hand, prices might rise sharply in boom times not owing to rising marginal costs, but by reason of speculative inventory accumulation resulting, for example, from crop failures, labor disturbances, or fear of war.[1] Or prices might fail to rise even though the marginal cost curves sloped upward, since increasing man-hour productivity (not offset by wage increases) might hold actual marginal costs (measured in a time series) constant.

Insufficient Capacity for Full Employment

It is to be noted that the late 1920's did indeed witness large profits. The high profits, it may be suggested, might not have been due to steeply rising marginal cost curves (with a wide gap between prices and total unit costs). High profits could equally be explained by a downward shift in horizontal cost curves due to the failure of wage rates to rise with rapidly increasing man-hour productivity. This down-

---

[1] In 1923 the prices of finished goods increased by 2.7 per cent compared with the preceding year; in 1926 they declined by 0.6 per cent compared with 1925; in 1929 they again declined compared with 1928 this time by 0.8 per cent; while in 1937 (a year of speculative inventory accumulation) finished goods prices rose by 5.7 per cent. In general there is apparently no consistent strong upward movement of the prices of manufactured goods up to the peak of production; though often at some earlier point in the boom phase a sharp rise in prices may occur. Thus in 1925 and again in 1928, prices rose considerably above those of the preceding year.

ward drift in the cost curves would necessarily widen the spread between prices and total unit costs. If this were the correct explanation, the remedy for the abnormal margin of profit in the boom 1920's would have been lower prices or higher wages. Submarginal firms might indeed not have been making profits, and higher wages or lower prices might (quite properly) have squeezed them out.

The special situation (unlike the usual cycle) growing out of the prolonged stagnation of the 1930's remains to be considered. It is quite possible that up to 1929, the United States was in general provided (taking an over-all view of the different branches of the economy) with fixed plant and equipment so adequate that even in boom periods output was at or near lowest unit cost—that cost functions were in general linear. In the 1930's, however, we added relatively little to our total capital stock; we never tested our "capacity" until the war brought full employment. It is true that the test did not appear to display any overwhelming serious deficiency in fixed capital. But it is also true that the large additions to plant and equipment made during the war were specialized, and much of it was not very useful for peacetime production. Thus we are probably not as well provided with fixed capacity, relative to full-employment requirements, now as we were in 1929 and in earlier peacetime booms.[1]

I have frequently called attention to the remarkable fact that of the 60 billion dollars of gross capital formation in business plant and equipment made in the decade 1931–1940, 90 per cent was replacement investment. Yet even though there was relatively little *net* investment, the productive capacity of American industry was enormously greater at the end of the decade than it was in 1930. Better and more productive equipment was installed in place of the worn-out and discarded equipment. Nevertheless, it is probable that in terms of the requirements of peacetime full employment there existed at the end of the war a condition of "undercapacity." Autonomous investment in the 1930's was inadequate to raise income to full-employment

---

[1] One finds in the literature of the business cycle a strange contradiction. On the one side, it is often alleged that there is a tendency toward a condition of "overcapacity" generally throughout the economy; on the other side, it is usually assumed that marginal cost curves rise steeply as output approaches boom dimensions.

levels. Had we by a positive program maintained full employment, a sustained high level of income would have induced far more net investment than we in fact experienced. Had this been done, we might have ended the decade with adequate capacity—adequate in the sense that full-employment output would be at or near the point of lowest total unit cost.

That this is a difficulty confronting us in the transition from the long stagnation of the 1930's to the goal of continuing full employment is certainly not improbable. And if these assumptions are correct, it means that we shall be compelled to operate for a period under conditions of high marginal cost with a wide spread between prices and total unit costs, and with abnormally large profits. Labor would have to choose between accepting this situation or experiencing considerable unemployment.

If we should find that we are suffering from "undercapacity," then high profits and a large volume of net saving would indeed be needed [1] and should be welcomed until we become sufficiently saturated with plant and equipment so that cost functions would again become linear. But we should still have to face the important question as to how rapidly we ought to move toward the new high plateau of capital facilities appropriate to our high postwar income and labor force. Should the transition be made at a high rate of capital formation over a short period or at a more moderate rate over a longer period?

It cannot be assumed that the investment in plant and equipment required to provide "optimum capacity" could be relied upon to be made automatically without a positive government program. It will be *induced* only on the condition that continuing full employment is maintained. The accumulated capital shortages caused by a total war may for some years provide sustained high levels of income and employment, with less need during this interval for a positive program.

Let me summarize the argument briefly, and add a postscript. Leaving aside (1) specific postwar scarcity situations, and (2) price increases brought about by general wage increases, we must still ask

---

[1] It is of course essential, in order to prevent a general income inflation, that investment shall not be allowed to exceed (by more than the normal growth in the active money supply) the savings from disposable income (using Robertson's definition) at full employment.

whether there is not, under full employment, a tendency toward inflation due to (3) general "undercapacity" with attendant rising marginal costs.

Is the allegation correct that marginal cost curves must rise prior to full-employment output and, in doing so, give rise to high prices and profits—profits so high as to endanger social and economic stability?

The answer is that such an impasse is not inevitable, and on two counts. First there is the tentative conclusion, based on empirical data, that when booms are sufficiently vigorous to produce full employment at the peak of the cycle, capacity tends to be adjusted to the "peak load," so that total unit cost curves, even at high output, are fairly flat. Second, if the autonomous factors fail to produce booms sufficiently vigorous to absorb the labor force, the condition of adequate fixed-capital capacity can nevertheless be induced by the maintenance of substantially full employment for a considerable period and on a basis such that people expect it to persist. If this is done, then (1) each firm will move along on its long-run cost curve—a curve in which plant is optimally varied to output and demand, and (2) new firms will be persuaded to enter the field with new capacity which will tend to put downward pressure on marginal costs, prices, and profits.[1]

There is, it might be suggested—and this is the postscript—still a fourth situation in addition to the three inflationary situations discussed above. Assume that postwar scarcities have been overcome, that wage inflation is under control, that capacity is adequate to prevent steeply rising marginal cost, does not labor scarcity at full employment per se imply an unstable situation? Fixed capacity may indeed be adequate, and aggregate demand may be kept under control, but *labor* itself at various points in the economy becomes the bottleneck. Thus growth and expansion are thwarted. There is no room, it is alleged, to move about: no flexibility.

This argument overlooks three things. (1) A margin of flexibility is provided by the 4 to 5 per cent "turnover" unemployment which

---

[1] Monopoly profits present, of course, a special problem, and this situation may require drastic state intervention whether in terms of antitrust action, special taxation, direct controls, or finally government ownership.

must be assumed in any full-employment program. If average un-employment is 2.5 million and each worker requires, on the average, 5 weeks to find a new job, then 25 million new hirings will take place in a single year. This should provide ample elbow room for a personnel manager operating in a well-organized labor exchange market. (2) Moreover, there are two factors of growth on the labor-supply side which afford scope for economic expansion, namely (a) the annual in-crease in the labor force, and (b) increasing man-hour productivity. These are of great importance for flexibility and adjustment to change.[1] Considerations such as these make it appear less convincing that full employment must inevitably run up against a rigid wall of perpen-dicularly rising costs owing to the needed labor factor at essential points being simply missing, or in other words, constituting an ab-solutely rigid bottleneck. (3) Finally in this connection is the im-portant suggestion that in practice the administration of job classi-fications and wage structures tends to "insulate the system in a variety of ways from the impact of an expansion in aggregate de-mand."[2] Adjustments, affecting an acute labor-shortage bottleneck, can be made at specific points without setting off a general cumula-tive process. Changes can be made, for example, in the job content of a particular job classification. Thus administration of the wage struc-ture and of job classifications can provide a large measure of flexibility —adjustments tending to ease bottleneck inflationary pressures.

---

[1] Also to be considered is the ease with which labor, at least in the United States, can move from industry to industry, owing to the semiskilled character of machine methods of production.

[2] John Dunlop, "Wage-Price Relations at High Level Employment," *American Economic Review*, vol. XXXVII, No. 2 (May, 1947), p. 249. See also Dunlop, "Productivity and the Wage Structure" in *Essays in Honor of Alvin H. Hansen*, W. W. Norton & Company, New York, 1948.

Chapter 8

Wages and Prices

Efficiency-wages and the Price Level

Wage rates per se are not especially significant. It is labor cost or efficiency-wages, which we shall denote as $\dfrac{W}{E}$, that is relevant to the problems of wages and prices. If labor productivity rises as rapidly as money wage rates, then efficiency-wages $\dfrac{W}{E}$ will remain constant.

A rise in money wage rates with no increase in productivity means that efficiency-wages $\dfrac{W}{E}$ are rising. This would be a condition of wage inflation—rapidly rising labor costs; a wage deflation means a fall in efficiency-wages.

Stability of efficiency-wages would indicate that every increase in productivity is matched by a corresponding increase in money wage rates. In such a society, *real* wage rates would rise along with increases in money wages; the price level would be relatively stable.

When money wage rates rise more than, equal to, or less than increases in productivity, then efficiency-wages will be rising, stable, or falling respectively. And the movement of efficiency-wages (labor costs) is likely to be associated with corresponding changes in the level of prices.

The level of costs is intimately connected with the price level, and efficiency-wages are closely bound up with the level of costs. If an inflationary price movement is allowed to develop, this will necessarily raise the level of money costs to a new high level. As a part of this process efficiency-wages will rise; in other words, a general inflationary movement involves in greater or less degree a wage inflation.

A new high level of costs is likely to leave the economy on a higher price plateau. This is true even though a major price collapse follows the inflationary peak. This, indeed, is what happened following the Civil War price upheaval—and even more after the First World War.

The whole inflationary movement in the First World War, including the postwar restocking spurt of 1919–1920, carried the wage level to a new high plateau, considerably more than double the prewar level. The collapse of 1921–1922 made only a slight dent in the new wage level, and by 1923 the wage index was back around the war peak. Wages, or more precisely *labor cost* or efficiency-wages, constitute the backbone of the cost structure. The efficiency-wage level $\dfrac{W}{E}$ is the pivot around which the whole price structure oscillates and revolves. Once labor costs have been pushed up in a wage-inflationary. movement to a new high plane, the price-making process tends to erect a new structure of prices around this central core.

This, I think, is the basic explanation for the new plateau of prices after the First World War. Wage rates (1914 = 100) had risen to an index around 220 in 1923 and to 230 by 1926. But man-hour productivity, while stationary in the war years, suddenly increased 30 per cent from 1919 to 1923, and rose to 53 per cent above 1919 by 1926. Thus the new level of *labor cost* or efficiency-wages (wage rates corrected for productivity) rose to a new plateau about 50 per cent above the prewar level. Accordingly, the new level of wholesale prices of finished products was adjusted to the new basic cost level, and settled at an index approximately in line with the new level of efficiency-wages.[1]

To a considerable degree, though varying greatly in detail, the same development is in process of unfolding following the Second World War. We are witnessing an upward shift in the structure of costs. Inflationary pressures are causing a cycle of price and wage increases, representing a rise in wages in excess of increases in productivity. The wage structure is rising to a new plateau, lifting *labor costs* (productivity increases considered) to a higher level. Accordingly, a new price plateau is likely to be established as an aftermath of the

---

[1] See Alvin H. Hansen, *Economic Policy and Full Employment*, p. 322; also Chap. XX.

Second World War, more or less similar to the development which occurred after the First World War.[1]

The Quantity Theory and the Income Theory

The sequence of events which logically could be expected in terms of the quantity theory of money and prices is as follows: Changes in the quantity of money lead to changes in prices, and this in turn, under the influence of competition, to adjustments of wage rates corresponding to the price changes. From the standpoint of the income

---

[1] The removal of price controls in July, 1946, among other factors, led to wage advances that have placed us on a new level of *labor cost*—the foundation for a new high plateau of prices. The world-wide shortage of food—in part a temporary situation caused by the destruction and derangement of the war and by exceptionally severe floods and droughts—could not fail to drive food prices up in the United States, once price controls and rationing were removed, even though there were no excess of general over-all demand in relation to total available output as a whole. Sharp increases in food prices, in turn, could not fail to incite demands for higher wages.

This analysis is confirmed in the statistical pattern of the years 1946-1947. Average hourly earnings in manufacturing averaged $1.02 in 1945. By February, 1946, despite numerous increases in basic wage rates, average hourly earnings had fallen to $1. Thereafter they rose slowly and stood at $1.08 in June, 1946. Thus average hourly earnings remained substantially stable until June, 1946 despite fairly sharp increases in basic wage rates in the first half of that year. This seeming paradox is explained by the following facts: (1) the return to a normal work week terminated penalty overtime pay for excess hours; (2) the shift of labor from highly paid war jobs to peace jobs meant a reduction in hourly earnings, even though no changes occurred within industries in basic wage rates; and (3) the process of downgrading (the reversal of the wartime upgrading) reduced hourly earnings, even though basic wage rates were unaltered. For all these reasons hourly earnings would have fallen drastically when the war was over, had it not been for substantial increases in the basic wage rates.

In the meantime food prices similarly remained substantially stable until June, 1946, the index being 139.1 in 1945 (1935–1939 = 100), 139.6 in February, 1946, and 145.6 in June, 1946. With the removal of price control, beginning in July, 1946, the record of substantial wage and price stability quickly vanished. Food prices rose rapidly from 145.6 in June to 165.7 in July and 187.7 in November. Wages measured in terms of earnings rose also, but in a lagging movement, from $1.08 in June to $1.09 in July to $1.14 in November. By June, 1947 food prices had risen to an index of 190 and average hourly earnings to $1.22.

This process of wage inflation (rise in $\frac{W}{E}$) in turn caused an excess of aggregate money outlay over total available output. Thus special situations (*i.e.*, food shortages) may affect wage movements and aggregate income, and so the over-all demand. In the normal situation it is more likely to be movements of aggregate demand which induce wage and price movements.

theory, however, the sequence is likely to run from changes in aggregate demand to changes in output, wages, and prices, and so to changes in the quantity of money.

These are short-cut statements of two theories of money, wages, and prices. The statements, being short and incomplete, are perhaps not much more than half-truths; but as such they are nonetheless helpful in focusing attention upon what is regarded, from each standpoint, as the more relevant factors. In the quantity theory M (and perhaps V) is regarded as the determinant of efficiency-wages and prices; in the income theory M and V are regarded as changing *in response* to changes in aggregate outlays, income, wages, and prices. Taking the two variables, wages and money, money is the significant determinant of wages according to the quantity theory; according to the income theory, it is believed more revealing to invert the relation and to regard wages as a determinant of the quantity of money.

Wage Rates, Demand, and Costs

An analysis of the role of wages in the determination of the level of prices requires a consideration of the relation of money wages to money-demand schedules and cost functions. Such an analysis constitutes a significant part of Keynes's *General Theory*. And from this has developed a considerable literature on wages, employment, income, and prices.

Aggregate money outlays, wage rates, and employment necessarily stand in a certain relation to each other. Given the wage rate, employment is fairly uniquely determined by the volume of aggregate outlays. A given volume of aggregate demand will provide more employment at a low wage rate than at a high wage rate.

The relationship between these variables can be stated in the form of the Pigouvian equation $N = q\dfrac{Y}{W}$.[1] N represents the number employed, Y the total money income (wage and nonwage), q the proportion of total money income going to wages, and W the average wage rate. Obviously $NW = qY$. The equation is an arithmetical truism.

Professor Pigou rightly warns us that we cannot assume that the

---

[1] See A. C. Pigou, *Agenda*, August, 1944.

three variables q, Y, and W are independent of one another. Rather, they are a complex which must be considered as a whole. Total money income is not independent of the wage rate.

The Classicals and neoclassicals tended to argue that total money outlays are determined by the quantity of money (or in the more refined version, by M and V) and are independent of the level of wage rates. This position was challenged by Keynes.

Keynes did not deny, other things being equal, that employment varies inversely with real wage rates. He accepted the proposition that the demand for labor is a function of real wage rates—the quantity of labor demanded increasing as real wages fall.

But Keynes denied that a cut in money wages, for the economy as a whole, would necessarily produce a cut in real wages. He believed that a cut in money wages would *tend* to produce a proportional decline in total outlay, demand, and prices, leaving real wage rates unaffected by the cut in money wages.

For the individual firm it is of course true that a cut in money wages (total outlays in the society as a whole being virtually unaffected thereby) will permit a cut in the prices charged by the firm in question, and so cause an increase in sales and employment. But when such wage cuts are generalized throughout the economy, other things will not stay put; demand schedules all around will fall. If *everyone* stands up in the bleachers, no one will be able to see any better than before. A cut in money wage rates will not necessarily reduce real wage rates.

Thus Keynes believed it necessary, in order to increase employment, to raise aggregate demand [1] while holding money wage rates substantially constant. Aggregate demand could be increased through monetary and fiscal policy; and he thought it possible that money wage rates could be held fairly stable under modern collective bargaining practices.

---

[1] In the preface to his *Lapses from Full Employment* (The Macmillan Company, New York, 1935) Professor Pigou says: "Professor Dennis Robertson, who has kindly read my proofs, has warned me that the form of the book may suggest that I am in favor of attacking the problem of unemployment by manipulating wages rather than by manipulating demand. I wish, therefore, to say clearly that this is not so." Reprinted by permission of The Macmillan Company, New York and London.

This procedure would (so he thought, at least in the *General Theory*) produce a necessary fall in real wage rates. Excluding (in the short run) changes in organization, equipment, and technique, he believed that any increase in employment and output would necessarily cause an increase in marginal cost and so raise prices. Thus an increase in aggregate demand would simultaneously raise output, marginal cost, and prices. Hence a fall in real wages would (so he argued) necessarily *accompany* an increase in employment. But the cut in real wages would come about through the increase in employment, not the other way around.

This analysis was based on Keynes's conviction that industry, even at low output, typically operates under conditions of rising marginal cost. This assumption he seems never to have abandoned. In his article on "Relative Movements of Real Wages and Output" [1] he did however suggest that businessmen often follow "full-cost" pricing policies, and therefore rising marginal costs may not be reflected in rising prices. On a "full-cost" pricing policy, prices can be lowered as output expands, up to the point at which rising marginal cost finally rises above total unit cost. Indeed, output may be pushed considerably beyond this point before total unit costs will equal the high unit costs (at low capacity utilization of the fixed plant) from which the expansion started. On this basis real wages (up to a point) need not fall as employment and output rise.

Keynes, moreover, placed unnecessarily severe limitations upon the efficacy of his method of expanding employment, by reason of the fact that he ruled out, in the short run, all changes in organization, equipment, and technique. In fact, however, changes in technology go on year after year with sufficient speed so that in any process of expansion real wages may remain constant even though we assume rising cost curves. This is so since improvements in technology may offset the increase in marginal cost springing from the shape of the cost functions.

Finally, contrary to Keynes's view, it is now widely held that the variable and marginal cost curves are substantially flat over wide ranges of output. If this is so, an increase of employment and output

---

[1] In the *Economic Journal*, March, 1939.

need not be accompanied by any fall in real wage rates, even though it is assumed that no improvements in technology occur in the short run. If in addition improvements in technique are assumed, there may even be an increase in real wage rates.[1]

As we have noted above, Keynes (in the *General Theory*) agreed with the Classicals and neoclassicals that real wage rates must fall as employment rises.[2] Current thinking, as we have seen, challenges this position, thereby offering a more optimistic view of the possibilities of expanding employment through raising aggregate demand. According to current thinking, prices need rise less, as employment and output rise, than Keynes had believed. But while Keynes stood with the Classicals with respect to the inverse relation between real wage rates and employment, he denied the efficacy of their remedy—namely, cuts in money wages.

Keynes believed (I think quite rightly) that wage earners are prepared to accept small increases in prices without demanding a corresponding increase in money wage rates.[3] Were this not true, every collective wage bargain would have to contain a clause providing for an automatic wage adjustment to changes in the cost of living. But this in fact is not the usual procedure.[4] On the other hand, it does not follow that wage earners are not price-conscious. If the cost of living persistently rises, wage demands will of course be made. This fact is not inconsistent with the acceptance of a decrease in real wage rates due to moderate price increases during the period of the labor contract.

On the other hand, Keynes was surely right when he argued that wage earners will vigorously resist cuts in money wages. Nor is this merely a "money illusion." A cut in money wage rates, for the individual union, means a cut in real wage rates if wages elsewhere (and

[1] Attention should be called to the fact that average weekly and annual earnings will increase more than wage rates owing to fuller employment and overtime pay.

[2] The demand for labor *is* a function of the real wage rate. But when the demand schedule is raised (for example by fiscal policy) employment will be increased *at the same real wage rate*.

[3] Since wage earners are prepared to accept more employment at current money wage rates, Keynes regarded labor as involuntarily unemployed if work was not offered at the current money wage.

[4] Many wage agreements have of course provided for such adjustments, and recently we have had fresh examples in the automobile industry.

prices in general) are not being cut. Moreover, many wage earners are confronted with debt obligations fixed in money terms. In addition, wage earners may refuse a wage cut even though prices fall proportionally, because they expect prices to return soon to what they regard as a "normal" price level—one to which they have become accustomed. Such expectations with respect to future prices cannot offhand be regarded as "irrational." Finally, wage earners may quite rationally resist money wage cuts even when prices are falling, simply because they are only vaguely conscious of the exact movement of the cost of living. Moreover, at best the measurement of the price index cannot be as precise as their knowledge of money wage rate changes.

Flexible Wages and Employment

Some writers have maintained that Keynes's underemployment equilibrium is based on the assumption of wage rigidity. Accordingly, it is held that in this respect there is really no difference between Keynes and the Classicals. The Classicals and neoclassicals had always held that, given rigid wages, unemployment would result from any falling off in demand. If, however, wage rates were flexible (so they believed) there could be only short-run unemployment, and this would be due to frictions and lags in the adjustment process.

It is, however, not correct to say that Keynes's analysis of underemployment assumes wage rigidity. Keynes in fact made a thorough analysis of employment assuming the condition of flexible wage rates. He did not regard this assumption as realistic, but he was prepared to make it in order to examine the economics of the case—in order to see whether in fact wage cuts could be an effective remedy for unemployment. But his conclusion is not (as with the Classicals) that under flexible wages the economy must tend toward full employment.[1] His argument runs in terms of the impact of flexible wage adjustments upon the determinants of income and employment—the schedule of the marginal efficiency of capital, the consumption function, and the liquidity preference function.

---

[1] Keynes suggested that the chief result of a policy of flexible wages "would be to cause a great instability of prices, so violent perhaps as to make business calculations futile in an economic society functioning after the manner of that in which we live." *General Theory,* p. 269.

Out of the debate has come a narrowing of the field of disagreement. Neoclassical theory formerly held that wage cuts would be highly effective in increasing employment, since it was assumed that the money-demand schedules would either remain unchanged by money wage cuts or else would fall proportionally much less than the induced decline in the supply or cost schedules. But it is now generally recognized that wage rates, aggregate outlay, and employment are an interdependent complex which must be regarded as a whole. One can not assume that aggregate money outlay is independent of the wage rate.[1] If the total outlay were independently determined (for example, by the quantity of money) then a cut in wage rates would indeed produce an increase in employment. But it is not that simple. A reduction in the wage rate may carry with it an equiproportionate reduction in money income and total outlay.[2] Indeed, very little has been said in the

[1] In a society pursuing a positive fiscal policy, aggregate demand can of course be increased while holding wage rates constant. The statement in the text refers to a society which does not consciously control aggregate demand.

[2] Professor Pigou accepts this view, but only in the special case in which the money rate of interest is prevented from falling whenever downward pressure is exerted on it through lower wage rates. This is the so-called Keynesian case in which the liquidity preference schedule is highly elastic with respect to the rate of interest, so that any release of money from the transactions sphere to the asset sphere is able to depress the interest rate little if at all. But even though the liquidity preference function were more or less interest-inelastic (for instance, an elasticity of $\frac{1}{2}$), thus permitting a fall in the rate of interest when the ratio of money to income rises, no expansion of employment could occur via investment, if the investment function were interest-inelastic. Some effect there might be via consumption, but this depends a great deal upon how widely over the community are distributed the liquid assets whose real value is enhanced under the downward pressure on income exerted through lower wage rates. See A. C. Pigou, *Agenda*, August, 1944, and *Lapses from Full Employment*, The Macmillan Company, New York, 1945.

Harrod, in an excellent review of A. C. Pigou's "Theory of Unemployment" in the *Economic Journal* of March, 1934, shows that prices must fall in the same proportion as wages if we assume that non-wage-earners simply *maintain* their former real level of purchases after prices have begun to fall owing to wage cuts. "If they do this the stream of purchasing power and the level of prices will be reduced by as much as the level of prime costs and wages." In other words as the volume of non-wage-earners' money expenditures falls *pari passu* with prices, then the fall in total expenditures (and in prices) will be controlled by the reduction in money wages.

If non-wage-earners *increase* their *real* level of purchases when prices begin to fall the prices will not fall proportionally as much as wages. But if we consider non-wage-earners' income as a part of factor cost then prices will tend to fall in the same proportion as total costs, though not as much percentagewise as wages.

controversial literature on this point which was not already anticipated by Keynes in Chap. 19 of the *General Theory.*

Direct and Indirect Effects of Wage Cuts

So long as it was possible to believe that demand (total money outlay) would be relatively little affected by wage cuts, it was possible to
place great stress on the efficacy of wage cuts as a means to raise employment. However, once it was clearly seen that what is true for the
individual firm is not true for the economy as a whole, this position
was no longer tenable.[1] Wage cuts are double edged: they reduce costs
but they also reduce money incomes and the expenditures of wage
earners. And it is possible (note Harrod's argument in the *Economic
Journal,* March, 1934) that this reduction in wage earners' outlays,
and so in prices, may induce a decline in the money expenditures of
non-wage-earners. Aggregate outlay would accordingly decline along
with wage cuts.

But demand may not necessarily fall off as much as costs. The very
process of falling incomes and a lower volume of monetary trans-

---

[1] Keynes stated the Classical and neoclassical thinking as follows: "In any given industry
we have a demand schedule for the product relating the quantities which can be sold to the
prices asked; we have a series of supply schedules relating the prices which will be asked for
the sale of different quantities on various bases of cost; and these schedules between them
lead up to a further schedule which, on the assumption that other costs are unchanged
(except as a result of the change in output), gives us the demand schedule for labor in the
industry relating the quantity of employment to different levels of wages, the shape of the
curve at any point furnishing the elasticity of demand for labor. This conception is then
transferred without substantial modification to industry as a whole; and it is supposed by
a parity of reasoning, that we have a demand schedule for labor in industry as a whole relating the quantity of employment to different levels of wages. . . . If this is the groundwork of the argument (and, if it is not, I do not know what the groundwork is), surely it
is fallacious. For the demand schedules for particular industries can only be constructed on
some fixed assumption as to the nature of the demand and supply schedules of other industries and as to the amount of the aggregate effective demand. It is invalid, therefore, to
transfer the argument to industry as a whole unless we also transfer our assumption that
the aggregate effective demand is fixed. . . . For while no one would wish to deny the
proposition that a reduction in money-wages *accompanied by the same aggregate effective
demand as before* will be associated with an increase in employment, the precise question at
issue is whether the reduction in money-wages will or will not be accompanied by the same
aggregate demand as before measured in money, or, at any rate, by an aggregate effective
demand which is not reduced in full proportion to the reduction in money-wages." See
Keynes, *General Theory,* pp. 258–260.

actions would sooner or later (so it was argued) bring its own corrective. The process of deflation would progressively operate to produce an expansion of demand relative to money costs. This would occur mainly through the rise in the real value of liquid assets.

This retreat to the *indirect* effects of wage cuts means, however, the abandonment of the strong position formerly held. Wage cuts would indeed be a highly effective method of increasing employment if total outlays remained unaffected by such cuts. But once it is granted that wage cuts bring falling money incomes and declining aggregate outlays, even businessmen will have no enthusiasm for wage cuts. If the road to expanding employment (via wage cuts) leads through the dangerous terrain of deflation, the enthusiasm for wage cuts vanishes.

Nonetheless, *in strict theory* the process of deflation may produce a new set of relationships favorable to employment. Wage cuts will cause money incomes to fall, and falling incomes will reduce money sales volume and so the transactions demand for money. The quantity of money, and indeed liquid assets in general, may therefore tend to become redundant—*relative* to the level of money income.[1] There follows from this a decline in the rate of interest, and this is favorable to investment. Moreover, an increase in liquid assets relative to income may raise the consumption function.

But if this is the method by which wage cuts will raise employment, the whole thing is patently absurd. If what is wanted is more money and more liquid assets (relative to income), the obvious method to achieve this result is through monetary policy. Indeed, according to Classical doctrine, there were two ways of increasing employment: (1) cut wages without reducing the quantity of money, and (2) increase the quantity of money, leaving wage rates where they were.[2]

---

[1] "If the quantity of money is itself a function of the wage- and price-level, there is indeed, nothing to hope in this direction. But if the quantity of money is virtually fixed, it is evident that its quantity in terms of wage-units can be indefinitely increased by a sufficient reduction in money-wages. . . ." See Keynes, *General Theory*, p. 266.

[2] "We can, therefore, theoretically at least, produce precisely the same effects on the rate of interest by reducing wages, whilst leaving the quantity of money unchanged, that we can produce by increasing the quantity of money whilst leaving the level of wages unchanged. It follows that wage reductions, as a method of securing full employment, are also subject to the same limitations as the method of increasing the quantity of money. . . ."

Recent shifts in wage theory amount in effect to an abandonment of the former method, leaving the field open for monetary policy.

The Modern Theory of Wages and Employment

Keynes himself thoroughly analyzed the employment effects of wage cuts under a variety of assumptions. His conclusion is that under certain conditions wage cuts may indeed increase employment, but the medicine may kill the patient (social revolution). This risk might, however, within reasonable limits be run if there were good reason to believe that the medicine would quite *certainly* cure the malady. But there is no such assurance.

The net effect of the whole discussion since the appearance of the *General Theory* is a state of agnosticism. There are few, if indeed any, economists now who will dogmatically assert *either* that wage cuts will surely increase employment *or* that such cuts cannot possibly have any favorable effects. There are too many unknowns that vary with special conditions and special circumstances.

The upshot of the controversy over the relation of wage rates to employment may be summarized briefly as follows: [1]

1. A general crumbling of wage rates, with successive cuts in one industry after another, is likely to arouse expectations which are unfavorable both with respect to investment and consumption outlays. The most favorable expectations may be assumed if a "once-and-for-all" wage cut could be engineered on a controlled nationwide basis.

In general, business confidence will be variously affected by wage cuts, partly by reason of the particular position of different industries

---

Just as a moderate increase in the quantity of money may exert an inadequate influence over the long-term rate of interest, whilst an immoderate increase may offset its other advantages by its disturbing effect on confidence; so a moderate reduction in money wages may prove inadequate, whilst an immoderate reduction might shatter confidence even if it were practicable. There is, therefore, no ground for the belief that a flexible wage policy is capable of maintaining a state of continuous full employment;—any more than for the belief that an open-market-monetary policy is capable, unaided, of achieving this result. The economic system cannot be made self-adjusting along these lines." Keynes, *General Theory*, pp. 266–267.

[1] See Chap. 13 in Alvin H. Hansen, *Economic Policy and Full Employment;* also see the exceptionally able statement by James Tobin in *The New Economics*, edited by S. E. Harris, Chap. XI.

in the economy as a whole, and especially with regard to the shape and flexibility of the demand schedule confronting each industry and firm. No general theory can predict how business expectations and business confidence will be affected by wage cuts. The conclusion on this score is decidedly agnostic.

2. A cut in wage rates may induce some substitutions of labor for other factors. But this will be true only if we assume flexible wage rates while the prices of other factors are assumed to be fairly rigid. If, however, one makes the heroic assumption that wage rates are flexible, it would seem more reasonable to assume flexible prices for the other factors as well. When this is done, no substitution will occur. A wage deflation will result in a general income deflation affecting all factors.

3. If a cut in money wage rates is not matched by a corresponding decline in the prices of other factors, income will be redistributed in a manner adverse to labor. Thus if rents and interest charges are not cut (debt obligations remaining in the short run at the same volume), the purchasing power of the *rentier* class is strengthened relative to that of the wage earners. Since the former is likely to have a lower marginal propensity to consume than the latter, the effect is to lower aggregate demand and to affect employment adversely. To prevent this, and also to achieve as nearly as could be an equitable adjustment between groups, Australia instituted in the Great Depression a controlled nationwide reduction of rents and interest charges along with wage cuts.

4. A wage cut *may* stimulate investment and employment. It may have this effect if a wage cut has the effect of reducing the rate of interest. A wage cut *may* reduce the rate of interest by reducing the transactions demand for cash. If, however, the schedule of the assets demand for money is highly elastic with respect to the interest rate, a wage cut will reduce the rate of interest little or not at all. Moreover, if the schedule of the marginal efficiency of capital is highly inelastic (as is likely in depression), any reduction in the rate of interest will have little or no effect on investment and employment. Finally, in so far as a lower rate of interest is effective in increasing employment, all modern nations equipped with central banks will certainly choose

the path of monetary expansion rather than the socially dangerous device of wage cuts and income deflation.

5. The increase in the real value of liquid assets in relation to income, consequent upon wage cuts and income deflation, entails also certain *unfavorable* effects upon employment. The fall in prices that raises the real value of liquid assets also increases the real burden of debt. This may unfavorably affect business investment decisions. However, as prices and incomes fall, private debts will decline, though not necessarily proportionally. While bank assets and deposits would decline under the impact of wage cuts and falling money incomes, on the other side public debt, treasury currency, and gold reserves would remain unchanged. Therefore the real value of *all* liquid assets would tend to rise relative to income, and the burden of business and other *private* debt would tend to fall relative to total liquid assets. Thus on balance, the net effect may be favorable to employment.

6. A wage cut *may* indirectly cause an upward shift in the consumption function, and so tend to increase output and employment. Wage cuts, by reducing incomes, will raise the real value of liquid assets in relation to income. An increase in the real value of accumulated savings will tend to raise consumption in relation to any given level of real income. Thus, having gone through a painful process of deflation, an improved ratio is reached between liquid assets and income that is favorable to employment. But the operation is dangerous to the general health of the social organism, everything considered. And it is a wholly unnecessary operation, since modern nations can easily, by appropriate monetary and fiscal policy, increase the real value of liquid assets in relation to income without resorting to wage cuts and suffering all the evil effects of income deflation.

7. A wage cut, especially for countries heavily dependent upon export trade, will tend to increase the net export surplus. The effect is equivalent to an increase in investment; output and employment will thereby be stimulated. Modern nations are, however, by international agreement committed to a policy of exchange rate adjustment through the International Monetary Fund, so that they are no longer compelled to resort to wage cuts and income deflation as a means of achieving a balance in their international accounts. Moreover, current international commitments look with disfavor upon either wage cuts or

exchange depreciation as means to increase a country's employment at the expense of its neighbors.

Wage Theory and Wage Policy

We thus reach the conclusion that modern economic theory is highly skeptical of the view that wage cuts can directly increase employment without first causing a decline in money income and consequently a fall in the money-demand schedules. It is agreed, however, that wage cuts and the attendant income deflation may eventually produce a new relationship between significant variables that is favorable to employment. This favorable relationship can, however, readily be achieved by appropriate monetary and fiscal policy, thus rendering it quite unnecessary to pass through the painful and socially dangerous process of deflation. Modern wage theory thus points to stability of efficiency-wages as the appropriate goal for wage policy. Indeed, modern nations are prepared to go further. If, in fact, through a mistaken policy or lack of socially responsible labor discipline, an increase in efficiency-wages (labor cost) has already occurred, it is now generally accepted that it is better to recognize the new situation as a *fait accompli* rather than to attempt to correct one mistaken policy (the increase in efficiency-wages) by another equally dangerous policy, namely, wage cuts and income deflation.

The net effect, to be sure, is that under modern wage theory and policy the cards are stacked in favor of a secular rise in efficiency-wages—in other words, a creeping but persistent wage inflation. A moderate secular increase in efficiency-wages (wages in relation to productivity) is perhaps of no great consequence. But too rapid an increase will cause serious distortions in wage and income distribution, throwing the advantage continuously toward the most strategically situated groups. The inequities caused thereby may be highly dangerous to the continued stability and social cohesiveness of a democratic society. Accordingly, stability of efficiency-wages, and therefore of the price level and the value of money, is a matter of great concern to the preservation and workability of a free society. Success or failure, within reasonable limits, with respect to this goal is one of the most crucial tests confronting our modern highly complex social and political democracies.

Chapter 9

The Keynesian Theory of Money and Prices [1]

Income, Output, and Prices

The general price level depends partly on the rate of remuneration of the factors of production which enter into marginal cost and partly on the scale of output.

If we assume that the rates of remuneration of the different factors all change in the same proportion as wage rates, then the price level would depend on the wage rate in relation to output.

The total remuneration of the factors of production is equal to the net national income. In terms of the income theory, the price level is determined by the relation of income or aggregate demand to total output.

Money and Aggregate Demand

The quantity of money may affect prices indirectly in the respect that it may affect total outlay or aggregate effective demand.

According to the quantity theory, any *increase* in the money supply is regarded as spendible and is spent on goods and services. It is assumed that people wish to hold money only for transactions purposes. Thus an increase in the quantity of money in effect amounts to a net addition to income. Outlays thus increase until the transactions demand for money is raised to the level of the new quantity of money. If we start from full employment, this means that prices will rise until the money value of transactions is in equilibrium with the quantity of

---

[1] This chapter is based primarily on Chap. 21 in Keynes's *General Theory*. While the analysis and interpretation are my own, I have followed in general Keynes's argument; at certain points I have made direct quotations, and at others I have made bold to paraphrase his statement.

131

money. If there is unemployment and the supply schedules are perfectly elastic, output will rise without an increase in price until total transactions reach a level consistent with the quantity of money.

In the former case, the rise in prices will lead to an increase in the prices paid the factors until the new money income will rise to a level commensurate with the quantity of money. At this point all prices will have risen so as to equate the demand for money with the quantity of money. In the latter case, employment will rise until income is in equilibrium with the quantity of money. In either case the demand for money is regarded as a function of the level of income.

But money is wanted not only for income purposes—*i.e.*, to transact the purchases of goods and services—but also to hold as an asset. In so far as the transactions demand is operative, an increase in the quantity of money will raise income—which means that either prices or output or both will rise. But the additional quantity of money may also be used for financial investment, in which case the rate of interest will fall until the extra money is desired as an idle asset. Financial investment will occur, when the quantity of money is increased, until the rate of interest is pushed down to a level at which the demand for money to hold as an asset is equal to the quantity of money not needed for transactions. The demand for money is thus regarded as a function of the rate of interest.

When an increase in money is regarded as a net addition to income, prices will rise (if employment is already full). When an increase in money is regarded as a means to add to one's liquid assets, the rate of interest will fall. It is the former case which commands attention in the quantity theory. The latter holds the center of the stage in Keynesian theory.

For Keynes, the quantity of money *may* be an important determinant of total outlay. The relevant question to be asked is always: how will a change in the quantity of money affect aggregate effective demand? A change in the quantity of money may affect (1) the schedule of the marginal efficiency of investment (through the psychological reaction of businessmen with respect to expectations of future monetary conditions), (2) the rate of interest, and (3) the consumption function. In any or all of these ways a change in the quantity of money may cause a change in aggregate demand.

Money and Prices

Having ascertained how changes in the quantity of money may affect aggregate demand, the next question is how such changes may affect prices. Changes in the effective demand will affect prices according to the effect of such changes on cost and on output. Here an analysis of cost functions becomes necessary. Effective demand will not change in exact proportion to changes in the quantity of money, and prices will not change in exact proportion to changes in effective demand. An increase in effective demand will spend itself partly in increasing the quantity of employment and partly in raising the level of prices. At first, starting from a depression situation, employment will tend to rise much faster than prices; but later, as full employment is approached, prices will tend to rise more rapidly than employment. The theory of money and prices is an analysis of the relation of changes in the quantity of money and changes in prices with a view to determining the elasticity of prices in response to changes in the quantity of money.

The Relevant Functions and Their Elasticities

The manner in which a change in the quantity of money may influence effective demand is very complicated. The effect of changes in the quantity of money operates through changes in the rate of interest, the marginal efficiency schedule, and the consumption function. But the process by which the changes spread is very complex, and varies at different levels of employment. There is first the question, how much of the new money is drawn into active circulation and how much into idle balances. There is further the question, how the increase in total outlay is divided between: (1) the rise in prices, and (2) the volume of output and employment. There is moreover the question, how the new income is divided between the different social groups—a matter which will affect the magnitude of the multiplier, and many other complicating interactions and relationships.

Given the various functions relating the variables involved, there will be a determinate amount of increase in the quantity of effective demand which will correspond to, and be in equilibrium with, the increase in the quantity of money. Something can be said about the elasticities of the functions in question, but only in a very general way.

On the supply side, in some industries the supply price will increase substantially as output is increased; in other industries the supply price will change very little if at all, at least until full employment is reached. In general, the supply curves for agriculture and mining are highly inelastic with respect to price; for many lines of manufacturing, highly elastic. But taking account of the inelasticity of the supply of raw materials, increasing output as a whole will typically be associated with some rise in prices.

The price-elasticity of output as a whole at different levels of output is conditioned in part by the presence and importance of "bottleneck" industries. Keynes was perhaps inclined to overstress their importance. The reader may at this point wish to refer to the chapter on Cost Functions, Employment, and Prices (Chap. 7) in this book, and also to Chap. 20 in my volume on *Economic Policy and Full Employment*. Adequate capacity or even overcapacity of plant and equipment appears to be the typical peacetime situation in modern industry. Cost functions are typically flat over wide ranges of output. Boom conditions, spontaneously springing from high autonomous investment or engendered by public policies, tend to induce the building up of plant and equipment in deficient areas. A good deal of slack ordinarily prevails in any business organization, and this can be taken up under emergency pressure. Bottleneck situations can more or less be broken (1) by a program of training and transfer of workers, (2) by emergency overtime, (3) by drawing on the minimum reserve of unemployed (allowed for in the technical concept of "full employment"), (4) by drawing upon that considerable fringe of the population which can at times be induced to enter temporarily the labor market, (5) by systematic stock piling in slack seasons, and (6) by increasing imports.

If the elasticity of prices with respect to the quantity of money is unity, then prices will change in the same proportion as the quantity of money. But this requires, first, a consideration of the elasticity of prices with respect to effective demand, and second, a consideration of the elasticity of effective demand with respect to changes in the quantity of money.

The elasticity of prices with respect to effective demand would be unity if (1) output were wholly inelastic with respect to effective demand, or (2) wage rates had an elasticity of unity with respect to effective demand. The elasticity of wage rates with respect to changes in effective demand depends primarily upon labor factors which determine the extent to which wage rates are raised as employment in-

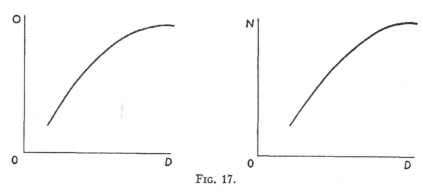

FIG. 17.

creases. The elasticity of output with respect to changes in effective demand depends primarily upon physical factors which determine the rate of decreasing returns (agriculture and mining) as more employment is applied to largely fixed natural resources and existing equipment.

The elasticity of effective demand with respect to changes in the quantity of money depends primarily upon the liquidity preferences which determine the demand for money.

Thus, both considerations, (1) liquidity preference on the one side, and (2) factors affecting efficiency-wages and the shape of the cost functions on the other, are the main factors determining how changes in the quantity of money affect prices.

It may be helpful to present the relevant relationships diagrammatically, even though the curves in the charts as here given represent vague guesses with respect to the shape of the functions. In Fig. 17, D means effective demand, N employment and O output. It is designed to show that (starting from a depression low) as effective demand rises, employment (and, to a slightly less extent, output) will rise at first approximately in proportion to changes in D.[1] As full employment and output are approached, however, increases in O and N become smaller and smaller relative to increases in D.

In Fig. 18, D stands again for effective demand, W for wage rates, and P for prices. The figure is designed to show that (starting from a low level of effective demand) as D rises, the price level P at first rises *slowly,* but eventually (as full employment is approached) *rapidly*

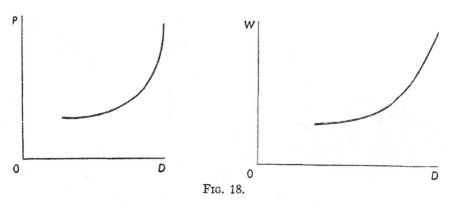

FIG. 18.

relative to changes in effective demand. Similarly, wage rates at first respond slowly to changes in effective demand but begin to rise steeply as full employment is reached.

In Fig. 19, M stands for the quantity of money, D for effective demand. Three curves are presented, showing alternative possible relationships of D to M. These alternatives merely suggest a variety of possibilities; they indicate a high degree of agnosticism with respect to

[1] The elasticity of output with respect to demand measures the rate at which output is increased as more effective demand is directed toward it. The elasticity of output with respect to demand may be expressed as follows: $\dfrac{dO}{dD} \cdot \dfrac{D}{O}$. Thus let $D = 200$, and $O = 100$; and let $dO = 5$, and $dD = 10$ (using finite increments). Then $\dfrac{5}{10} \cdot \dfrac{200}{100} = \dfrac{1,000}{1,000}$, or $\dfrac{1}{1}$, an elasticity of unity. If $dO = 5$ and $dD = 40$, then $\dfrac{5}{40} \cdot \dfrac{200}{100} = \dfrac{1,000}{4,000}$, an elasticity of ¼, or far less than unity. In Fig. 17, the elasticity is about unity at low levels of D and approaches zero at high levels of D.

the effect of changes in the quantity of money upon effective demand. The significant factors determining the relationship are (1) the income and interest elasticities of the demand for money, and (2) the interest-elasticity of the marginal efficiency of capital schedule. With respect to these relationships various assumptions may be made.

Curve A suggests that at first the injection of more money will raise effective demand rather rapidly, but eventually, as more new money is added, its potency in raising demand becomes progressively weaker.

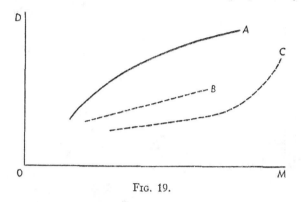

FIG. 19.

This would indicate either that an increase in money is regarded by the public as a net addition to spendible funds, or else that the liquidity preference schedule L is interest-inelastic while at the same time the investment function is interest-elastic. As more and more money is injected, however, a point is reached on the liquidity preference schedule at which the function becomes highly interest-elastic while the investment function becomes interest-inelastic. Thus the curve flattens out at the top.

Let us suppose that in consequence of monetary expansion the rate of interest is reduced and that this causes some upward shift in the consumption function. This may induce the public to "cash in" some savings bonds, the proceeds being spent on consumers' goods. The lower rate of interest may, however, induce the sale to banks of securities held by the well-to-do, who now simply hold their wealth in the form of money. In the first instance the injection of money will raise effective demand, while in the latter case it will have little ef-

fect. Thus under conditions such as those last stated we may assume
that curve *A* flattens out as the quantity of money is increased.

There is no assurance that monetary policy will increase demand.
The mass of the population may have only negligible holdings of savings bonds to be "cashed in"; and in a depression the mere monetization of securities held by the well-to-do is not likely to increase investment significantly. Monetary policy alone, under these circumstances,

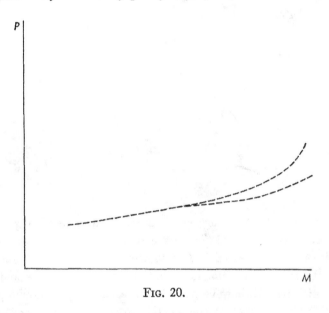

FIG. 20.

can accomplish very little. These conditions are reflected in curve *B*.
Fiscal policy, under which (1) additional spending is undertaken by
the government, or (2) private spending is stimulated, for example
by the reduction of the basic income tax (the rate affecting a large
part of the population), or possibly by subsidies or other forms of aid
to consumption, may be necessary in order to raise effective demand.

Yet if the volume of securities in the possession of the public is very
large, and if it were monetized on a wholesale basis, it is possible that
eventually speculation in commodities and securities would start an
inflationary spiral. This possibility is suggested in the sharp upturn
of curve *C* when the quantity of money has reached a high volume.

In Fig. 20, *M* represents the quantity of money and *P* the price
level. According to the quantity theory, the curve would be a straight

line, showing an increase in prices proportionate to the increase in the quantity of money. The curve in the figure, however, is intended to suggest that no such proportionate relation can be suggested. And while only two curves appear in the diagram, it must not be thought that the relationships indicated can in any sense be regarded as typical. The curves are intended merely to illustrate some plausible relationships between increases in the quantity of money and prices.

The curves, however, are intended to suggest that *in so far as* changes in the quantity of money may produce effects on aggregate demand, the influence on prices will at first be relatively slight (output being mainly affected), although as larger money volume (and fuller employment) is reached, prices may rise more rapidly. Also the curves are intended to show the combined influence of the relationships depicted in Figs. 17 and 18, together with the relationships depicted in curve *C* in Fig. 19. In short, all of the elasticities discussed above influence the relation of the price level to changes in the quantity of money.[1] More than anything else, this discussion of elasticities is designed to show the uncertain character of the relationships involved—in short, there is "many a slip 'twixt the cup and the lip."

Short-run and Long-run Considerations

Keynes emphasizes [2] the point that the complex relationships which he elaborates in Chap. 21 involve primarily considerations of the short-run effect of changes in the quantity of money on prices. From the long-run standpoint he suggests that some simpler relationship may perhaps be found.

But he thinks that this is a question for historical generalization rather than for pure theory. He suggests that over the long run there may well be some sort of rough relationship between the national income and the quantity of money. Over and above the quantity of money required in the active circulation, he suggests that there may be "some fairly stable proportion of the national income more than

[1] Keynes's discussion of elasticities expressed in algebraic symbols (pp. 304–306 in the *General Theory*) may profitably be studied in connection with the charts presented in this chapter.

[2] *General Theory*, p. 306.

which people will not readily keep in the shape of idle balances for long periods together, provided the rate of interest exceeds a certain psychological minimum." [1] Fluctuations in the quantity of "surplus money" (*i.e.*, money in excess of the requirements of the active circulation) will tend to raise and lower the rate of interest (possibly down to the minimum), and such fluctuations in the rate of interest will tend to influence the volume of effective demand. "Thus the net effect of fluctuations over a period of time will be to establish a mean figure in conformity with the stable proportion between the national income and the quantity of money to which the psychology of the public tends sooner or later to revert." [2]

As we have seen (Chap. 1) the ratio of money to national income in the United States has risen (but at a varying rate of increase) from 1800 to 1947. It will be recalled that the money supply was (in round numbers) about 5 per cent of national income in 1800, 15 per cent in 1850, 50 per cent in 1900, and 80 per cent in 1947. Correcting for the secular trend in the ratio, one could possibly speak of a "stable proportion between the national income and the quantity of money," but this is probably not what Keynes intended to say. If, however, by "stable proportion" one merely means that the ratio of income to money does not simply behave capriciously and in a wholly random fashion, then we are thrown back again to a consideration of the behavior pattern of the community with respect to the quantity of money and its influence on effective demand and all the other relationships which we have been analyzing in this chapter.

Keynes believed that the long-run fluctuations and tendencies referred to above would probably work with less friction in the upward than in the downward direction. If the

"quantity of money remains very deficient for a long time, the escape will be normally found in changing the monetary standard or the monetary system so as to raise the quantity of money, rather than in forcing down the wage-unit and thereby increasing the burden of debt. Thus the very long-run course of prices has

[1] *Ibid.*, p. 306.
[2] *Ibid.*, p. 307.

almost always been upward. For when money is relatively abundant, the wage-unit rises; and when money is relatively scarce, some means is found to increase the effective quantity of money." [1]

"During the nineteenth century, the growth of population and of invention, the opening-up of new lands, the state of confidence and the frequency of war over the average of (say) each decade seem to have been sufficient, taken in conjunction with the propensity to consume, to establish a schedule of the marginal efficiency of capital, which allowed a reasonably satisfactory average level of employment to be compatible with a rate of interest high enough to be psychologically acceptable to wealth owners." [2]

The monetary system, particularly the development of bank money, was adjusted so as to ensure a quantity of money sufficient to satisfy normal liquidity preference at rates of interest seldom much below the gilt-edged rate of 3 or $3\frac{1}{2}$ per cent. Wage rates tended steadily upward, but were largely balanced by increases in efficiency so as to allow a fair measure of stability of prices. This was not an accident. It was due to a

"balance of forces in an age when individual groups of employers were strong enough to prevent the wage-unit from rising much faster than the efficiency of production, and when monetary systems were at the same time sufficiently fluid and sufficiently conservative"

to provide on balance a quantity of money adequate to establish the lowest rate of interest readily acceptable by wealth owners in view of their liquidity preferences. "The average level of employment was, of course, substantially below full employment, but not so intolerably below it as to provoke revolutionary changes." [3]

The contemporary problem arises out of the "possibility that the average rate of interest which will allow a reasonable average level of employment is one so unacceptable to wealth owners that it cannot be

[1] *Ibid.*, p. 307.
[2] *Ibid.*, p. 307.
[3] *Ibid.*, p. 308.

readily established merely by manipulating the quantity of money." [1]

The nineteenth century could find its way because, under the conditions stated above, it could achieve a tolerable level of employment merely by assuring an adequate supply of money in relation to the level of wages. "If this were our only problem now . . . we, today, would certainly find a way." [2]

> "But the most stable, and the least easily shifted, element in our contemporary economy has been hitherto, and may prove to be in future, the minimum rate of interest acceptable to the generality of wealth-owners. If a tolerable level of employment requires a rate of interest much below the average rates which ruled in the nineteenth century, it is most doubtful whether it can be achieved merely by manipulating the quantity of money." [3]

From the prospective rate of return on new investment has to be deducted (1) an allowance for risk and uncertainty, (2) the cost of bringing borrowers and lenders together, and (3) income taxes, before we arrive at the *net* return required to tempt the wealth owner to sacrifice his liquidity. "If, in conditions of tolerable average employment, this net yield turns out to be infinitesimal, time-honored methods may prove unavailing." [4]

Thus it is that modern countries place primary emphasis on fiscal policy in whose service monetary policy is relegated to the subsidiary role of a useful but necessary handmaiden. This aspect of the problem we shall discuss in some detail in Chap. 12.

[1] *Ibid.*, pp. 308–309.
[2] *Ibid.*, p. 309.
[3] *Ibid.*, p. 309.
[4] *Ibid.*, p. 309.

Chapter 10

Historical View of Prices: Factors Making for Stability

PRICES FLUCTUATED considerably, and at times rather violently, throughout the nineteenth century. Nevertheless, in the United States and Great Britain at any rate, viewing the matter broadly, price fluctuations were sufficiently moderate so that the value of money remained reasonably stable from 1800 to 1914.

Considering the whole period from 1800 to the present, some interesting facts emerge. For the United States, wholesale prices (1926 = 100) stood at 102 in 1800 and at 103 in 1943. In the intervening 150 years the average for any one year never fell below 47,[1] and never rose, even in war years, above 155.[2] The average index by decades from 1800 to 1940 was as shown in Table 10.

Table 10.   Wholesale Prices in the United States

(1926 = 100)

Period	Prices	Period	Prices
1800–1809	100	1880–1889	60
1810–1819	110	1890–1899	51
1820–1829	72	1900–1909	61
1830–1839	75	1910–1919	88
1840–1849	65	1920–1929	104
1850–1859	65	1930–1939	77
1860–1869	94	1940–1946	100
1870–1879	76	1947	152

In 1789, the year the Federal government began to function, the index of wholesale prices stood at 68. In 1914, the beginning of the

[1] Only the 5 years 1894–1898 dropped below an index of 50.

[2] The index for 1814 was 155; in 1865 it was 132; in 1920, 154; and in 1947, 152.

143

First World War, the index again stood at 68. Apart from the Napoleonic War years (including the War of 1812), the Civil War years, and the years immediately following these wars, the index fluctuated between 47 and 85. Indeed, in 72 out of the total of 125 years (1789–1914) the index fell within the rather narrow range of 55–75.

Automatic Stabilizing Factors

This record, in a period of *laissez faire* when there was relatively little control, is, to say the least, remarkable. In a free market, and operating largely under automatic forces, the system apparently tended to produce reasonably stable prices. This could scarcely be purely accidental. What, probably, were the most significant factors involved?

In the preceding chapter some aspects of this interesting problem have already been suggested. In this chapter we shall elaborate upon these, and discuss in addition such other factors as appear to be relevant.

First and foremost, it is important to stress the role of labor cost or efficiency-wages $\frac{W}{E}$. As we have already noted, the wage structure, or more precisely the cost structure, is the central pivot around which the system of prices fluctuates. The cost structure has tended to be relatively stable under the conditions prevailing in the period under consideration. On the one side, management is continuously under pressure to reduce costs by means of better organization, improved processes, and more efficient techniques. But lower costs raise profits. Wage earners working in plants making large profits may demand a share in the proceeds. If prices are cut, however, aggregate gross sales will rise if the elasticity of demand is greater than unity. Since this is typically the case with all new products, there is, in a dynamic society in which many new products are continuously coming on the market, a persistent tendency toward a secular fall in prices. For this reason we should expect a long-run downward trend in prices (apart from the impact of wars), were it not for the counter tendency of rising money incomes.

Rising money incomes result more or less automatically from the processes inherent in a dynamic society. Cost-reducing improvements raise profits, and this leads to the sharing of the gains of progress with all those employed in the industry in question. This in turn leads, through the competition of the labor market, to wage-rate increases in industries less progressive or even stagnant with respect to organization and technique. These nonprogressive industries are therefore compelled to raise prices in order to cover mounting money costs. Thus while the new and dynamic industries are continually lowering prices in order to expand sales (and at the same time passing a part of the gains of progress to their employees), the stagnant industries are compelled to raise prices. The balance of these forces tends to produce a fairly stable general level of prices.

The Cumulative Process

So far, so good. But now we encounter a difficulty which has perennially pestered economists—namely the tendency of the economy to fluctuate, especially the tendency of any movement, whether upward or downward, to develop in a cumulative, self-perpetuating fashion. The record discloses these fluctuations. Once an upward (or downward) movement is started, why will it not go on and on, feeding on itself until the end result turns out to be either a progressive inflation or deflation?

There are two answers to this question. One runs in terms of classical doctrine and the other in terms of the Spiethoff-Robertson investment theory of the cycle, supplemented by the Keynesian consumption function.[1]

According to classical doctrine, any flow of income (and outlays) tends to perpetuate itself into the future—a rising income tends to keep rising, and a falling income tends to keep falling. In other words, the elasticity of expectations tends to be unity. If sales are rising, businessmen will expand production, thus raising incomes further; or if full employment and full output for the economy as a whole has been reached, they will compete among themselves for the limited factors of production, thus raising money incomes. All income earned

[1] In a general way one may also say that the two explanations run in terms of (1) the quantity theory, and (2) the income theory.

tends (so the argument runs—Say's law) to be spent. There are therefore no leakages from the income stream—and moreover the income stream is continually being fed from the spring of rising expectations. The converse is true in the case of a cumulative, self-perpetuating process of contraction.

Thus an expansionist process

"was believed to be reinforced by optimistic expectations. . . . And since Say's Law (supply creates its own demand) was generally accepted, it was difficult to see how producers' expectations, in the aggregate, could be disappointed. . . . The cumulative movement of income and prices was thus regarded as an obvious process; the real difficulty lay in an explanation of the turning points." [1]

Exogenous Limiting Factors

That an upward movement did not continue indefinitely in a self-reinforcing, cumulative fashion was typically explained by introducing certain limiting factors, once the expansion had reached fairly high levels of activity. The factor most commonly stressed was the limits imposed by the gold standard. In the final analysis it was the limited quantity of gold reserves (so ran the argument) which checked the otherwise limitless expansion of bank credit, and thereby held the boom in leash, short of running away into a spiral of inflation.

This was the thesis of the quantity theory and currency school from Ricardo on. Ricardo believed that unless note issues were limited by "calling for bullion or specie" there was no limit to the inflationary process. If banks "charge less than the market rate of interest [2] there is no amount of money which they might not lend."

---

[1] Lloyd Metzler, "Business Cycles and the Modern Theory of Employment," *American Economic Review*, June, 1946.

[2] Elsewhere in the same paragraph, Ricardo explains that the market rate of interest is independent of the bank rate, and is regulated by the "rate of profit which can be made by the employment of capital." Accordingly the gap between the two rates might be closed not merely by an increase in bank rate (the monetary "reining-in" effect), but also by a fall in the rate of profit. In the latter case, Ricardo could be classified with Spiethoff, Robertson, and others emphasizing the real factors. David Ricardo, *Political Economy and Taxation* (Everyman's Library), p. 246.

Later, the monetary-investment school of business-cycle theorists explained the upper turning point in terms of the "reining-in" effect of a limited supply of bank credit. Thus Tugan-Baranowsky believed that the boom came to an end by reason of the exhaustion of previously accumulated idle balances and the limitation of bank credit. Investment, having far outrun the funds continuously made available out of planned current savings from income, was now "reined in" when these supplementary sources of financing petered out. Only planned savings from income could continue on indefinitely, and these were far below the level of the investment outlays reached in the peak of the boom. Hayek similarly argued that the boom was fed from "forced saving," artificially wrung out of the community by means of monetary expansion, and that this process must inevitably come to an end by reason of the limitations of bank reserves. Once this artificial source of funds—monetary expansion—was exhausted, it would be discovered that capital formation had been overextended. Investments which had been planned on the basis of expectations of, say, a 3 per cent rate of interest, were now discovered to be excessive, since on the basis of voluntary saving the rate of interest turned out to be, say, 5 per cent. There would therefore necessarily ensue a "shortening of the process of production"—a "reining in" of investment. Similarly with Hawtrey, it is the depletion of bank cash (as currency is pulled into active circulation by rising prices, wages, and sales volume) which "reins in" the otherwise self-perpetuating and cumulative upward movement. Finally, Ragnar Frisch, in his celebrated essay on "Propagation Problems and Impulse Problems in Dynamic Economics," [1] introduced "the Walrasian idea of an *encaisse désirée.*" During a period of expansion the *"encaisse désirée"* will increase, but the total stock of money, or money substitutes, cannot be expanded *ad infinitum"* by reason of "limitations of gold supply, the artificial rigidity of the monetary systems," etc. There is thus "created a *tension* which counteracts a further expansion"—the "reining-in effect of the *encaisse désirée.*" [2]

Increasingly, however, the view gained ground that the explanation

[1] In *Economic Essays in Honour of Gustav Cassel*, George Allen & Unwin, Ltd., London, 1933.

[2] *Ibid.*, pp. 179–180.

of the upper turning point in terms of *money* as the limiting factor overlooked important *real* factors on which the expansion process was founded. It became apparent that the expansionist process contained *within itself* self-limiting factors which brought the upward movement to a close.

Self-limiting Factors

Were it not for the inner imperious necessity by which every period of rapid advance *halts itself*, it is probable that the cumulative process would have continued more or less indefinitely. Mere limitation of the money supply is no very serious obstacle if there is the will to expand. Ways and means would have been found to adjust the money supply to the requirements of a continued upward spiral of perpetual prosperity. If money were all that was lacking, the business community would have seen to that. For this there are historical examples. Thus when the Peel Bank Act was passed with its rigid limitations on note issues, Deposit money was introduced to take the place of the notes. Monetary and banking institutions have had a way of adjusting themselves (not always without serious frictions and sometimes serious social strain, it must be admitted) to the deeper *real* requirements of a dynamic community. If *self-limiting* factors had not been present throughout the 150 years here under examination, it is highly doubtful if monetary limitations alone would in fact have given us the relatively high degree of price stability that we have witnessed both in England and in the United States.

Within the dynamic process of expansion three *self-limiting* factors have been disclosed by various writers: (1) the boom "dies a natural death," since the very process of investment on which it rests progressively drives the marginal efficiency of capital lower and lower; (2) the *acceleration* of the boom via induced investment necessarily fades out as the *rate of increase* of physical output tapers off when full employment of factors is approached; and (3) the expansion is necessarily halted by the functional relation of consumption to income, account being taken of the first two factors mentioned above.

Let us consider these three factors in combination. As real income rises, there develops (until a full-employment output is reached) an ever widening gap between consumption and income. Thus the shape of the consumption function places an upper limit to the expansion. For some months or even years, the gap between consumption and income may have reached its maximum level—consumption and income both continuing at high levels with a substantially constant spread between them, as in the boom 1920's. This situation could continue so long as investment, both autonomous and induced, proved adequate to fill the gap.

But the longer this situation continues, the more precarious it becomes. This is true for two reasons. In the first place, when the *rate of increase* of output has begun to decline, as it must as full employment is approached, the *induced* investment in inventories and in fixed plant and equipment will fall. It must always be remembered that *induced* investment depends upon the *rate of increase* of final output (the acceleration principle—Aftalion and J. M. Clark). When the rate of increase slackens,[1] the absolute level of induced investment falls off. Induced investment rests on a highly temporary and shaky foundation, which is inevitably swept away the closer the economy approaches full employment. Second, the available volume of *autonomous* investment depends upon the investment outlets opened up by new advances in technique, the development of new resources, and the opening up of new territory. The exploitation of these new investment opportunities takes place by spurts, by intermittent surges of growth (Spiethoff, Cassel, Robertson, Schumpeter). For a while the accumulated volume of *autonomous* investment plus the *induced* investment is adequate to fill the consumption–income gap. But this cannot, in the nature of the case, last. Once the new and enlarged [2] "bucket of capital formation" (Spiethoff) has been filled, the boom dies a natural death. Once the new fixed plant and equipment, corresponding to the prevailing level of technique, has been built, one does not proceed to build it all over again, but only to maintain it by replacements, small

---

[1] It is true that this may for a time, under certain given conditions which however are not very realistic, be offset by increases in the rate of replacement-investment. See Alvin H. Hansen, *Full Recovery or Stagnation?* Chap. II.

[2] The new and enlarged "bucket" is the product of technological developments and the opening up of new natural resources.

improvements, and repairs. But mere replacement investment fills no part of the gap between consumption and net income. The gap must be filled by *net* investment—autonomous and induced. And when these recede (as explained above), income falls by a magnified amount, by reason of the induced decline in consumption (the multiplier) as employment in the investment industries falls off.

The self-limiting and self-terminating inner nature of the expansion process operates to hold peacetime booms in check. Apart from a *fiscal* inflation (fed progressively by vast government deficits from outside the production system itself), it is not true, as is often loosely alleged, that an expansion *progressively* "feeds on itself," continuously reinforcing itself in a cumulative fashion. On the contrary, the internal self-limiting factors inherent in the process of expansion operate to halt the advance and usher in a decline. Thus we have never had a pronounced inflation in the whole history of the United States except those fed by large wartime government deficits (and their aftermaths) which fed the income stream until it had swollen far beyond the flow of available output.

Some Historical Cases

Nor can it be convincingly shown that inflationary booms have typically been halted by limitations of the money supply.[1] In support of the monetary thesis the strongest case can perhaps be made out for the 1919–1920 postwar inflation, which it is often alleged was checked by monetary means. But even here the monetary explanation is far from conclusive. More plausible is the explanation which runs in terms of the internal self-limiting factors inherent in the expansion process itself.

Let us consider the 1919–1920 case in some detail. The role of the self-limiting factors seems to me decisive. The boom was fed by a vast volume of autonomous and induced investment. The volume of invest-

---

[1] It is not intended to suggest that no instances can be found in the history of various countries in which drastic curtailment of the money supply played an important role in terminating hyperinflation. Such examples can certainly be found in Europe both after the First World War (the Schachtian stabilization of the mark) and the Second World War (the Belgian monetary reforms).

ment exceeded the savings (given the prevailing consumption function) which could be generated *at a stable level* of prices. Accordingly, the money income was, by an inflationary process, driven up to a point high enough to generate the required savings. This is what necessarily occurs when there is a general over-all excess of effective demand in relation to the available supply of goods and services. In the circumstances the required savings exceed the savings which would be forthcoming if prices remained stable.

Gross private investment in 1920 ran at the rate of 18.5 billion dollars, or 22.7 per cent of the Gross National Product. In the non-inflationary 1929 boom (noninflationary in the sense that there was no substantial increase in the price level), the gross private investment was only 16.0 per cent of the Gross National Product. It was the vast excess of investment outlays which caused the inflationary pressure witnessed in 1919–1920. But this high volume of investment could not last for long. And the reason is that both *autonomous* and *induced* investments are by their very nature precarious and short-lived.

The inventory situation in 1920 well illustrates the precarious character of induced investment. Net inventory accumulation was running at the rate of 4.9 billion dollars, or 5.6 per cent of the Gross National Product. Such a rate of net additions to inventories could only be continued if the *rate of increase* in output continued to rise. This of course was not possible, once full employment was approached. Thus we witnessed a decline in net inventory accumulation from 4.9 billion dollars in 1920 to 0.1 billion in 1921.

Investment in equipment (machinery and capital equipment of all kinds other than plant) illustrates well the role of *autonomous* investment, though a part of the 1920 volume was doubtless *induced* investment. The gross investment in producers' durable equipment was 6.7 billion dollars both in 1919 and in 1920. This high rate of investment in equipment was the result of an accumulation of technological developments over the war years. But it could not last, since at this rate of new installations the investment opportunities which had been opened up by the new advances in technique were rapidly being exhausted. Accordingly, gross investment in producers' equipment fell by 3 billion dollars in 1921.

The combined *decline* in the investment in inventories and in producers' equipment from 1920 to 1921 was 7.8 billion dollars out of a total decline of private gross capital formation as a whole of 9.3 billions. Thus it is possible to find in the inventory and producers' equipment situation the key to the end of the inflationary boom of 1919–1920.

The decline in investment, moreover, induced a 7-billion-dollar decline in consumption expenditures from 1920 to 1921. Since government outlays for goods and services remained substantially constant, the entire decline (18 billion dollars) in Gross National Product can be accounted for by the fall in private investment and private consumption.

This analysis, in terms of the internal self-limiting factors inherent in the process of expansion itself, is believed to be more fundamental than the explanation which runs in terms of monetary limitation.

Similarly the monetary explanation is inconclusive and inadequate with respect to the expansion terminating in 1929. Here again the decline of autonomous and induced investment is impressive. Gross private investment fell from 15.8 billion dollars in 1929 to 0.9 billion dollars in 1932. Inventory accumulation fell off by 4.1 billion dollars, producers' equipment by 4.6 billion, construction by 5.1 billion, and net foreign investment by 0.6 billion. The investment decline was clearly both autonomous and induced. But it was probably especially the falling off of autonomous investment which characterized the 1929 collapse. The upward surge of innovational investment associated with the rise of vast new industries, new products, and new processes, which characterized the boom of 1923–1929, produced a volume of gross private *domestic* investment which averaged 15 billion dollars from 1923 to 1929 inclusive. The optimism engendered by the prolonged surge of autonomous investment doubtless induced a not inconsiderable volume of unwise investment born of the excesses of a boom psychology. But it was fundamentally the temporary exhaustion of autonomous investment (Spiethoff, Robertson) which explains the collapse in investment. And this in turn induced a drastic curtailment of consumption expenditures. It is in *real*, not monetary, factors that one must search for a satisfactory explanation.

Thus the boom ran out more by reason of the internal nature of the expansion process than because of limitation of the money supply. It was the decline in the marginal efficiency of capital which terminated the boom as more and more investment progressively exhausted the list of opportunities which the then level of technique had opened up for profitable exploitation. Given the wide spread between consumption and income at high levels of employment, it required a continuous surge of *autonomous* investment, together with the *induced* investment caused by the *rate of increase* in output itself, to maintain prosperity. This could not last. Regardless of the monetary situation, the internal nature of the expansion itself necessarily brought the development to a close and precipitated a downward movement.

Upper and Lower Limits in the Internal Adjustment Process

And just as the consumption function, together with the marginal efficiency schedule and the acceleration principle, explains the upper limit (and so the cessation of an inflationary movement), so also these factors—inherent in the expansion and contraction process itself—explain the lower limit (and so the cessation of a deflationary tendency). As real income falls, consumption declines proportionally less, until eventually consumption equals income. Should consumption for a while fall below real income, this would mean that current output was being supplemented by the disinvestment of inventories and of fixed capital. In other words, consumption would exceed current production. This could not last. Net investment would soon rise from a minus quantity to at least zero.

Thus the *shape* of the consumption function, together with its *level* (both together establishing the "break-even" point at which consumption equals income), sets a lower limit to the process of contraction. Moreover, since there is typically some net autonomous investment in considerable sections of the economy, the lower limit, in the usual case, tends to be somewhat above the minimum.

We conclude then that there are internal self-limiting factors inherent in the process of expansion and contraction which tend to set upper and lower limits to any movement which is started in either direction. Thus the consumption function, together with the autonomous and induced investment functions (which functions relate investment to the interest rate and to changes in income respectively), are offered as significant factors explaining the relatively high stability in the value of money and the level of prices which (apart from wars) the historical record reveals. These self-limiting factors appear to be, by and large, adequate *unless* outside factors—notably inflationary fiscal operations of government in wartime—intervene to overthrow the tendency toward stability.

Conclusion

This analysis again emphasizes the point that it is basically the volume of *expenditures* which controls the quantity of money M and the intensity of its utilization V, not the other way around.

When the volume of government outlays is greatly expanded as in wartime, inflation typically occurs, and with it an increase in the quantity of money. Historically, except for wartime, the fiscal operations of government have not been inflationary—in fact, have contributed quite inadequately to the maintenance of full employment. Moreover, the fiscal operations have hitherto typically moved along with the fluctuations in private outlays, though usually with a smaller amplitude. It is true that there has often developed a treasury surplus in good times and a deficit (usually unplanned) in bad times. Thus fiscal operations have sometimes dampened, in a very limited degree, the fluctuations. But virtually no effort has, until recently, been made deliberately to *offset* fluctuations in private investment and consumption outlays. Accordingly, rather wide fluctuations in income and aggregate outlays have occurred over 150 years. But, except for wartime, these fluctuations have been kept within fairly well-defined limits, restricted by the self-limiting factors inherent in the internal nature of the expansion and contraction process itself. The system is so constituted that within these limits it is essentially stable. No external limiting, or "reining-in," factors are needed to explain this stability.

The more income expands, the more investment must rise to fill the ever widening gap between consumption and income. Thus the schedule of declining marginal efficiency of capital, the acceleration principle, and the consumption function constitute a self-limiting adjustment mechanism by which expansion comes to a close. The system is within limits internally and inherently stable. The degree of stability we have witnessed over a century and more cannot be credited mainly to institutional arrangements such as money and banking. Rather, it is to be explained in terms of the nature of the process itself as disclosed in the variables involved in the investment and consumption functions.

With respect to the future, however, two factors are emerging which raise the question whether the outlook may not point toward a continuous secular rise in prices. One is the vastly increased power of labor in its bargaining relation with employers; and the other is the powerful drive in all modern democratic societies to carry out a program of full employment. Under the conditions of continuing full employment, is it likely that efficiency-wages (labor cost) will be kept stable? If efficiency-wage rates $\dfrac{W}{E}$ are allowed to rise, the price level must rise also.

All these are long-run problems quite distinct from the immediately pressing problems of inflation, cast up by the war upheaval, which are now upon us. To these current inflationary developments we turn in the following chapter.

Chapter 11

Monetary and Fiscal Policy in Postwar Inflation

EXCLUSIVE RELIANCE upon monetary policy as the means to cope with inflation is a dangerously one-sided weapon. A many-sided attack on the problem is necessary.

Even nowadays, despite the fact that the quantity theory has been pushed off the stage, one sometimes encounters the view that variations in the general price level are in the main determined by variations in the quantity of money. This is partly an oversimplification, partly a half-truth, and partly just wrong. It would be much nearer the truth to say that variations in the general price level are mainly determined by variations in the total outlays of business, consumers, and government.

But there is no direct relation even here. Under conditions of unemployment and unused resources, variations in total outlays may largely affect output with little effect on prices; under conditions of full employment, increases in total outlays will be reflected in a general rise in prices. To control inflation, it is then necessary to control total outlays.

Bottlenecks and Specific Shortages

Moreover, it is not simply a matter of aggregates. In periods of inflationary pressures, the economy may suffer from bottlenecks in steel and transportation, and from serious shortages of certain raw materials and foods. The aggregate approach alone will not do. Specific and direct measures may be needed.

The central fact, often overlooked, about the postwar inflation following the Second World War is the world scarcity of food and the extraordinary rise in food prices. The wholesale prices of foods in the

United States increased from an index of 70.4 in 1939 (1926 = 100) to 190.3 at the end of November, 1947, an increase of 170 per cent. Meanwhile the consumers' price index for food rose from 95.2 (1935–1939 = 100) in 1939 to 201.6 in October, 1947, an increase of 122 per cent. Farm products and food prices (and also hides and leather products, and building materials) had risen far out of line with the prices of all other commodities. From 1945 to the end of 1947, whole-sale food and farm prices have risen 70 per cent. And food accounts normally for about 35 per cent of the total expenditures of wage earners' families in the United States.

In a free market, under the conditions following the Second World War, a sharp rise of food prices *in relation to other commodities* was inevitable. It should especially be noted that policies directed at the over-all aggregate demand, including monetary and fiscal policy, could not possibly cope with this problem of *relative* price distortion. The current world food shortage is the result of the destruction caused by the war and unusually severe floods and droughts; and on the demand side it is due to full-employment incomes, especially in the United States.

In its present aggravated form it is certainly a temporary situation. Agricultural reconstruction and development all over the world will in a few years bring relief from food shortages. Food prices, we can be sure, will fall in relation to the prices of other commodities, though they are not likely to fall to the abnormally low ratio prevailing in the 1930's.

Rationing and price control are the only measures which could have prevented the drastic rise in the prices of food *relative to other com-modities*. Over-all reduction in aggregate demand might indeed have kept the general level of prices lower, but it could not prevent the rise in food prices relative to other commodities.

These considerations are important, since they emphasize the fact that the postwar inflationary problem, at least in the United States, is not merely one of excess aggregate demand in relation to available supply.

It is indeed true that aggregate demand has been, and continues to be, in excess of the available supply. But this also is in no small measure an indirect consequence of scarcities in special areas—food, steel, certain transportation facilities, specific kinds of machinery and materials. In the period of reconversion from a vast war effort to peacetime production, bottlenecks will inevitably develop. It takes time to fill the pipe lines and restock inventories all along the way, including the kitchens, closets, and storerooms of the consumers. Such shortages at numerous strategic points in the economy tend to generate (as we shall see later in this chapter) a condition of excess over-all demand in relation to available supply.

But this situation is surely very different from the normal peacetime condition of an over-all excess of aggregate demand. It is indeed a part of the war experience. It cannot be dealt with by ordinary peacetime methods.

Yet it does not necessarily follow that wartime rationing and price control should be extended beyond the immediate transition period into the longer period of reconversion. That depends a great deal, in a democratic society, upon the attitude of the public. In the First World War the political complexion of democratic countries was such that they preferred wartime inflation to rationing and price control. In the Second World War, impressed by the experience of other countries and mindful of the experience of the First World War, a New Deal administration in the United States was indeed able to undertake rationing and price control. But the political complexion of the country did not permit its continuation for long in peacetime. Without the cooperation of business and a large section of the consuming public, controls were apparently no longer workable.

Without going into the *theoretical* merits of rationing and price control as means to cope with the *temporary* and *strategic* shortages, it is sufficient to point out that the choice lay in fact between continuing the controls or accepting as inevitable a very considerable general price inflation. The latter is indeed what has occurred. And I do not believe it could have been altogether prevented by any indirect attack on the problem, such as monetary and fiscal policy. These indirect methods could at best only limit the extent of the inflation. Had we been prepared to maintain the controls through the period of the restocking boom, we could I think have entered the more normal peacetime period with a substantially stable price level at around an index of, say, 110. In the meantime real income would progressively have grown until the volume of money and liquid assets would no longer have been excessive.

Over-all Control Measures

Theoretically we could, of course, imagine so drastic a tax program that private spending on investment and consumption, even in the absence of controls, would have prevented any *general* price rise. But a cutback of business and personal incomes, after taxes, sufficiently drastic to produce this result would surely have prevented the vast expansion of production which actually occurred.

Those who argue that the "miracle of peacetime production" (despite serious bottlenecks) could not have occurred had the controls been maintained are perhaps right, when one takes into consideration the political complexion and general public attitude. But some have argued that the price inflation following the removal of controls could have been prevented by monetary or fiscal measures, without curtailing production. This would, however, have required a drastic deflation of income, whether by fiscal measures or by monetary and credit contraction, far more serious, I believe, for production and employment than any reasonably efficient system of controls.

The plain fact is that in the condition of special scarcities and bottlenecks prevailing in 1946–1947, a considerable inflation of the prices of foodstuffs and materials in short supply (once a free market was restored) was inevitable. Only a drastic deflation of income could, in a free market, have prevented it. And if we were determined to reestablish prematurely a free market, some considerable price inflation was certainly to be preferred to the deflation and unemployment which would have been necessary to check inflation in the absence of rationing and price control.

Moreover, it was inevitable, in the absence of rationing and price control, that these special scarcity situations (especially in food) should themselves contribute to the excess of over-all, aggregate demand. We have already noted (Chap. 8) that the sharp rise in food prices, once the controls were removed, could not fail to incite demands for higher wages. The statistical record, as we have noted, supports this view. The sharp advance in average hourly earnings since June, 1946 raised aggregate demand in relation to the available output. Thus the specialized shortages (especially in foodstuffs), in the absence of rationing and price controls, contributed to an income inflation which magnified the over-all inflationary problem.

We were thus confronted with an excess of aggregate demand in relation to available output. We were caught, as so often, in a vicious circle. Since we were unwilling to exercise direct controls in the special scarcity areas where they were needed, the over-all problem was necessarily aggravated.

Monetary Control Measures

The fiscal remedy for an over-all excess of demand is more effective and less dangerous than the monetary one. Indeed, the monetary weapon to curtail an over-all excess of effective demand has the peculiar characteristic that it is scarcely at all effective unless the brakes are applied so vigorously as to precipitate a collapse. It would be interesting to know how high the interest rate would have to be pushed, in a period of inflationary pressure, before it could have any substantial effect on investment and consumption outlays. Indeed, once the measure did take hold, it would probably be found to operate indirectly via a general shattering of confidence (through the effect on the securities market) rather than in terms of the direct effect of higher interest rates on investment and consumption decisions. Those who glibly talk about controlling the inflation by monetary policy have failed to consider that moderate monetary measures by themselves alone are relatively ineffective, while drastic measures may easily turn the economy into a tail spin.

Historical experience does not justify the belief that monetary measures can effectively control over-all inflationary pressures. High rates of interest did not check the inflationary movement of prices in 1919–1920 or the speculative tendencies in the real-estate and security markets in the late 1920's. Nevertheless, while it is not likely to prove *single-handed* an effective method, in conjunction with fiscal and other policies monetary policy can play a significant role in helping to bring the economy through to more stable conditions.

A Many-sided Program

First and foremost, in order to control inflation it is necessary to produce a very substantial budgetary surplus. Government expenditures should be held down to what is urgently necessary. And if we have learned anything from both theory and experience, it should be that a period of strong inflationary pressures is not the time to reduce taxes. We should use the cash surplus to retire government securities held by the Federal Reserve Banks and the commercial banks, thereby reducing the volume of reserves and deposits.[1]

Second, it is necessary to resist wage inflation, by which I mean an increase in wages in excess of productivity. Until the removal of price control we had substantial wage stability in terms of average hourly earnings. A substantial wage inflation—an increase in wage rates in excess of productivity advances—followed the decontrols after June, 1946. That this would occur could easily have been foreseen in view of the sharp increases in food prices following the abandonment of controls. Thus the country moved into a vicious spiral of price–wage increases—both a symptom and a further cause of inflation.

Third, restriction of consumer credit. Fourth, an intensive campaign to sell savings bonds. Fifth (apart from reasonable provisions for housing for veterans and low-income groups as far as urgent necessity dictates), control of inflation will not permit lax standards of appraisal on such easy credit terms as to encourage the development of a speculative real-estate market. Sixth, limited allocations, rationing, and price controls in special areas.

[1] A *voluntary* reduction of deposits (once the pressure for active and precautionary balances is relaxed) is by no means impossible. Suppose the public wishes to hold less deposits and more securities. This means a shift to the left in the L function. If the function has an intermediate interest-elasticity, the effect of a downward shift in the L function is partly to lower the rate of interest and partly to decrease the volume of deposits. The interest rate will be lowered because the public will be bidding against the banks for securities; and to the degree that they succeed in pulling securities away from the banks, the volume of deposits will decline.

Money and "Near-money": General Liquidity

There are many who become quite impatient with anyone who assigns a secondary role to monetary policy in the control of inflation. Yet in the nature of the case it cannot be the primary measure. This is so because the monetary and banking system, if it is to perform its normal function, must necessarily be highly flexible. The conception that the rate of spending can be rigorously controlled by increasing and decreasing the money supply, extending and curtailing credit, is based on a very primitive notion of the role of money and liquid assets in modern societies. In primitive societies wealth could easily be classified, on the one hand, into real estate and commodities, and on the other, into money. In the modern community tangible wealth is typically represented by claims (securities). Thus there is a vast volume of liquid assets that shade off into near-money. Moreover, the growth of the public debt has added enormously to the liquid assets, of which the short-term obligations are very close to being money. In addition there is a vast volume of savings deposits. "Money" is no longer an easily separable and distinctively marked-off category of wealth. In these circumstances it is no simple matter to control the rate of spending by controlling the quantity of money. Under the postwar conditions of high all-around liquidity, government bonds would have to fall to intolerable levels if even a beginning toward control were to be sought by monetary means alone.[1]

It would be an easy matter to stop a man from becoming excessively corpulent simply by strangling him to death. A sufficiently sharp curtailment of the money supply could indeed quickly end an inflation. No one denies that. But a program to stop an inflationary development merely by reducing the quantity of money is a dangerous device. Moderately used, it courts the failure of ineffectiveness; pushed to the needed fanatical extremes, it courts disaster.

Consumption and Investment

The high volume of current consumer spending is primarily due to the current high level of income. No one wishes to deflate this income

[1] It is one thing to talk about credit restriction when banks are fully loaned up (as in the 1920's) and when neither the public nor the banks hold large quantities of securities; it is quite another matter when the community is possessed of a large volume of liquid assets.

level. And there is no convincing evidence that *consumers as a whole* are spending beyond their income, though it is certainly possible that one would find this to be the case if farmers and unincorporated business units could be segregated. The total holdings of Series "E" savings bonds has remained at the stable level of 30.8 billion dollars in January, 1946 and 31.7 billion dollars in June, 1948, though lower income groups held less at the end of the period while upper income groups held more. In the first half of 1948 consumers were saving out of disposable income (income after taxes) 11.6 billion dollars, or 6.2 per cent of disposable income, compared with 4.4 per cent in 1929. (Against this there was the offset of an increase in consumer credit of 2.9 billion dollars from May, 1947 to May, 1948.) During this period the government had a substantial cash surplus. Thus both consumers and the government spent substantially less than income. Accordingly, the basic source of the inflationary pressure came from private investment outlays and net foreign investment, which together ran around 40 billion dollars per annum. Put in another way, gross investment outran the volume of planned gross saving. Monetary expansion filled the gap. During 1947 the loans and investments of all commercial banks to private enterprise and consumers increased by around 7 billion dollars.

Merely to choke off (even though this were a simple matter, which it is not) the excess of investment over available savings [1] would be a shotgun method of dealing with the problem. Much investment of a type which would contribute to available output would be hit, while much speculative investment—investment which would contribute little to increase available supply—might not be affected. Use of allocations and construction permits would be far more effective and they could be applied at the points needed.

---

[1] The excess of investment over available planned savings tends to drive income up until savings (Keynesian terminology) equal investment. Thus it is the inflationary process itself (and the redistribution of income which it brings about) which generates a flow of savings out of current income equal to investment. The income stream has of course been fed by new money and the activation of idle money; so that Robertsonian savings plus the increment in MV equal the volume of investment. Compare in this connection, William Fellner, *Monetary Policies and Full Employment*, pp. 183–186, especially p. 184.

Government Cash Surplus

Highly essential as a means of controlling inflation is the maintenance of a surplus of government cash receipts (other than borrowing) over cash payments. In the calendar year 1947 the cash surplus was 5.7 billion dollars and in the first half of 1948 it was 7.6 billion dollars. The 1948 reduction in income taxes, enacted just when expenditures for defense had to be increased, added substantially, especially when account is taken of the multiplier, to the prevailing inflationary pressures.

Cash taken from the public (mainly taxes) in excess of cash payments to the public has the effect of reducing private expenditures. This is particularly true if personal income taxes [1] are collected from a large part of the consuming public. Moreover, when these surplus cash funds are used to retire bonds held by the commercial banks the effect is to reduce demand deposits; [2] and when used to retire bonds held by the Federal Reserve Banks, the effect is to put a continuous pressure on member-bank reserves. It is true that the banks can replenish their reserves by selling securities to the Federal Reserve Banks, or by borrowing upon them, but the pressure on reserves nonetheless operates to restrain bank credit expansion. The continuous pressure on reserves, incident to the use of Treasury cash surplus to retire securities held by the Federal Reserve Banks, is much to be preferred to the "jerky method" of raising reserve requirements.

[1] An excess profits tax is antiinflationary in two respects. By reducing the corporate profits after taxes (1) wage demands stimulated by high profits will tend to be less insistent and (2) dividend payments (and so consumption) will be more or less curtailed.

[2] Sometimes it is alleged that the retirement of debt held by the public is not antiinflationary, since the extra tax money is paid over to bondholders who will put the funds to work. But the conclusion reached is erroneous for the following reasons. When tax money collected from the masses of citizens is paid over to bondholders, funds are by and large transferred from consumers to savers. Bondholders are not likely to increase consumption merely because some of their liquid assets have been transferred from bonds into cash. Some will simply hold the cash idle; others will seek a financial investment and this will tend (slightly) to lower the rate of interest. The net effect, of the receipt of cash by the bondholders whose securities are repaid, on total expenditures for goods and services is likely to be negligible. In contrast the effect of the extra taxes (from which the cash surplus is derived) on consumption expenditures is likely to be substantial. Thus the net effect of the retirement of bonds held by the public is antiinflationary.

Moderate Monetary Restraint

Any attempt to control inflation by monetary means alone is likely to turn the economy into a nose dive. Nonetheless, some monetary restraint is necessary and desirable. In a period of inflationary pressures it does not make sense to feed the inflation with easy credit. Monetary restraint can, in conjunction with other measures, play a useful role.

We have already mentioned the importance of control of consumer and real-estate credit. Margin requirements on the stock exchange could be raised to 100 per cent. Moreover, banks could be prevented from shifting out of government securities into private loans and investments by imposing a security reserve in addition to the cash reserve. An increase in the yield on short-term government obligations operates to a limited extent in the same direction. A stiffening of interest rates all around is perhaps more an indication of a high rate of investment activity than a deterrent to the volume of investment.

Summary

These proposals having to do with monetary restraints cannot be regarded as in any sense a "solution" to the problem of inflation. There is needed instead a many-sided attack on the problem, including the following:

1. Judicious use of monetary policy. Moderate control of the use of credit.

2. Fiscal policy—maintenance of high tax rates, scrutiny of expenditures, and postponement of all capital outlays not justified on strong grounds of national policy. A large Treasury cash surplus must be the core and center of an antiinflationary program.

3. In addition to the judicious use of monetary policy and a firm use of fiscal policy, minimum direct controls, including allocation of scarce materials for essential uses, construction permits, and rationing (for example, of important foods). Over-all monetary and fiscal policy alone cannot cope with bottlenecks and special scarcities.

Moderation and self-restraint are essential for the survival of free democratic government. But this suggests the willingness to use controls when emergency conditions require such measures—and also the capacity to use them judiciously.

Chapter 12

The Role of Money in Fiscal Policy

FISCAL POLICY and deficit financing are to many people merely different terms for the same thing. This is, however, an erroneous conception. An increase in government outlays will tend to increase the flow of national income, whatever the method of financing; but the expansionist effect will vary according to the method used.

Financing Methods

In general there are four methods of financing: (1) borrowing from the banking system, (2) borrowing from the public, (3) a progressive system of taxation, and (4) regressive taxes.

If an increase in government outlays is financed by borrowing from the banks, the quantity of money is increased. If financing is done by borrowing from the public, deposits already in existence will be spent which might otherwise remain idle balances. If the outlays are financed by progressive taxation, the effect is mainly to tap the savings of the wealthy without encroaching significantly upon consumption. If financing is by regressive taxation (for example, sales taxes), income may indeed expand by the amount of the increased outlays, but not by a magnified amount. Thus the expansionist effect of government outlays will vary according to the method of financing.

We have noted the (mistaken) view that government outlays can have an expansionist effect only if they are deficit-financed. Others have advanced the view that no favorable effects can be expected unless the deficit is financed by new money. Both these positions are untenable. From Keynes's *General Theory* on, it was always recognized that expenditures financed by progressive taxation (effecting a re-distribution of income) may raise income and employment.[1] More

[1] See Alvin H. Hansen, *Fiscal Policy and Business Cycles*, pp. 182–184; also Hansen, "Three Methods of Expansion through Fiscal Policy," *American Economic Review*, June, 1945.

recently it has been shown that an increase in expenditures, tax-financed, may be expansionist even though the system of taxation has no redistributional effect upon income.[1]

Monetary and Fiscal Policy: Independent Use of Each

For our purposes here, we are concerned specifically with the relation of the fiscal operations of the government to the *money supply*. Those who hold with Hawtrey that "variations of effective demand . . . must be traced to movements of bank credit"[2] will deny that fiscal policy could be effective except in so far as it serves to increase the quantity of money.[3]

Two questions relating to the role of money in income generation present themselves. On the one side, will an expansion of government outlays (or private investment, for that matter) financed by methods which do not increase the quantity of money raise aggregate demand and so the level of national income? On the other side, will an increase in the quantity of money by methods which are not directly related to outlays on goods and services (such as gold inflows, or open-market operations of the Central Bank) raise the level of aggregate demand?

The answers to these questions depend upon the facts with respect to the prevailing interest-elasticities of the liquidity preference function and the investment function, and whether the consumption function rises or falls in response to changes in the rate of interest.[4]

---

[1] See Hansen and Perloff, *State and Local Finance in the National Economy*, pp. 245–246, where the expansionist effect of *regressively* financed government outlays is discussed; also Trygve Haavelmo, "Multiplier Effects of a Balanced Budget," *Econometrica*, October, 1945, together with the literature there cited; also Haberler, Goodwin, Hagen, and Haavelmo in *Econometrica*, April, 1946.

[2] *Readings in Business Cycle Theory*, p. 341.

[3] See the able criticisms of this point of view by James Tobin, "Liquidity Preference and Monetary Policy," *The Review of Economic Statistics*, May, 1947. I have relied heavily upon his analysis.

[4] An increase in the money supply resulting from open-market purchases of securities by the banking system merely has the effect of monetizing a part of the liquid assets held by the nonbanking investors. It does not involve a change in the volume of *total* liquid assets in the possession of the public. Only the composition of the assets is affected. An increase (or decrease) in the volume of total liquid assets held by the public *would* tend to raise (or lower) the consumption function. But this situation is not involved in the case of pure monetary policy.

Case A

If the liquidity function L is completely interest-inelastic (Fig. 21), it follows that the investment function must be more or less interest-elastic (say an elasticity of unity), and/or the consumption function must shift upward as interest rates fall. In these circumstances an increase in the quantity of money will raise income. Accordingly, monetary policy by itself alone will prove effective in raising income. There will be no need of direct fiscal policy in the form of government

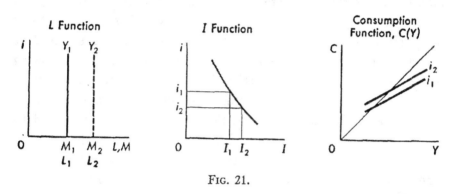

FIG. 21.

outlays or income-generating expenditures. Under the conditions given above an increase in the quantity of money will either flow *directly* into the market for goods and services or *indirectly* (financial investment) via the impact of lower rates of interest upon investment [1] or consumption expenditures. Either way, additions to the money supply (from M_1 to M_2, Fig. 21) will be *spent* until income and sales volume rise to a level sufficiently high so that the additional stock of money will be needed for transactions purposes.[2] At this point the public will no longer regard the extra money as a net addition to spendible income, or as "spare" or "unwanted" cash. *Desired* cash will have risen until it again equals the *actual* quantity of cash.[3]

[1] In Fig. 21, as interest rates fall from i_1 to i_2 (the spare cash having been used to buy securities) investment rises from I_1 to I_2. Similarly the fall in the rate of interest will raise the consumption function from the level labeled i_1 to that labeled i_2.

[2] The L function will shift from the schedule labeled Y_1 to that labeled Y_2.

[3] In Fig. 21 *desired* cash will increase from L_1 to L_2. Thus a new equilibrium is reached at which $L_2 = M_2$.

Under the given assumptions with respect to the L function, the I function, and the consumption function, income-generating expenditures by the government unsupported by an increase in the quantity of money would be wholly ineffective. This is so since any incipient increase in total outlays would require an increase in money for transactions purposes. Since, under the assumptions as given, no such increase is provided by the monetary authorities, an effort would be made to obtain the money through the sale of securities (causing an increase in the rate of interest) or by cutting down on consumption expenditures. By these means the necessary "working balances" could be obtained. But by this process the increased government outlays would be offset either by reduced private investment outlays (owing to the rise in the rate of interest) or by reduced private consumption outlays. Thus the income-generating expenditures of the government, unaccompanied by an increase in the quantity of money, would be self-defeating, since they would induce, under the conditions here assumed, a corresponding reduction in private expenditures. It is assumptions such as these outlined here that underlie the pure monetary theory of the business cycle and the quantity theory of money and prices.

Case B

If the L function is fairly interest-elastic (say an elasticity of $\frac{1}{2}$ to 2) while the I function is similarly interest-elastic,[1] an increase in the quantity of money (unaccompanied by income-generating fiscal outlays) will be *partially* effective in raising the level of income. But in this case the increase in income will be relatively less than in Case A. This is so because the L function is more or less interest-elastic. Accordingly, not *all* the new money will be regarded as a net addition to spendible income; a part will be held as idle balances. Thus income will not rise in proportion to the increase in the money supply.

Also, under the assumption given in Case B income-generating expenditures of the government unaccompanied by any increase in

---

[1] The consumption function may also, possibly, be responsive to changes in the rate of interest.

the quantity of money will prove only *partially* effective in raising income. This is so because such outlays will, in these circumstances, in some measure, be counterbalanced by some offsetting decline in private investment (and perhaps consumption) expenditures, since the rate of interest will rise. Total spending will be increased, but not by the full leverage (multiplier and accelerator) effect, since the rise in the rate of interest will have a damping influence on private investment (here assumed to be interest-elastic) and possibly also on consumption expenditures.[1]

Case C

In this case it is assumed *either* that the L function is infinitely interest-elastic *or* that the I function and the consumption function

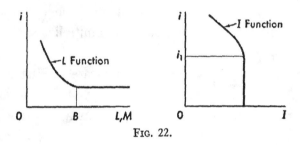

FIG. 22.

are both wholly insensitive to a reduction in the rate of interest. Under either of these conditions an increase in the quantity of money unaccompanied by income-generating fiscal outlays will prove wholly ineffective in raising income.

Let us consider each assumption separately. If the L function is infinitely interest-elastic (Fig. 22, horizontal part of curve), then an increase in the quantity of money alone (not backed up by fiscal policy) will only add to the volume of idle balances. The increased quantity of money will not raise the level of private expenditures.

If, on the other hand, the investment function [2] and the consumption

---

[1] The relevant diagram would be similar to those given in Fig. 21, except that the L function, being moderately interest-elastic, would have a falling slope similar to the I function curve in Fig. 21.

[2] See the vertical part of I function in Fig. 22.

function are both wholly insensitive to changes in the rate of interest, an increase in the quantity of money would not affect private outlays, even though the L function had an interest-elasticity of less than infinity (downward-sloping part of curve, Fig. 22). This is so since in these circumstances the increased quantity of money will not be used directly to buy investment or consumption goods, but instead will be used for *financial* investment. This will reduce the rate of interest. But according to the assumptions here made, such reduction will have no effect on either investment or consumption.

Accordingly, under either one of these two sets of assumptions monetary policy *alone*, unsupported by fiscal policy, would be wholly ineffective. This is Case C. Fiscal policy however (even though un-supported by any increase in the quantity of money) would in this case be fully effective (including both the multiplier and acceleration effect) in raising income.

Again, let us take the assumptions separately. First assume that the L function is wholly interest-elastic. It will then be possible for the income-generating outlays by the government to draw the needed money for transactions purposes from idle balances without raising the rate of interest. Accordingly, no adverse effect will be felt on private investment or private consumption expenditures even though these were more or less sensitive to the rate of interest.

Assume, second, that the investment and consumption functions are wholly *insensitive* to changes in the rate of interest. Then no adverse effects would follow from some increase in the rate of interest, incident to the increased demand for "transactions" cash. Such needed cash would be drawn from idle balances, but at the cost of higher rates of interest, since the L function is in this case assumed to be sloping downward (see Fig. 22). But the increased rate of interest would not reduce private investment or consumption outlays, since these func-tions are here assumed to be wholly insensitive to interest changes. Accordingly, fiscal policy (income-generating outlays), even though entirely unsupported by monetary policy (there being no increase in quantity of money), would nevertheless be wholly effective in raising income.

General Conclusions

The rigorous assumptions made in each of the three cases under consideration above are helpful in isolating clearly the factors involved and thereby appraising the efficacy of monetary *or* fiscal policy, each unaided by the other.

In the real world the assumptions made in Case A describe more or less the conditions in a country rich in natural resources, but industrially undeveloped and rapidly expanding. Here the quantity theory and pure monetary policy come into their own; and indeed it was under such conditions that the quantity theory held the field.

The assumptions made in Case C describe more or less accurately the conditions in a highly developed industrialized country well equipped with modern and efficient capital facilities. More particularly, this case describes the conditions of temporary saturation of investment opportunities following a pronounced upward surge of investment.

The assumptions made in Case B are perhaps, on the whole, most likely to prevail under normal circumstances. The L function, while fairly elastic, is regarded as having some downward slope; and investment and consumption are thought to be more or less responsive to changes in the rate of interest. In these circumstances fiscal and monetary policy are both needed to reinforce each other—the one without the other can only be partially effective.

In the usual case governmental outlays are likely to affect the capital market adversely unless accompanied by monetary policy designed to increase the quantity of money, thereby preventing a rise in (or even lowering) the rate of interest. A low rate of interest can be achieved by financing a portion (how much is needed will depend upon the interest-elasticity of the L function) of the income-generating outlays by borrowing from the banking system. For the rest, borrowing from the public will restrict consumption outlays less than tax financing, even though a progressive system of taxation is applied. In so far as the outlays are tax financed, progressive taxation will restrict consumption less than regressive taxation, but may adversely affect investment. Thus it is usually safer to supplement fiscal policy with monetary policy.

Chapter 13

A Managed Compensatory Fiscal Program

IN GENERAL THREE types of fiscal programs can be applied in an economy experiencing cyclical fluctuations of income and employment. These programs are outlined in a recent report of the Committee for Economic Development entitled *Taxes and the Budget*.

The Balanced Budget

First there is the balanced-budget program; second, the CED plan of "built-in flexibility"; and third, the managed compensatory program.

The balanced-budget program could be carried out either on the basis of fixed public expenditures over the cycle, or (in accordance with past practice) on the basis of an increase in expenditures in boom years as tax revenues rise, with reduced expenditures in depression years as tax revenues fall. If the expenditures were fixed over the cycle, tax rates would be lowered in boom years and increased in depression,[1] so as to make revenues just sufficient to balance the fixed budget. In actual practice the goal arrived at by so-called sound finance has in fact not fully been realized. In severe depression periods it has not been possible to balance the budget. Thus under the Hoover administration, despite strong efforts to balance the budget, insistent emergency demands raised expenditures from 3.2 billion dollars in 1930 to 4.6 billion dollars in 1932, while revenues declined from 3.9 billion dollars in 1930 to 1.9 billion dollars in 1932.

---

[1] This is so because a fall in income, with constant tax rates, results in a decline in total revenues. The fall in revenues will exceed, percentagewise, the fall in income if the income-tax structure is progressive in character. Conversely when income rises total revenues will rise, on a percentage basis, more rapidly than income.

The CED Program

Second, there is the budgetary program prepared by the Committee for Economic Development, perhaps somewhat too optimistically referred to as the "stabilizing budget policy."

This calls for fixed public expenditures over the cycle, determined on the basis of social needs in accordance with the values placed on public services by a democratic society. Moreover, it calls for fixed *tax rates*, so adjusted as to balance the budget when, say, 93 per cent of the labor force is employed. It is assumed that an employment of 96 per cent of the labor force represents "full employment." At full employment the fixed tax rate structure should yield a budgetary surplus [1] of, say, around 3 billion dollars. At employment levels below 93 per cent a deficit would develop, since tax revenues would fall as income declines. Indeed, tax revenue would fall much faster than income (a rough estimate [2] suggests a ratio of perhaps 1.5 to 1), with fairly high progressivity in rates.

Deficits in depression years are welcomed, since deficit financing reduces private spending less than tax financing. In boom years budgetary surpluses are welcomed, since an excess of taxes over expenditures tends to curtail excessive private spending. There can be no question that a fixed budget combined with fixed tax rates tends to promote stability *in contrast with* the balanced-budget procedure.

The CED report represents an important advance in fiscal thinking compared with the tenets of so-called sound finance. Income-generating outlays are indeed to be held constant, but in boom years more tax money will be taken from the public than the government spends; in depression years government spending will exceed the tax money taken from the public, thereby contributing to the total stream of outlays, governmental and private.

Critique of the CED Proposals

The CED program is excellent as far as it goes, but it falls short of being adequate. The report takes a somewhat too optimistic view of

---

[1] It is the "cash budget," not the "conventional budget," to which reference is here made. See *Midyear Economic Report of the President*, July, 1948, pp. 18–19, for definitions of these terms.

[2] No estimate is made by the CED.

the manner in which the modern complex economy functions. It promises too much when it suggests that its program is a "stabilizing budget." It is indeed more a stabilizing than a balanced budget; but the phrase, and indeed the whole tenor of the report, suggests much more than that. The plain fact is that under the CED plan we could have not only prolonged unemployment, but also drastic and precipitate declines in income and employment.

There are two things fundamentally wrong with the CED report. First, it assumes too optimistically that (given its budgetary plan, its tax structure, and in general a healthy balance in the cost-price structure, in labor-management relations, and the like) the economy would automatically tend toward full employment. Second, it fails to recognize the precarious foundation upon which boom conditions rest, the speed with which a recession can develop, and the difficulty of checking it once the cumulative downward process is under way.

In the decade of the 1920's an unwarranted optimism spread abroad in the land under the banner of what came to be known as the "new era" philosophy. Prosperity, it came to be believed, was here to stay. And when it suddenly vanished, very many, including the more sophisticated, were mystified. It was assumed that prosperity was somehow "natural." Why, then, should it so tragically elude us, try as we might to hold it in our grasp? Nothing more vividly illustrates (despite the fact that the 1920's were the decade in which the "business cycle" had become, so to speak, a popular fad) how little we had learned about the nature of booms and depressions.

"New era" talk has been reviving in recent years under a new banner. We are told that if we will but make our society "healthy" we shall not need to worry about depressions and unemployment. A good tax system, good labor-management relations, a good balance in the price structure [1] (*et hoc genus omne*) will ensure continuing full employment.

This is Say's law all over again. It does not even take account of all we have learned from business-cycle theory. It is true that business-cycle theory, until the advent of Keynes's *General Theory* in 1936, leaned to the view that the economy automatically tends toward full

---

[1] While these conditions will not *ensure* stability, they are nevertheless important on their own account; and they can *contribute* to stability.

employment *in the boom phase* of the cycle. So strong was this view that a well-known American business-cycle analyst could not believe, in the autumn of 1937, that the downturn might really develop into a depression. Why not? Forsooth, because we had not yet reached full employment!

Nevertheless, business-cycle theory, from Tugan-Baranowsky, Spiethoff, Cassel, Robertson, and Schumpeter on, has taught us, or should have taught us, that fluctuations, even violent fluctuations, in the rate of investment can be expected in the modern economic order, even though it is a "healthy" society with respect to the tax structure, wage–price balance, industrial relations, etc. And under the impulse of the cumulative process a deep recession can quickly turn into a rapidly moving collapse. Such mild and gentle stabilizers as a fixed budget and fixed tax rates will in these circumstances prove to be hopelessly ineffective. The business cycle is an unruly behavior characteristic of the modern economy. It will be no easy task to bring it under control. *And it is not a pathological behavior pattern.* It is an inherent characteristic of a dynamic, progressive society, which can only be understood by analyzing the factors underlying the intermittent surges of investment activity. These will occur, more or less, even though the society is "healthy" with respect to such structural arrangements as those cited above.

But this is not all. The CED report fails to take adequate account of the pattern of consumption in relation to income—the consumption function. The prevailing consumption function in the United States is a product of very deep and fundamental behavior patterns and institutional arrangements, which can indeed over time be modified, but are not likely (except for terrific disturbances such as a global war) to be quickly or easily altered. There is good reason to believe that it is not easy to change the consumption function, in the short run, with a speed which could even approximate (were this the only policy) the requirements of continuing income and employment stability over the various phases of the investment cycle. Accordingly, it is necessary to make vigorous use of an anticyclical fiscal program, since it is not to be expected that consumption can or will offset such fluctuations as may occur in the rate of investment.

The CED budget and tax program provides that *if* there is full employment the budget will be slightly overbalanced. The program offers no assurance that the system will reach full employment even in boom years, or that in special circumstances there may not be over-full employment.

The *size* of the public budget and the *method of financing* it are determinants of the level of income that modern societies cannot overlook; it cannot be assumed that under automatic forces the economy will naturally tend, despite some oscillations around this norm, toward full employment. Such a view overlooks the consumption function together with the role of continually changing and often volatile forces —new discoveries, technological developments, population movements and shifts—together with the responses of entrepreneurs (waves of innovations, optimism and pessimism) to these external shocks—upon the rate of autonomous investment.

The CED program would be reasonably adequate if the modern economy tended always, with mild oscillations around the norm, toward full employment. But that is not the kind of society we live in. Rather, it is one of intermittent surges of growth, with spurts of capital formation lasting precariously only so long as autonomous outlets for investment hold out. When these become exhausted the leverage effect operates swiftly in reverse, with induced investment and induced consumption rapidly dwindling along with the decline in autonomous investment. At times these upward surges, with full leverage effect, drive the economy up to full employment, and occasionally even beyond; but often the expansion is halting and inadequate.

Thus in place of smooth and dependable oscillations around a full-employment norm we are actually confronted with widely different situations—bulges of investment, as in 1920 and 1947, with inflationary pressures; hyperdeflation, as in 1932; and partial recoveries and stagnation, as in 1936–1939. These intermittent surges and cumulative collapses, varying widely from cycle to cycle, can only be met by a managed compensatory program. "Built-in flexibility" is highly desirable as far as it goes, but it could only be adequate in a society experiencing mild oscillations. A managed program is necessary in the rough-and-tumble world we live in. Our economy can quickly take a nose dive.

The CED report is indeed not altogether oblivious of this problem, as will be evident from the following quotation:

> "The recommendations of this report are presented in the belief that, if they are combined with appropriate measures in other fields, economic fluctuations can be confined to moderate departures from a high level. Yet it would be foolhardy to ignore the possibility that we may again confront an economic crisis of great magnitude—either severe depression or major inflation. Some extraordinary action must and will be taken if such a crisis appears. An emergency Congressional reduction or increase in tax rates (perhaps with a fixed, automatic termination date) would then be one of the most effective and least dangerous of the available courses." [1]

This again is excellent as far as it goes. But there lies behind this statement the assumption that emergency situations are likely to be rare and exceptional. This view, against the background of history and theoretical analysis, appears to be unrealistic. It is not a question of smooth and gentle oscillations with occasional crises. It is rather a question of continuous surprises—ups and downs that are quite irregular. This is the picture which the record of the American economy discloses. Indeed, the older terminology—"crisis" and "stagnation," "boom" and "slump," "upheaval" and "collapse"—would seem to be more accurately descriptive of the kind of world we have lived in throughout the last 100 years than such terms as "oscillations" or even "cycles." The "cycle" has been pretty much swamped by the titanic upheavals which have swept the economy, notably in the present century.

A Managed Compensatory Program

An adequate compensatory program—one which can quickly be put into motion, highly flexible and subject to quick adjustment

---

[1] *Taxes and the Budget,* Committee for Economic Development, Research and Policy Committee, New York, November, 1947, p. 25.

and change—is impossible without long-range plans and preparations involving improvement and development projects, housing, and public works (Federal, State, and local). In one important area, the Taft-Wagner-Ellender Urban Redevelopment and Housing bill illustrates the kind of planning needed.

There has been a disposition of late to minimize the anticyclical possibilities in a public investment program. There are indeed great difficulties which have often been slurred over. But the pendulum has swung too far. We need to reexamine the possibilities of flexible adjustment in a comprehensive and varied long-range public construction and development program. Unless this is done we shall, in fact, engage in wasteful expenditures, once a serious depression is upon us. For we shall discover that it is not possible to meet the onrush of a rapidly cumulating depression without a large expansion of public outlays. Such outlays can be wisely implemented not merely in public works, improvements, and development projects, but also in low-cost housing and, indeed, in other kinds of durable consumers' goods. The last item in particular has been explored at some length in the postwar programs of Great Britain, the British Empire countries, and the Scandinavian countries.[1]

A flexible, long-range expenditure program, however, is not enough. Urgently necessary, if we are going to implement a really effective anticyclical policy, is a flexible tax system. Nothing is more immediately important than a wider public understanding of this important issue. With a vast Federal budget in the neighborhood of 40 to 45 billion dollars, the anticyclical possibilities in a flexible tax system are enormous. The modern fast-moving economy, with its tendency toward violent fluctuations, cannot be managed effectively on the basis of an unchanging tax structure fixed for two or more years or worse yet over an entire cycle.

Just as Congress has (within limits established by law) empowered the executive to make adjustments in tariff rates, and just as Congress

[1] See Alvin H. Hansen, "Needed: A Cycle Policy," *Industrial and Labor Relations Review*, October, 1947; also Hansen, *Economic Policy and Full Employment*, 1947. For a different point of view see Milton Friedman, "A Monetary and Fiscal Framework for Economic Stability," *The American Economic Review*, June, 1948.

in the Federal Reserve Act allocated.to the monetary authority (within limits established by legislation) the power to raise and lower reserve ratios, so also it now becomes highly important, and indeed essential, to permit executive adjustment of the basic income-tax rate within limits imposed by Congress. Only in this manner is it possible to get quick timing and adequate flexibility in our tax structure. It is possible that certain guideposts could be laid down by Congress to strengthen the President's hands—such as a schedule of rates stepped up or down according to percentage changes in the volume of unemployment.[1] But it will not do to tie the executive down rigorously to mandatory rules. Judgment on a wide range of indicators is necessary, as in the case of monetary policy.

The President should periodically report to Congress—annually in his Economic Report, and probably quarterly—on action which he may or may not have taken, together with reasons for his action. In the final analysis the power would always reside in Congress not only to lay down the basic pattern within which the executive could operate, but also to intervene if it so chooses. Thus Congress would in no sense abdicate its power, but would only make possible an implementation of the tax system as an effective anticyclical device.[2]

Despite the general agreement about the dangers ahead, there is a disposition to take a chance, to hope for the best, to let well enough alone, and to improvise if and when necessary. The fact is that we

[1] Recent literature contains much discussion of "built-in-flexibility," "automatic stabilizers," and "automatic timing" devices. See, for example, the able discussion of these problems by Hagen, Hart, Galbraith, Higgins and others in the *Papers and Proceedings* of the *American Economic Review*, May, 1948, pp. 417–451; also Albert G. Hart, *Money, Debt and Economic Activity*, Prentice-Hall, 1948, pp. 475–514. Something useful along these lines can certainly be accomplished, and already the social-security program and the tax system operate in a measure as automatic stabilizers. But there is a danger of too great a reliance on automatic devices.

[2] "In keeping with our constitutional traditions, a procedure must be found which enables the Executive to make quick decisions under prior authority from Congress. There is not space here to enlarge upon what might be the legislative ingredients of such a program, but the items which I would most stress would be: provision for flexibility in tax rates at the discretion of the President but in conformity with a formula laid down by Congress, and an enlargement of the powers of the Federal Reserve authorities to regulate the volume of bank credit on an over-all basis." Jacob Viner, "Can We Check Inflation?" *The Yale Review*, copyright Yale University Press, Winter, 1948, p. 211.

have not been able to resolve the basic problem of the role of government in our modern world. Particularly we have not learned how to make government an effective, flexible, and responsive instrument in a fluctuating and highly complex society. This society embraces activities and institutions that are voluntary and noncoercive—a society functioning mainly through private enterprise, cooperative action, and numerous private institutional arrangements. Yet it is also a society in which the state should function not only as a balance wheel (offsetting fluctuations in the private sector), but also as the provider or important community services and for basic developmental projects which underlie and support private industry. Such a society needs a teering gear—a managed compensatory monetary and fiscal program

Chapter 14

Monetary Expansion and National Income

IN EARLIER CHAPTERS (especially in Chaps. 1, 3, 4, 6, 9, and 12), in this book we have explored in some detail, both historically and analytically, the relation of the quantity of money to the national money income. On the one side we have seen that, as national income has grown, the money has grown also, but at a more rapid pace. Thus the ratio of money to income has increased, though not at the same percentage rate in all periods.

Quantity Theory and Expansion

According to the so-called neutral money theory,[1] it is assumed in general that a constant money supply would result in a constant money income, with increasing productivity forcing a decline in prices. This accords with the quantity theory. Any change in the quantity of money will produce a corresponding change in money income, with consequent fluctuations in prices, except as corrected for changes in productivity.

According to the quantity theory, an increase in the quantity of money will tend to raise income proportionally, and there could be no increase in income without an increase in the quantity of money.

These two propositions are not the same. An increase in the national income may need to have associated with it an increase (more or less) in the money supply; yet an increase in the quantity of money may nevertheless have little effect in raising the money income. To repeat the homely analogy we have used before, an increasing waistline re-

---

[1] For a discussion of neutral money, see Alvin H. Hansen, *Full Recovery or Stagnation?* Chaps. III and V, and the literature there cited; also Hansen, *Economic Stabilization in an Unbalanced World*, Chaps. XVIII and XIX.

quires trousers with a larger girth, but the mere wearing of larger trousers will not increase one's weight.

We have seen, however, that an increase in the quantity of money *may* raise the national income in varying degrees according to a variety of circumstances (especially the interest-elasticities of the liquidity preference, the investment, and the consumption functions). Thus the national income is indeed a function of the money supply; but the relation is devious and complex, and varies according to changing circumstances and conditions. There is no simple, direct route between money and income.

The Need for Monetary Expansion

On the other side, any increase in the national income [1]—the consequence of an increase in total outlays—is likely to encounter restraining obstacles to further expansion unless the money supply is increased. Eventually a point is reached at which further income-generating expenditures will become wholly ineffective unless there is an increase in the quantity of money. These conditions we have examined above, particularly in Chap. 12.

Thus in general we may set down the proposition that the national income cannot be raised effectively and in the most advantageous manner without some increase in the money supply. Under certain conditions it may be advantageous and desirable to accompany an increase in the national income by a less than proportional increase in the quantity of money; under others, by a *more than proportional* increase.

Consider the period from 1933 to 1937, a period of rapid advance in output and employment. The national income increased from 39.6 billion dollars to 73.6 billion dollars, or 86 per cent; demand deposits (adjusted) increased from 14.4 billion dollars to 25.2 billion dollars, or 75 per cent; the money supply (demand deposits plus currency) increased from 19.2 billion dollars to 30.7 billion dollars, or 60 per cent.[2]

---

[1] We are here thinking mainly of an increase in employment and output, with some incidental increase in prices.

[2] The June figures, the mid-point of each year, are taken for the money supply.

If we include time deposits, the total money supply increased from 41.7 billion dollars to 57.3 billion, or 37 per cent.

These increases in money income are compounded of both price and output advances. Wholesale prices increased 31 per cent from 1933 to 1937. Agricultural production increased only 10 per cent from 1933 to 1937; industrial production increased 64 per cent.

Viewed realistically, a growth of money income in excess of the increase in output is necessary in view of the inelasticity of the supply schedule, especially in the case of agriculture—the industrial supply functions are in general highly elastic—and in view of the role of the price mechanism in directing unemployed factors into the productive process. Taking account of the supply and cost factors, an expansion of employment and output cannot easily (without serious frictions and almost insurmountable obstacles) develop in a market economy unless money income rises faster than real income—in short, without some rise in prices. On the other hand, if the money income advances too rapidly in relation to output, the effect is distortion and confusion. Varying according to circumstances, there is some optimum rate of increase in money income in relation to real income which would best promote employment and productivity.

Expansion is normally initiated through an increase in private investment or governmental outlays. These in turn induce, via the multiplier process, an increase in consumption expenditures. Now a sharp increase in private investment or governmental outlays is likely to require borrowing from the banking system. A net increase in inventory accumulation in particular is likely to be bank-financed. And a substantial increase in government outlays cannot at once be financed from taxes. Nor is it easy to *borrow* from the public while incomes are still at a low level; under these circumstances there are net advantages in borrowing from the banking system.

A *rapid* expansion of private investment (or government outlays) must normally be financed from new money or from idle balances. These new funds are thrown into the market to buy goods and services. Accordingly, income rises. But consumption for a time lags behind. However, the new higher income minus consumption (namely savings) equals the new flow of investment. $(Y - C) = S = I.$[1] But the net additional expenditures are likely to have come from new money or from the use of idle balances.

If the net additional outlays on investment are financed from idle balances, the rate of interest will rise more or less, according to the interest-elasticity of the liquidity preference function. Any increase in the rate of interest will have more or less a dampening effect on investment and consumption, according to the prevailing interest-elasticities of the I and C functions. Thus in general the *full* leverage effect of an increase in private investment or governmental loan expenditures cannot take place unless there is an increase in the money supply.

New Money and "Excess Savings"

It is highly important to emphasize again at this point that there is no contradiction between (1) the proposition that a given society has too high a propensity to save—savings in relation to income, at different income levels, being too high in view of the limited investment opportunities (marginal efficiency schedule), and (2) the proposition that an expansion of investment, to be fully effective, must be financed from new money.[2] This is sometimes erroneously regarded as a contradiction. In popular language, "Why," it is said, "must the increase in investment (public or private) be financed by new money, if there are excess savings? Why not use all these excess savings?"

But these questions reveal a serious misunderstanding of the savings-investment analysis. In a period of depression there are in fact no "excess savings." In a deep depression both investment and savings may indeed be zero. In the Robertsonian sense (period analysis), savings may indeed exceed investment, and so income is driven down still further; but the difference is a day-to-day difference and is never at any time large; and the excess of savings over investment may completely disappear at a stabilized low depression level. In the

[1] All these flows—Y, C, S, and I—apply to the same period of time (Keynesian terminology). In Robertsonian terminology, investment exceeds savings.

[2] Or equally well from the use of idle balances, provided the liquidity preference function is wholly elastic with respect to the rate of interest.

Keynesian terminology savings and investment are necessarily always equal, since they apply to the *same* period of time. Here the savings-investment problem arises only in the sense that, given the *savings function*, investment may be too low to provide full employment.[1]

In general, savings (in the Robertsonian sense) are low relative to income *while* income is rapidly rising; after income has reached a high and fairly stable level, savings (from yesterday's income) will rise to a normal ratio to income. Thus when income is rising rapidly a high proportion of private investment and government loan expenditures is likely to be financed by the creation of new money; after income has reached a high and stable level, investment and government loan expenditures will tend to be financed mainly by borrowing from the public and not by monetary expansion.

Historically this tendency is apparent in the record of typical periods of rapid advance. Thus from 1933 to 1937, while income was rapidly rising, the government deficit was heavily financed by borrowing from the banks. Commercial bank holdings of United States government securities from June, 1933 to June, 1936 increased from 7.5 to 15.3 billion dollars. This was the period of the most rapid rise of income. From June, 1936 to June, 1939—a period in which income rose relatively little—commercial bank holdings of United States government securities increased only from 15.3 billion dollars to 15.7 billion dollars. Bank financing—the creation of new money—ran high while income was rapidly rising. When income had substantially stabilized at the new high level, the government financed its deficit by borrowing from the public—a method of financing which does not involve any increase in the quantity of money. Similarly, during the war, in the earlier phase when income was rapidly rising, a larger proportion of government outlays were bank-financed. After income had risen and become somewhat stabilized, a larger proportion could be, and in fact was, financed by taxes and by borrowing from the public.

An increase in income means necessarily an increase in MV. Now an increase in V cannot be obtained except at the cost of a rise in the rate of interest, unless the liquidity preference is *wholly* interest-elastic. It follows, accordingly, as we have noted above, that the *most*

[1] See Appendix B, "A Note on Savings and Investment."

effective expansion of the national income can only be achieved when accompanied by an expansion of the money supply.

This in fact was what occurred in the period of rapid expansion and recovery of 1933–1937. Member-bank assets (loans, investments, and reserve balances) increased by 12.6 billion dollars from 1933 to 1937, while deposits (demand adjusted, plus time) increased by 12.8 billion dollars. Federal Reserve gold assets increased by 5.6 billion dollars, reflected in an increase in Reserve money (Federal Reserve notes and member-bank reserves) of 5.5 billion dollars. Thus as total outlays increased (initially through increases in private investment and government loan expenditures and then, via the multiplier process, through private consumption expenditures) the money supply increased also, though not in an exact proportion to increases in the national income.

The Cyclical Pattern

Consider also the cyclical pattern of monetary adjustment. The income velocity of money (demand deposits adjusted, plus currency in circulation) fell from 3.2 in 1919 to 2.5 in 1921, and rose again to 3.1 in 1923. These data disclose the pattern with which we were formerly familiar—namely, a cyclical fluctuation in velocity correlated more or less closely with the fluctuation in the physical volume of trade. In these earlier cycles, in the periods of deflation and decline in output, two developments typically occurred simultaneously: (1) a decline in the quantity of money (mainly demand deposits), and (2) a decline in velocity (an increase in idle balances). Similarly, on the upswing, characterized in part by rising prices and in part by increased output, there normally occurred (1) an increase in the money supply, and (2) an increase in velocity, or, in other words, a decline in the volume of inactive balances.

This familiar cyclical pattern was again evident in the decline of income velocity from 3.3 in 1929 to 2.1 in 1933. But it was scarcely visible in the upswing following 1933, when the income velocity of money rose only slightly from the depression low of 2.1 to 2.4 in 1937— far below the previous boom figures. There was a large increase in the supply of money, but only a slight rise in velocity. Why did the familiar cyclical pattern with respect to the income velocity of money not occur from 1933 to 1937?

The increase in the money supply from 19.2 billion dollars in June, 1933 to 30.7 billion dollars in June, 1937 sprang from two main sources: (1) the great inflow of gold (5.6 billion dollars of gold added to Federal Reserve assets) and (2) government borrowing from the commercial banks (7.1 billion dollars). Of these two sources of additional money, the gold inflow was the novel and unusual factor; the increased deposits springing from expansion of bank credit were a normal source of new money in a recovery period, though in this instance the increased bank credit was based on government borrowing instead of on commercial loans. Bank credit, thus made available to the government, was at once paid out by the government to private individuals and business firms for further spending after the initial use. Thus the effect, as far as cash holdings were concerned, was essentially the same as if the bank credit had been made available to private individuals and business in the first instance.

Had it not been for the large import of gold and the consequent unprecedented increase in member-bank reserves, the familiar pattern—increase in velocity along with expansion in business activity—might very probably have recurred from 1933 to 1937.

Liquidity Preference after 1930

What happened is in fact a vast laboratory demonstration of the high elasticity of the liquidity preference function at low rates of interest. The huge gold inflows placed extra cash in the hands of the banks. Naturally they wished to turn these unearning assets into earning assets. Loans not being available in any volume, the banks turned to investment in gilt-edged securities. This pushed the rate of interest down. But as the rate fell, the risk of loss of principal (in the event of even a slight fall in the bond market) deterred further purchases. Hence the continued piling up of excess reserves. No explanation of the phenomenon of excess reserves other than the liquidity preference analysis has been advanced which is at all plausible.

This analysis, moreover, offers a satisfactory explanation for the continued low income velocity of money. The high liquidity of the banks led to an expansion of bank assets (and so to an increase in the money supply) over and above the normal expansion of bank credit in a period of recovery. Thus the public became possessed of an excess of cash beyond the transactions requirements or the "income demand" for money. Accordingly, the public and the banks competed for securities. Thus the rate of interest was driven down until an equilibrium was reached that satisfied the market and at which the advantages of holding cash (complete liquidity together with no risk of loss of principal) were balanced with the advantages of holding earning assets (near-liquid, but not wholly so, and carrying the risk of a market decline). A margin was reached in the allocation of assets between cash and earning assets at which it was a matter of indifference whether to hold cash or to make a financial investment.[1]

Thus it is the shape of the liquidity preference function—its high elasticity at low rates of interest—which explains the low income velocity of money in the two periods of rapid expansion of output, 1933–1937 and 1940–1945. And it was the large gold inflows, together with the wartime purchases of government securities by the Federal Reserve Banks, which provided the commercial banks in the first instance, and so indirectly the public, with cash resources adequate to push the community far down the liquidity preference schedule into the area of low interest rates. The low income velocity *and* the low rate of interest are interrelated. They are both explained by the shape of the liquidity preference function and the vast quantity of money created by the gold inflows, the wartime expansion of Federal Reserve credit, and the deficit financing (both during the depression and the war) through the commercial banks.

The income velocity reached 1.7 in 1946—an all-time low. Interest rates similarly reached an all-time low for this century. Moody's Aaa bonds fell from 2.72 in 1944 and 2.62 in 1945 to 2.53 in 1946. Both the

---

[1] Put in another way, the lack of any earnings in cash amounts to a sort of insurance premium—the opportunity-cost "paid" for the advantages of holding cash. When the interest rate is high, the opportunity-cost of holding cash will be high, and one will feel less inclined to pay the price of holding cash. When, however, insurance premiums are cheap, one feels more inclined to take precautions against loss. Holding assets in the form of cash represents an insurance against loss of principal. At each interest rate, each individual will decide how much insurance, in the form of cash, he wishes to hold.

income velocity of money and the rate of interest turned upward slightly in 1947—velocity to 1.9 and Moody's Aaa to 2.77.

The Future Outlook for Interest Rates

What of the future? Are we on our way back to the 1929 interest rates and income velocity of money? [1]

This is scarcely probable but not impossible. But if indeed we should reach these levels, the circumstances bringing it about are likely to be very different from those prevailing in the late 1920's. An aggressive labor movement (demanding wage increases which outrun increases in productivity) combined with a full-employment program could give us a continuing (though perhaps moderate) efficiency-wage and price inflation. Under these circumstances a penalty would be placed upon the holding of inactive cash. This penalty would be the "invisible tax" that a rising price level would impose upon holders of idle balances. The expectation of continually rising prices promotes speculation in commodities, in real estate, and in common stocks. Rising prices eat away the purchasing power of cash holdings in relation to that of many other forms of wealth. There would thus be a tendency to move out of cash and bonds into equities.

In a period in which the secular rise of prices is upward, the "nominal" rate of interest (in money terms) will tend to rise, but the "purchasing-power" rate of interest (the "real" rate in Fisher's sense) may still be low.

But we might also have a situation in which the balance of forces—wage pressures, investment opportunities in relation to the savings function, governmental fiscal policies, etc.—yielded a substantially stable price level, or a moderately declining one. In these circumstances we should not likely return to the income velocity of money or the rate of interest of the 1920's. This at any rate is true unless we follow a restrictive monetary policy—one that would not permit an increase

[1] It may be argued with reason that any society which wishes to enjoy the advantages of a low rate of interest must expect individuals and business firms to hold a larger proportion of their assets in the form of cash. It follows from this that if we anticipate low rates of interest, we must also anticipate a low income velocity of money. There is no reason to suppose that the income velocity of the 1920's could be regarded as in any sense normal, irrespective of the rate of interest.

in the quantity of money more or less commensurate with the increase in the national real income which one may reasonably expect if our society continues to be dynamic and progressive.

Future Growth of the Money Supply

Our real national income in 1948 was roughly five times greater than in 1900. In other words, it has nearly doubled every 20 years. Let us suppose a doubling of real income in the next 25 to 30 years. What would this imply with respect to the appropriate quantity of money?

As we have seen, the total money supply (including time deposits) has increased *relative* to income, without abatement (but at varying rates) throughout the last 150 years. This secular trend cannot, however, be projected with confidence into the future. The more rapid growth of total deposits and currency relative to national income may possibly have come to an end. But we may nevertheless wish an increase in the money supply at least equal to the growth of income.

In the more restricted sense of demand deposits and currency, the quantity of money remained fairly constant (in the ratio of about one to three) relative to income, from 1892 to 1930. Thereafter the ratio rose until in 1948 the money supply, so defined, was a little over one-half the annual money income.

Without a growth in the money supply more or less commensurate with the growth in real income, income-generating investment and governmental outlays would sooner or later be restricted to less than their full leverage effect. Adequate liquidity is a necessary condition for the full play of the expansionist process. Monetary policy is needed to supplement, and to provide a favorable environment for, fiscal policy.[1]

---

[1] Adequate liquidity is a necessary *condition* for the best functioning of the mechanism which generates the flow of income. But monetary policy is not a good cyclical-compensatory device for regulating the *volume* of the income flow. So long as currency (and later demand deposits) constituted the only form of liquid wealth, and so long as money played a role *merely* for transactions purposes, monetary policy could be used (even though a somewhat clumsy device) for cycle control. But under modern conditions the vast volume of liquid wealth (near-money) makes monetary control ineffective unless indeed the screw is turned to a point which is not only painful but disastrous to the health and subsequent recovery of the economic organism. The Classicals were quite right when they looked upon "money" as a contrivance to facilitate the *effective functioning* of the productive process Other devices, notably fiscal policy, and in emergency conditions direct controls, are how ever the appropriate tools for *cyclical control*.

A doubling of real national income by 1975 would give us a national income at approximately current prices (allowing for some decline in the prices of those commodities which are quite out of line with the general price structure) of around 400 billion dollars. Assuming a roughly commensurate increase in the money supply or a constant *ratio* of money to income,[1] this would mean an increase in demand deposits and currency of about 100 billion dollars. Commercial-bank assets would have to grow by this amount in 25 years. It is not probable that this could happen without a substantial increase in the public debt.[2]

Bank assets consist of loans, United States government securities, and "other investments." In October, 1947 total loans (including commercial, agricultural, real-estate, consumer, and other loans) of all commercial banks were only 36.9 billion dollars, compared with 28.1 billion dollars in June, 1920 and 29.5 billion dollars in June, 1925. Investments in securities other than United States government securities stood at only 9 billion dollars in October, 1947, compared with 4.4 billion in June, 1920 and 7 billion in June, 1925. On the other hand, commercial bank investments in United States government securities stood at 70.5 billion dollars in October, 1947, compared with 3.7 billion in June, 1920 and 4.6 billion in June, 1925.

[1] A constant ratio of money to income would mean that the *increase* in this ratio (witnessed over the past 150 years) had come to an end. Having reached a high degree of liquidity, this is not unreasonable. On the other hand, there appears to be no good reason for supposing that the ratio of money to income should decline.

[2] I am indebted to Professor Jörgen Pedersen for some comments at this point which lead me to add the following note: If the public debt were small, competitive bidding for the limited volume of corporate bonds would tend to drive down the rate of interest. If the rate of interest on bonds were, in consequence, reduced relative to the dividend-yield on common stocks, concerns floating new securities would find bond issues a cheaper method of financing. Moreover, rental housing projects might be induced under these circumstances to raise funds through the sale of real-estate bonds. Thus the volume of outstanding securities available for bank purchase and "monetization" would be increased.

Accordingly even though there were only a small public debt, no insuperable banking difficulties would be encountered in controlling the rate of interest or the money supply. However, the total volume of liquid assets would, in these circumstances, be limited to the volume of private debt—whether monetized by the banking system or held as claims directly by the public. But the community, as it grows richer in real wealth, may wish to hold a much larger volume of liquid assets (debt claims) than that represented by private debt.

From 1920 to 1947 commercial bank holdings of United States government securities increased by 66.8 billion dollars; loans and other investments had increased by only 13.4 billion. During this interval it would plainly not have been possible to have matched the growth in real national income—output increased nearly 2½ fold in this period—with a corresponding increase in the money supply without a large increase in the public debt. The money supply cannot grow, under our prevailing monetary institutions, without a growth in bank assets. And if loans and other investments are not available in any considerable volume, this means that United States securities must be available for bank purchases.

During the next quarter-century the commercial banks could, of course, increase their assets considerably (and so increase the volume of deposits) by purchasing the 60 billion dollars of marketable public issues not already held by the commercial banks and the Federal Reserve Banks. But the life insurance companies, savings banks, and private trust funds (not to mention corporations and the public generally) would not likely be content to see all their investments in government securities absorbed by the commercial banks. Indeed, over the long run, they may wish to increase their holdings. If this is so, the commercial banks will need new government issues if the money supply is to be increased in large volume.

These matters are quite overlooked by people who talk glibly about a continued reduction in the public debt, taking no cognizance whatever of the implications of such a policy with respect to the money supply. An expanding economy needs an increasing money supply, and under current business financing practices, together with the prevailing monetary and banking institutions, this implies (as experience shows) an increase in the public debt.

It is, of course, true that we could radically change our monetary institutions. We could resort to the old-fashioned but now outmoded method of printing paper money. The modern and more rational procedure to achieve the same end is to resort to Central-Bank purchases of government securities. The Federal Reserve Banks could create Reserve money (Federal Reserve notes and member-bank balances) by increasing their holdings of Treasury bills (perhaps interest-free).

This procedure has some advantages, and also many disadvantages, compared with the orthodox procedures used during the war, in which both the Federal Reserve Banks and the commercial banks participated in the purchase of government securities.[1]

Since 1939 the real national income has increased by perhaps two-thirds.[2] This increase represents the potential which the economy could achieve under existing techniques, once full employment was reached. It is interesting to speculate how we could have managed the requisite *monetary* expansion commensurate with this increase in output, had there been no war. Political opinion prevailing in this country would scarcely have accepted, in peacetime, an expansion of the money supply via the necessary increase in the public debt, and certainly not the more novel proposals for increasing the money supply, involving direct issues of new money. It is very difficult to see how one could have gotten (short of a vast increase in the public debt or radical modifications of our monetary and banking institutions) an appropriate increase in the money supply.

As a nation our economic thinking was not then, and is not now, up to the needs and requirements of our productive potentialities. In the 1930's we were unwilling to adopt either the fiscal policies or the monetary policies needed to give us full employment. Social and economic institutions have a way of getting frozen and fixed—deeply embedded in prejudices which are well-nigh insurmountable. Time and again in human history, wars and revolutions have broken through the crust of outworn institutions. The accident of vast gold inflows and the exigency of wartime financing have provided us this time with a money supply commensurate with (indeed, for the present somewhat in excess of) our productive potential.

Human beings are, however, not easily satisfied. On balance, we are happy about our liquid assets, our deposits, and our savings. But we are unhappy about the condition which has made it possible—the vast increase in the public debt. And some among us would like to have our cake and eat it too. Many would like to wipe out the debt

[1] These matters I have discussed fully in Chaps. XVIII and XXII in my *Economic Policy and Full Employment,* to which the interested reader is referred.

[2] See *The Economic Report of the President,* January, 1948, p. 122.

over the next 25 years, without giving a thought to the effect of such action upon our money supply.

The current postwar inflationary pressures make it sound policy to reduce the public debt, and particularly to retire the bank holdings of government securities. But there is little evidence that any clear distinction is being made in public thinking between what is appropriate now and what may be appropriate monetary policy over the long run. There are many signs that we are again settling down into a frozen mold from which it may be difficult to escape. A dynamic and expanding economy will need a monetary policy flexible enough to give us a money supply commensurate with our growing productive potentialities.

An adequate money supply is a *necessary*, but not a *sufficient* condition, for economic expansion.

Chapter 15

International Monetary Developments

The Gold Standard Corrective Mechanism

Under the old international gold standard the balance of payments presented no great difficulties. About this there was no great mystery. When imports exceed exports, a quite simple remedy is at hand, if a country is prepared to use it. Let income and employment fall; the effect will necessarily be to reduce imports. How effective this remedy is, will of course depend upon the income-elasticity of imports, and this varies with different countries. In general, however, imports are relatively sensitive to changes in income.

A fall in income can scarcely fail to improve the balance of payments. Imports will be sharply curtailed; exports, on the other hand, may be stimulated by lower costs.[1]

Formerly all this was taken as a matter of course. Depression was in more ways than one a "corrective" mechanism by means of which unbalancing tendencies were checked and a new balance restored. If prices and wage rates in certain parts of the economy tended to get out of line during the boom, the ensuing depression could be counted on to restore the balance. If the money market got tight in the boom, the depression would relieve the tension and restore easy credit conditions. If speculators tended in a burst of excess optimism to undertake unwise ventures, the depression would surely call them ruthlessly to account for wasteful misuse of the productive resources. If a country was losing gold, a deflation of income and employment could quickly restore the balance.

[1] Indirectly, and after a time lag, exports may in some measure be unfavorably affected, since the decline in imports adversely affects the income of other trading nations, which in turn may therefore buy less from the country in question. The effect on exports (except for the stimulus from lower costs) is indirect and uncertain, while the effect of a fall in income on imports is direct and certain.

The International Cycle

In the nineteenth century England stood at the center of international trade. The gold standard was basically a British standard. In the boom phase of the cycle England's demand for imported foodstuffs and raw materials rose. This raised the prices (and quantities) of the exports of primary producing countries.[1] The ensuing rapid rise in prosperity opened rich prospects for profitable investment in the underdeveloped countries. Capital thus flowed from England abroad. The net effect of all these tendencies was, in the usual case, to increase the gold and foreign exchange holdings of the primary producing countries. As the boom advanced, England lost gold to the outside world, while internally an increasing volume of currency was being drawn into hand-to-hand circulation. The consequent credit restriction tended to dampen the boom in England, while the rising tide of international reserves flowing to the primary producing countries tended to carry them into a wave of inflation. Conversely, in the inevitable deflation which followed, the back flow of gold cushioned the depression in England and intensified the deflation in the primary producing countries.[2]

Germany and the United States, with growing industries but still largely agricultural, occupied in the last half of the nineteenth century an intermediate position. In the first half of the century the United States was preponderantly a primary producing country.

Income inflation and deflation in England (and in Germany and the United States as they became industrialized) took the form mainly of cycles of employment and unemployment. For the primary producing countries the income cycle took the form mainly of price inflation and deflation. But in the interwar period following the First World War serious unemployment and price deflation made all countries, whether advanced or undeveloped, increasingly rebellious against the income inflation-deflation balancing mechanism.

[1] For advanced industrial countries, fluctuations in investment are mainly responsible for fluctuations in income and employment; for primary producing countries, it is "net exports" which is the main dynamic factor whose oscillations cause expansion and contraction, typically with price inflationary and deflationary consequences.

[2] See Robert Triffin, *Post-war Economic Studies*, No. 7, Board of Governors, Federal Reserve System, 1947.

A Revolution in Monetary Thinking

Since the Great Depression of the 1930's a profound change has occurred both in monetary thinking and in monetary institutions. The disturbing forces springing from the First World War, the Great Depression, and finally the Second World War hastened a development which probably has deep roots in the inner nature of the modern industrial society—a development which would have come anyway, sooner or later, as industrialization spread over the globe from the more advanced to the primary producing countries. In the nineteenth century it was taken for granted that the economy would adjust itself (in terms of income, employment, output, and prices) to automatic forces—particularly gold flows—over which the community, as an organized entity, had little or no control.

Nevertheless, substitutes for gold, in greater or less degree, played a role all through the nineteenth century—silver, bank notes, government legal-tender notes, demand deposits. All these were ways and means of adapting money to the requirements of the economy. These substitutes for gold—"national" forms of money—represent the beginnings of a "managed currency."

Yet despite the growth of "substitutes," gold ruled the roost in two respects: first, the superstructure of money and credit was tied to gold; and second, net international balances were paid in gold. Thus the ebb and flow of gold in and out of the country affected the internal money supply, except in so far as ingenuity, within the limits of the gold standard, could devise compensatory offsets. These, indeed, were never wholly lacking. The nineteenth century could, however, be characterized more or less as one in which countries were prepared for the most part to surrender their national monetary sovereignty and to submit to the dictates of the automatic gold standard. Nations were accordingly not altogether masters of their own economic fates. They were ruled in no inconsiderable measure by movements of gold in response to fluctuations in the balance of payments.

After the First World War orthodox monetary thinking continued to control international conferences. Countries were urged to return to gold and find their "international level" via the gold standard adjustment process. But in the interwar decades a new standard for monetary policy increasingly won its way—emancipation from the adjustment process dictated by the gold standard; freedom to pursue a program of internal stability and full employment without regard to the balance of payments.

The Significance of Balance-of-payment Problems

Money, as we have noted in earlier chapters, cannot alone ensure an expansion of income. Yet a shortage of money may adversely affect investment and consumption. Moreover, a prosperous economy may be strangled by a sharp curtailment of the money supply. Accordingly, it was a matter of no little concern for a country to find itself closely geared, in its monetary system, to fluctuations in its balance of payments. Internal stability and full employment are not compatible with domestic monetary dependence upon uncontrolled gaps and surpluses in the international account.

Excessive inflows of gold and foreign exchange were particularly serious for primary producing countries. In such countries the quantity theory was (and in large measure still is) pretty much applicable without much modification. This is true (1) partly because the *slope* of the consumption function is steep; and moreover the *level* of the schedule of consumption is high relative to income (the margin of saving even at full-employment levels being very thin); (2) partly because the investment function, in undeveloped countries, tends to be highly elastic with respect to the rate of interest; (3) partly because the liquidity preference function tends to be interest-inelastic (increases in the money supply are regarded as net additions to spendible income and are quickly applied to purchases of goods and services); and (4) finally because of inelasticity of the supply of goods in primary producing countries.

Thus many Latin-American countries experienced, in consequence of the inflows of international monetary reserves in the boom 1920's, strong inflationary movements. When the turning point came in the cycle, their monetary reserves were quickly drained off, with deflationary consequences. It was with a view to checking these tendencies that Argentina, for example, eventually undertook a program of monetary "insulation." The inflow of foreign exchange in 1936–1937 was sterilized partly by open market operations by the Central Bank [1] and partly by the sale of Treasury bonds and certificates against purchases of foreign exchange by the Central Bank on government account.[2] The total accumulation of foreign exchange thus absorbed and sterilized on government account amounted to 1 billion pesos by June, 1937. When the turning point came in the cycle, in 1937, the sterilized Treasury holdings were released, thereby supplying needed funds for international payment without causing a drain on the domestic monetary reserves. At the same time the Central Bank offset the decline in commercial bank reserves, due to the outflow of gold, by open market purchases of government bonds.[3]

Advanced industrial countries (unlike the experience of less developed countries) may be quite capable of absorbing vast gold inflows without inflationary consequences. This was the experience of the United States in the 1930's. The explanation is to be sought basically in the high interest-elasticity of the liquidity preference function in rich countries, partly in the interest-inelasticity of the investment function that tends to prevail in advanced industrial countries, and partly in the high propensity to save. Under the conditions of the 1930's, at any rate, the vast gold inflows indeed brought low interest rates, but relatively little expansion of income and prices. Accordingly (except for a limited period in 1936–1937, later reversed), the United States did not find it necessary to sterilize the gold inflows. On balance, it appears quite clear that the country welcomed the increased liquidity of the commercial banks, together with the increased liquidity of the public that followed from the gold inflows.

There are three choices open to a country confronted with a state

---

[1] Thus as commercial bank reserves were increased by the inflow of gold and foreign balances to the Central Bank, these *increased* reserves were mopped up by the sale of Treasury bonds (held by the Central Bank) to the commercial banks. Thus bank reserves tended to remain constant, despite the gold inflow.

[2] The operation was equivalent to setting up an exchange equalization account in the Treasury whereby foreign exchange was absorbed and sterilized by the Treasury; thus the inflow of foreign exchange was kept out of the banking system. Similarly, the British Exchange Equalization Account sold Treasury bills to the banks, thereby acquiring deposit balances with which foreign exchange and gold could be purchased and kept out of the banking system.

[3] See League of Nations, *International Currency Experience*, p. 85.

of disequilibrium in its balance of payments. First, it may accept without resistance the effect of the flow (in or out) of gold and foreign exchange upon its domestic money supply. The deflationary effect of an outflow is likely to be more or less serious for any country, whether advanced or undeveloped; the inflationary effect will be most pronounced in a primary producing country. Second, it may take steps to neutralize the impact of gold and foreign exchange flows—sterilizing the inflow and releasing the accumulated hoards when an outflow movement begins. Third, steps may be taken to stop the flow, in or out, by various measures, including (1) refusal to receive or pay gold, with consequent appreciation or depreciation of the foreign exchange value of the currency (flexible exchanges), and (2) direct control of the balance of payments by means of exchange control, import quotas, or other quantitative restrictions.

In the 1930's the United States could have refused to take the gold inflow, but the effect would have been a sharp appreciation of the dollar. This would have had a seriously deflationary effect upon agricultural prices (which were already low, even in the late 1930's) relative to industrial prices.

This brief survey of alternative programs is sufficient to show how important the balance of payments is, even for so self-sufficient a country as the United States. The United States has, however, never been seriously confronted with the problem of inadequate international monetary reserves. Yet in 1934, had we adhered to the old gold price, a vigorous internal expansion might well have encountered serious monetary limitations. Indeed, it is difficult to see how an expansionist fiscal policy, requiring large funds from the capital market and even from banks, could successfully have been pursued under the restraints of a tight money market such as a loss of gold, actual or prospective, would have imposed. Sooner or later the increasingly threatening European situation might have driven gold here, even at the old gold price; but this would scarcely have been possible in 1934 or even in 1935. As events actually unfolded, it was a combination of the dollar devaluation, the profitable opportunities for investment in the American security and real-estate markets (once recovery was under way), and later the war scare that drew gold to the United States.

Living, as we have been in recent years, under conditions of high and indeed superabundant liquidity, we are likely to forget the profound monetary revolution which has occurred within the last two decades. And holding, as we do, two-thirds of the world's gold supply and being accustomed to a strong favorable balance in our international account, it is difficult for Americans to appreciate how important the balance of payments is for most of the nations of the world.

International Balance and Domestic Full Employment

Everywhere nations are at long last (after prolonged theoretical controversy and painful deflationary experiences in the interwar years) committed to the proposition that the balance of payments shall no longer control their internal monetary policy. Accordingly, we have witnessed a growing tendency toward national independence with respect to the control of the domestic money supply. Countries everywhere have developed ways and means of insulating their internal monetary systems from fluctuations in their international balances.

To this end various methods have been devised: (1) the development of central banks all over the world, (2) stabilization funds (England, the United States, France, and others) and similar devices to offset international monetary reserves, (3) exchange control, and (4) adjustment of exchange rates. In addition to these monetary devices there have been added direct controls of the trade balance—import quotas, export subsidies, etc.

The development of central banking placed a flexible control mechanism between the basic monetary reserves (fed or denuded by the ebb and flow of international balances) and the domestic money supply—deposits and currency. The Central Bank became the custodian of the basic monetary reserves (gold and foreign balances). As such, it stood between the basic reserves and the commercial banks. Thus the internal money supply could be regulated without regard to the fluctuations in the gold supply, according to the requirements of internal stability.

During the 1930's stabilization funds were set up as special accounts in various government treasuries. Through these accounts or funds foreign exchange could be bought or sold without affecting the domestic monetary reserves.

Exchange control permitted countries to undertake internal anti-deflation or income-expansion programs without losing their monetary reserves to the outside world.

And finally, exchange depreciation often enabled a country to reach a balance between its cost and price structure in relation to other countries without having to go through the painful process of deflation.

So long as countries were prepared to rely upon income-deflation as the main means of adjusting their international accounts, relatively small gold movements, supplemented by short-term lending, were adequate. Once countries became determined to stabilize their internal economies irrespective of their international position, large gold reserves for international settlement became necessary—unless, indeed, *direct* measures such as exchange control were adopted to control the balance of payments, or *indirect* measures such as exchange depreciation. Short of such measures the policy of internal stability, in the face of disequilibrium in international account, might involve a heavy loss of gold and foreign exchange balances; and such losses eventually would eat into the internal monetary reserves.

The Role of Gold

Thus it was that the trend toward "monetary nationalism" led straight toward an increased demand for gold for international payments. Whereas formerly relatively small gold reserves proved adequate, now that domestic policies looking toward internal stability might produce wide gaps in the balance of payments, a large volume of international monetary reserves became necessary.

The total amount of monetary gold and foreign exchange reserves was estimated for 1929 at 14.7 billion dollars, of which about 10.7 billion was gold. Of this 7.7 billion dollars were legally required "cover" for the domestic currency and credit structures, while 7 billion were "free" international monetary reserves.[1] Thereafter the gold supply rapidly increased, partly by reason of the upward valuation of gold in

[1] See *International Currency Experience*, League of Nations, 1944, p. 12; also *Banking and Monetary Statistics*, Board of Governors of the Federal Reserve System, 1943, p. 544.

the 1930's (in the United States, by about 70 per cent) and partly by reason of a large increase in gold output. By 1948 total monetary gold amounted to about 33 billion dollars, of which two-thirds was held in the United States. In the meantime many countries (notably England) have virtually dispensed altogether with gold as "cover" for the domestic currency.[1]

Countries are no longer willing to take the income-deflation route to equilibrium in their balance of payments. The result is that gaps in the balance of payments have become an increasingly serious problem. Accordingly, countries are more and more acutely "gold-conscious." They want gold for international payments. Managed currencies mean that gold is less needed for internal reserves, but all the more needed for international reserves.

The United States continues to adhere to the principle of gold cover for its internal monetary system. A gold reserve of 25 per cent is required against Federal Reserve notes and deposit liabilities. Thus of the 22 billion dollars of monetary gold in the United States in 1948, 11 billion was "cover" gold legally required as domestic reserves and 11 billion was "free" gold available for international payments.

Moreover, the United States stands ready to buy gold at $35 an ounce. So long as this is the case, and so long as the dollar remains the leading international currency, gold will continue to be in demand for international monetary reserves.

Since 1934 the United States has purchased over 14 billion dollars' worth of gold from abroad. Of this about 3 billion dollars has been added to our domestic monetary reserves and about 11 billion dollars, as we have noted above, is available for international payments. This

---

[1] In general the primary producing countries (Latin America, the Far East, Eastern Europe) require no gold "cover," but many do require a reserve of foreign exchange. Countries still requiring a gold reserve against Central Bank liabilities include France, Belgium, Holland, Switzerland, Denmark, Argentina, Union of South Africa, and a few others. Norway has a limited fiduciary issue, the remaining notes (nearly four-fifths of the total) being covered by gold. Sweden requires a small *absolute* gold reserve, currently equal to only 5 per cent of all notes outstanding. The United Kingdom has a fiduciary issue (now authorized up to 1.4 billion pounds sterling) which constitutes all but a negligible fraction of the notes in circulation. Increases in the fiduciary issue may be authorized by the Treasury at the request of the Bank of England. See *Federal Reserve Bulletin*, January, 1948, pp. 34–38.

gold represents, so to speak, a short-term international credit. It has placed that much dollar-purchasing power in the hands of foreigners, which will not be repaid until such time as we need to use our international reserves. That time does not appear imminent. Indeed, it seems highly probable that we shall continue to buy gold from abroad. These gold purchases can best be regarded as amounting to interest-free loans. And it may turn out that we shall never call for repayment.

International Lending

International lending institutions have been set up with a view to supplementing (and perhaps minimizing) gold movements. One of the functions of the International Monetary Fund is to provide short-term loans to countries experiencing temporary gaps in their balance of payments. These loans pay interest, and it may be some years before they are repaid. Long-term loans are provided by the International Bank for Reconstruction and Development and by the United States Export-Import Bank.

In the main it is dollars (even in the case of the international institutions) that are wanted. In addition, there are the large United States loan to Britain and smaller loans to other countries, and now the contemplated loans and grants to sixteen European countries under the European Recovery Plan. Add up these sums and they appear large. But they are small, indeed insignificant, compared with the vast war expenditures. The loans we have made and which are in contemplation are a small price to pay for a peaceful world.

The International Monetary Fund and the International Bank for Reconstruction and Development were established not merely to make loans, but also to promote international equilibrium with a view to minimizing the need for settling balances by means of gold and foreign exchange. To this end the International Monetary Fund is designed to study, promote, and institute a system of foreign exchange rates which will tend to provide equilibrium in international accounts. And the International Bank for Reconstruction and Development is expected to strengthen, by means of investment in developmental projects (industrial and agricultural), the structure of the various economies with a view to making them more productive and to help bring their exports and imports into balance.

When these institutions were organized, it was hoped that an international equilibrium could be established on a multilateral trade basis, with free convertibility of foreign exchange into the currency of any member country. This goal is still far away, and may not ever be wholly reached. We are likely to witness in the visible future a "mixed world" in which the international price system indeed plays a large role, but which is subject nevertheless to a considerable measure of continuing controls of different kinds. The control of capital movements is here to stay. Groups of countries, where intercountry trade is fairly balanced, may at first provide interconvertibility, without extending it to all countries. Wider convertibility of exchange may be facilitated if in times of temporary stress a country is permitted to institute a system of selective exchange control (perhaps better described as partial currency depreciation) as advocated by Dr. Robert Triffin [1] and already incorporated as established procedure in some Latin-American countries. This system provides that when there is a shortage of foreign exchange, importers of commodities which are not on the "preferred" or necessary list must purchase foreign exchange in an auction market. The auction rate will be a depreciated rate. All "necessary" imports and all exports will be traded in terms of the official exchange rate. As soon as the emergency is over and sufficient exchange again becomes available to meet all requirements, the auction rate would then tend to move toward the official rate and might eventually disappear altogether.

Monetary Management and International Disequilibrium

The battle for managed currencies is over; there will be no futile attempt this time to reconstruct the automatic gold standard. Nevertheless, independent monetary management [2] may be tempered in part by new "rules of the game" pragmatically worked out in the various international institutions such as the International Monetary

---

[1] *Op. cit.*

[2] The recent foreign exchange developments in France, carried through without the sanction of the International Monetary Fund, underline the point that independent monetary action is far from over. How France may finally work out her problem in relation to the Monetary Fund is not altogether clear. But this experience (and probably others to follow) may lead to modified procedures and methods of adjustment between countries and the Monetary Fund.

Fund. On the most essential point of all, no limitation is tolerated—no nation will be required to correct an international imbalance by means of deflation of income, employment, and prices, and no nation will be denied a readjustment of the foreign exchange value of its currency, even though the fundamental disequilibrium to be corrected has been caused by domestic policies. No country will be required to force its domestic price, wage, and income structure into line with the existing exchange rate. It is the purpose of the new international institutions to promote equilibrium without forcing any country to go through the painful process of deflation.

But independent monetary management, designed to support programs for economic stability and full employment, offers no assurance that equilibrium will be achieved in the balance of payments. Indeed, unless all countries "keep in step," independent action will greatly intensify the balance-of-payments problem.

This poses the central question for the future. Will it prove possible to maintain fairly stable conditions with high levels of employment in all countries (at least the important ones), or will fairly wide *fluctuations* recur in income and employment, together with divergent tendencies between countries with respect to prices and costs? If the latter should prove to be the course of events, it will not be possible to maintain interconvertibility of currencies on a free exchange basis.[1] Neither the augmentation of international monetary reserves which the Fund provides nor the Fund machinery for adjustment of exchange rates can effectively achieve that purpose, unless countries succeed reasonably well in "keeping in step" and in maintaining a high degree of internal stability at high levels of employment.

Divergent movements of cost and price levels between different countries may well produce *fundamental* disequilibrium in the balance of payments. This was the type of problem to which the Classical analysis relating to the gold-standard adjustment process addressed itself. For price level disparities the Classical remedy was income deflation until costs and prices had been brought into line with other countries. The modern remedy—for which provision is made in the

---

[1] This is true at any rate unless there are frequent adjustments of exchange rates; these, if too frequent and drastic, are likely to be disturbing to international equilibrium.

International Monetary Fund—is to adjust the exchange rate so as to bring international costs and prices into line. However, it is hoped that countries will for the most part "keep in step" so as to minimize the need for exchange-rate adjustment.

But there is also the problem of cyclical disequilibrium resulting not from cost- or price-level disparities, but from loss of export markets in a depression period. For this situation the Classical remedy (income deflation) would indeed serve to choke off imports and thus restore a balance in the international accounts, but it could help little to restore exports to a depressed market. Nor is exchange depreciation the appropriate remedy. The difficulty in this case is not an excessively high cost-price structure relative to other countries, but simply a loss of markets owing to depression abroad. The fundamental remedy is to reduce cyclical fluctuations to a minimum by compensatory fiscal (and monetary) policy, especially in the large industrial countries. To the extent that this fails, countries suffering from cyclical decline in export markets need large international reserves (including access to the International Monetary Fund) to tide them over. Should the drain on gold and foreign exchange balances prove to be too great, then either exchange control or Dr. Triffin's auction market (selective exchange control or partial depreciation) are to be preferred to outright exchange depreciation. A permanent revaluation of the currency is not the appropriate remedy, since the disequilibrium is not *fundamental* but is cyclical or temporary in character.

Apart from the divergent tendencies referred to above, the evolution of modern industrialism tends to create conditions unfavorable to international equilibrium. The increasing industrialization of more and more countries means that world trade runs relatively less in terms of raw materials and semifinished products, and more in terms of an exchange of finished goods. But the latter do not respond easily to slight price differentials. Finished goods are sold under trade-marks and brands, and each seller builds up a clientele of buyers that limits the effect of price competition. Very large price differentials (often quite impractical in terms of costs) may be necessary in order to invade a foreign market. Under these conditions the price elasticity of the demand for imports tends to be low, and this makes it difficult, and sometimes impossible,[1] to reach an equilibrium in the balance of payments via the process of price (or exchange) adjustment.

The current large-scale volume of bulk purchases by state trading monopolies is not likely to disappear in the visible future. It is estimated that more than 60 per cent of Britain's imports (1947) came under state-trading or government-sponsored bulk-purchase and sale arrangements.[2] These arrangements often cover precisely the commodities and raw materials that are most responsive to the equilibrating adjustment process. The remaining private trade consists heavily of goods, as indicated above, where trade volume is not easily adjusted to the requirements of balance on international account. Thus the range within which the mechanism for the restoration of equilibrium can operate is narrowed—on the one side, by the volume and character of government-controlled trade, and on the other, by the special conditions (monopolistic competition and oligopoly) of much of the remaining private trade. The effect is a strong tendency toward direct measures to control the trade balance—exchange control, import and licensing systems, bilateral arrangements,[3] and limited or regional payments agreements.

Dollar Scarcity and the Structure of Exchange Rates

The fundamental problem of dollar scarcity remains more or less an inscrutable enigma. It remains the major obstacle to the free convertibility of currencies and the general restoration of multilateral trade. It is partly a matter of technology—the immense superiority of American mass-production techniques in a wide range of products eagerly sought for in the modern world, including automobiles, electrical appliances, machinery, etc. It is in some measure related to the high American tariff. It is partly due to the strong preference (except for luxury and specialty products, the value of which can never loom

---

[1] If the sum of the elasticities of imports *and* exports is less than one, price reductions (and exchange depreciation) cannot achieve equilibrium.

[2] See Raymond F. Mikesell, "The Role of International Monetary Agreements in a World of Planned Economies," *Journal of Political Economy*, December, 1947.

[3] In 1947, it is estimated that 60 per cent of western European trade was covered by bilateral trade and payments agreements. See J. Polk and G. Patterson, "The Emerging Pattern of Bilateralism," *Quarterly Journal of Economics*, November, 1947.

large) of the mass of American consumers for American-made products, continually reinforced by advertising campaigns. Domestic goods produced under the conditions of monopolistic competition or oligopoly are not likely to be supplanted in volume by the inroads of foreign competition. It is partly a matter of wrong valuation of many foreign currencies. And finally, it cannot be denied that the trade policies of many nations contribute to the imbalance.

In the period of reconversion and reconstruction following the ravages of the Second World War, it was natural that countries would desire overvalued currencies. Most countries were confronted with inflationary pressures which an overvalued currency would tend to dampen. And in a world of pent-up, unsatisfied postwar demand, there was no difficulty in exporting as much as it was possible to produce. More and more as these accumulated demands are met, however, countries will find it increasingly difficult to export at the high prices which must be charged to cover costs if the currency is greatly overvalued.

Accordingly, as inflationary conditions are brought under control and (on the other side) as the export situation begins to tighten up, we may expect a movement on the part of several hard-pressed countries toward a revaluation of currencies. This will present a difficult problem for the International Monetary Fund.

The general goal toward which we should strive is the optimum international division of labor. This has of course never in fact been reached, not even in the nineteenth century; and we shall fall far short of attaining it in the visible future. But it must nonetheless remain the fundamental criterion for the determination of a system of exchange rates. Statistical studies will be helpful, but an experimental and flexible approach to the problem will be necessary. More than anything else, we cannot afford to freeze into a rigid mold the current grossly distorted structure of exchange rates.[1]

[1] This in no way implies a criticism of the action of the Fund in accepting as initial parities the prevailing rates. Under the disturbed postwar conditions, the rates adopted were perhaps as good as any. What is now needed is a flexible policy looking toward exchange-rate adjustment as soon as more normal peacetime conditions disclose serious cost and price differentials.

Appendix A

Hume and the Quantity Theory

DAVID HUME, in his *Political Discourses* (1752) skillfully exposed fallacies then current. By and large, his analysis was a good corrective, and, moreover, it fitted passably well the conditions of his time.

Put in technical terms, Hume denied that the demand function for money was interest-elastic. In his view the demand for money was elastic only with respect to the "price of labour and commodities."

He begins his discourse "Of Interest" by denying that the "lowness of interest" can be ascribed to "plenty of money." Money, however plentiful, will have no other effect than to "heighten the price of labour and commodities." He allowed that in the process of adjustment "the augmentation may have some influence [1] by exciting industry." But the rate of interest is not derived from the quantity of money.

High interest, he says, arises from three circumstances: (1) a high rate of profit, (2) a large volume of investment—a "large demand for borrowing," and (3) a low volume of saving—"little riches to supply the demand." Landlords are typically prodigal, and beggarly peasants have no means. Merchants alone—"the most useful races of men"—compose a great monied interest. Thus there arises a great number of lenders, which tends to reduce the rate of interest. But money in the hands of landlords and peasants "could never gather into sums, and would only serve to increase the prices of everything." Thus it depends

---

[1] In his essay "Of Money" he says it is of no consequence "whether money be in a greater or less quantity. The good policy of the magistrate consists only in keeping it, if possible, still increasing; because by that means he keeps alive a spirit of industry in the nation. . . . In my opinion, it is only in the interval or intermediate situation, between the acquisition of money and the rise in prices, that the increasing quantity of gold and silver is favourable to industry. . . . The farmer or gardener, finding that all their commodities are taken off, apply themselves with alacrity to the raising of more. . . . It is easy to trace the money in its progress through the whole commonwealth; where we shall find that it must first quicken the diligence of every individual, before it increase the price of labour.":

upon who it is that gets the "plentiful" money supply; if it gets into the hands of merchants, it will be gathered into large sums to be lent out and so will tend to reduce the rate of interest; if it gets into the hands of landlords and peasants, it will be spent and so raise prices.

The rate of interest, says Hume, depends upon (1) industry, and (2) frugality—or in other words, upon productivity and thrift. Commerce increases industry. "Commerce alone assembles it [money] into considerable sums." The increase of commerce "raises a great number of lenders." But the great increase in commerce also diminishes profit. This is due to the "rivalry among merchants, which diminishes the profits from trade." Low interest and low profit both arise from extensive commerce. Thus if we consider the whole connection of causes and effects, interest is the barometer of the economy, and its lowness is a "sign almost infallible of the flourishing condition of a people." Translated into modern terminology, he means to say that a high development of industry and commerce tends to promote the expansion of investment and capital formation to a point at which the marginal efficiency of capital is low.

Now the expansion of industry and commerce "will require a great quantity of these metals (money) to represent a great quantity of commodities and labour." Thus "low interest and plenty of money are in fact almost inseparable." Both are concomitant effects of a high state of industry and commerce.

"[A sudden] new acquisition of money will fall into a few hands, and be gathered into large sums, which seeks a secure revenue, either by the purchase of land or by interest. . . . The increase of lenders above borrowers sinks the interest. . . . But after this new mass of gold and silver has been digested, and has circulated, through the whole state, affairs will soon return to their former situation. . . . The whole money may still be in the state, and make itself felt by the increase of prices."

Thus in the end the increase in the money supply affects the price level, but not the rate of interest.[1]

---

[1] Changes in the quantity of money "are not immediately attended with proportionable alterations in the price of commodities. There is always an interval before matters can be adjusted to their new situation. . . ." But in the end he thinks that "prices of commodities are always proportional to the plenty of money. . . ."

The reduction of interest might indeed prove to be permanent, but not "from the increase of money, considered merely in itself." The natural effect of an increase in money "in that interval, before it raises the price of labour and provisions" is to increase industry.[1] And this increase in industry concentrates large sums in the hands of merchants and lowers the rate of interest; on the other hand, it pushes investment to a low profit rate. Thus in so far as the increase in the money supply in the *short run* stimulates industry, the effect is to promote fundamental *long-run* conditions favorable to a low rate of interest.

"Suppose four-fifths of all the money in Great Britain to be annihilated in one night. . . . Must not the price of all labour and commodities sink in proportion?" Or suppose the opposite—money "multiplied five-fold in a night. . . . Must not all labour and commodities rise to such an exorbitant height, that no neighboring nation could afford to buy from us; while their commodities . . . would be run in upon us, and our money would flow out." Thus the money supply of each nation will be "nearly proportional to the art and industry of each nation." The level of money is always in "proportional level to the commodities, labour, industry, and skill, which is in the several states."

Industry and commerce may indeed "be promoted by the right use of paper money. It is well known of what advantage it is to a merchant to be able to discount his bills. . . ." As "his bank credit is equivalent to ready money, a merchant does hereby in a manner coin the goods in his ware house . . . and can, upon occasion, employ them in all payments, as if they were the current money of the country." Thus Hume regards the monetization of private credit as advantageous to industry and commerce. Here we have an early statement of the banking principle.

Money and bank credit are useful institutions. But their importance is secondary.

"In short, a government has every reason to preserve with care its people and its manufactures. Its money, it may safely trust to

---

[1] This comes to much the same thing as the Wicksellian analysis: investment is stimulated when the market rate of interest falls below the productivity rate.

the course of human affairs, without fear or jealousy. Or if it ever give attention to this latter circumstance, it ought only to be so far as it affects the former."

Here are the root ideas that permeated monetary thinking in much of the nineteenth century. Thrift and productivity determine the rate of interest; the money supply determines the level of prices. The demand for money is interest-inelastic. Internationally, gold and silver are distributed in proportion to the level of industry and commerce in each country and thereby the price levels of different countries are kept in line.

Appendix B

A Note on Savings and Investment

IN HIS RECENT book *The Keynesian Revolution*,[1] a significant contribution to current literature, Lawrence Klein says that there are
"two Keyneses in the matter of the savings-investment equation."
This statement has frequently been made before, and although much
has been written about it, perhaps something useful can still be added.

In Klein's exposition savings and investment as *observables* are
always equal, being the point of intersection of the *schedules* of savings
and investment. There is, of course, as Klein points out, no inconsist-
ency between (1) the definition which makes *actual* or *observable* savings
and investment always equal, and (2) the concept of savings and investment as intersecting schedules. Nevertheless, the question remains
whether these schedules are to be regarded as (1) *very* short-run
schedules which might at times shift about violently and capriciously
in response to temporary conditions, or (2) longer run schedules determined by fairly stable factors involving the behavior pattern of a
community with respect to the ratio of savings to income at different
income levels.

A related, but distinct, terminological matter should be mentioned.
While the Keynesian theory of income determination can indeed be
formulated in terms of savings and investment schedules, I am increasingly convinced that the presentation as given in the *General
Theory* is more useful. In the *General Theory* Keynes in fact did not
explicitly work with savings and investment schedules,[2] even though
it is perfectly true that his analysis can be put in these terms. The
General Theory, however, makes (1) *actual* investment, and (2) the

[1] L. R. Klein, *The Keynesian Revolution*, The Macmillan Company, New York, 1947, p. 91.
[2] The marginal efficiency schedule is of course an investment schedule, but it relates investment to the rate of interest. In the schedules referred to above, savings and investment
are related to income.

consumption function, the determinants of income. "The propensity to consume and the rate of new investment determine between them the volume of employment. . . ." [1]

The savings schedule formulation (while entirely correct) is, it seems to me, a back-door approach; the consumption function formulation gets at the problem directly through the front door. This is true because income is generated by *outlays* on investment and consumption. [2] It is the volume of *expenditures* that determines income and employment. All we need to know is the actual rate of investment and the consumption function. The savings schedule can, it is true, easily be derived from the consumption function, but in fact we do not need it.

The choice between the use of the consumption, rather than the savings, function has, however, nothing to do with the problem of actual (observable) quantities versus schedules. $Y = C + I$ is merely a definitional equation; but $Y = C(Y) + \bar{I}$ is a determinate equation which includes the consumption function. Thus the concept of a schedule is as essential for the "front-door" formulation as for the "back-door" formulation, and the problem of observables versus schedules is still present.

But now there remains the confusion to which Keynes himself refers on page 122, and which Klein does not consider. If *actual* investment and savings are always equal, what does Keynes mean when he says: [3] "Thus their effort to consume a part of their increased incomes will stimulate output until the new level (and distribution) of incomes provide a margin of saving sufficient to correspond to the increased investment." Savings and investment are not here conceived of in terms of schedules; they are actual savings and investment. But if actual saving is always equal to investment, then why must income rise to a certain level before actual savings will equal actual investment? Are there not here, at any rate, two Keyneses?

Evidently there are two concepts with respect to the relation of actual savings to investment: (1) that they are always identically equal, and (2) that actual savings equal investment when the "multi-

[1] *General Theory*, p. 30.

[2] For simplicity, government tax-financed outlays are here included in C, loan-financed outlays in I.

[3] *General Theory*, p. 117.

plier" process has raised income to a level sufficient to induce that much saving. These two concepts are, however, not contradictory or inconsistent. What is true is that *actual* savings may or may not be at a point corresponding to the *normal* relation of savings to income.

Precisely the same kind of problem arises in the familiar demand and supply analysis. Assume an upward movement of the demand schedule. Momentarily price will rise sharply, and only gradually will it settle at the point of intersection of the short-run "normal" supply and demand schedules. Suppliers cannot at once adjust themselves to the new demand situation; the supply schedule becomes momentarily inelastic with respect to price. Gradually, as suppliers adjust themselves, the supply schedule becomes more and more elastic until, after the time lag has been worked through, it reaches a "normal" elasticity.

So also with the process of income determination. If actual investment rises, savings will always rise by an equal amount. But the ratio of savings to income may not be "normal." Assume a given increment of investment. Consumers may not instantly respond to the rise in income; there is then a time lag. The consumption function becomes momentarily inelastic with respect to income. As income rises, consumption lags. The marginal propensity to consume is far below normal; indeed, it may in the first interval be zero. Thus at first $\Delta I = \Delta S = \Delta Y$, and $\Delta C = 0$. But before long consumers adjust themselves to the new, higher income; the marginal propensity to consume rises until, after a time lag, it becomes "normal." In the interval between zero elasticity and "normal" elasticity, consumption keeps rising. At any point in this interval $\Delta I = \Delta S = (\Delta Y - \Delta C)$, with ΔC continuously rising. At first (at zero marginal propensity to consume) $\Delta S = \Delta Y$; gradually $\dfrac{\Delta S}{\Delta Y}$ will approach a ratio corresponding to the "normal" marginal propensity to save.

Not until the expansion process has raised income to a level corresponding to the "full" or "normal" multiplier [1] will it be possible for

---

[1] "The multiplier tells us by how much their employment has to be increased to yield an increase in real income sufficient to induce them to do the necessary extra saving, and is a function of their psychological propensities." *General Theory*, p. 117.

consumers to achieve an increase in consumption corresponding to their normal propensity to consume and at the same time to save an amount equal to the given increment of investment.

But all this does not mean that income has to rise by the "full" or "normal" multiplier before actual savings equal investment. Actual savings always equal investment, whatever the momentary marginal propensity to consume and whatever the income level. But actual savings will not hold a *normal* relation to income until income has risen by an amount which permits a normal propensity to consume.[1]

Starting with the initial impulse given by an increment of investment, it is the striving of consumers to satisfy their normal propensity to consume which raises income to the point at which it is possible not only to satisfy this desire, but also to save an amount equal to investment. At any other income level actual savings indeed equal investment, but the normal propensity to consume is not satisfied. Only at the "normal multiplier" income level will actual savings correspond to the normal marginal propensity to save and to consume.

Keynes puts in as follows:

> "In general, however, we have to take account of the case where the initiative comes from an increase in the output of the capital goods industries which was not fully foreseen. It is obvious that an initiative of this description only produces its full effect on employment over a period of time. I have found, however, in discussion that this obvious fact often gives rise to some confusion between the logical theory of the multiplier, which holds good continuously, without time-lag, at all moments of time, and the consequences of an expansion in the capital goods industries which take gradual effect, subject to time-lag and only after an interval." [2]

---

[1] So long as the momentary marginal propensity to consume is below normal, very little of the actual new savings are savings in the Robertsonian sense. In other words, nearly all of the new investment will be financed not from savings in the common-sense meaning, but from new money (or perhaps from money formerly held idle). But in the Keynesian terminology, this new money was paid out to create income in the current period and was saved out of current income. Thus $S = Y - C$, all terms applying to the same period.

[2] *Ibid.*, pp. 122–123.

The relationship between "these two things," he continues can be cleared up by pointing out that an imperfectly foreseen expansion in the capital goods industries "may cause a temporary departure of the marginal propensity to consume away from its normal value, followed, however, by a gradual return to it." [1]

Moreover,

> "there is no reason to suppose that more than a brief interval of time need elapse before employment in the consumption industries is advancing *pari passu* with employment in the capital goods industries, with the multiplier operating near its normal figure." [2]

When Keynes says that "income must necessarily change in just that degree which is necessary to make a change in saving equal to the change of investment," [3] he means that the *normal* relation of saving (and consumption) to income has been realized. Not until this *normal* relation has been established can you say that saving is, in a meaningful sense, in equilibrium with investment.

This, however, does not mean that the marginal propensity to consume will necessarily behave in a capricious manner during the interval of the time lag while it is approaching normal. Thus even during the period of the time lag the multiplier equation $\Delta Y = \left(\dfrac{1}{1 - \dfrac{\Delta C}{\Delta Y}} \right) \Delta I$

may not be a mere tautology, since we may be able to formulate definite empirical hypotheses concerning the time behavior of $\dfrac{\Delta C}{\Delta Y}$. If, indeed, it were true that whenever the system is out of equilibrium the consumption function shifted about in a wholly capricious manner, then in such periods the multiplier equation would in fact be tautological. But it is reasonable to suppose that this is not the case. If investment

[1] *Ibid.*, p. 123.

[2] *Ibid.*, pp. 124–125. See in this connection Lloyd Metzler's chapter in *Essays in Honor of Alvin H. Hansen* (W. W. Norton & Company, 1948) where he argues that the lag in consumption is negligible.

[3] *Ibid.*, p. 184.

suddenly expands, consumption will for a time lag behind, but not capriciously or in an unpredictable manner. The tendency that is expressed in the normal consumption function will progressively assert itself more and more until the normal relationship between consumption and income is approached. Any departure from equilibrium sets forces in motion which tend toward the equilibrium relation.

When the marginal propensity to consume is "normal," $I = S$ in an equilibrium sense. But this does not mean, as is sometimes inferred, that in such a situation income necessarily has no tendency to change over time. It may be a moving equilibrium in which investment and income are ever rising, but in which consumption is continuously in a normal relation to income. This assumes that the community has adjusted its expectation to a continuous expansion process, so that the marginal propensity to consume is continuously normal. It is reasonable to suppose, as Keynes does, that the marginal propensity to consume would have its normal value not only when "the community has settled down to a new steady level of aggregate investment," but also when a continuous process of "expansion had been foreseen." [1]

A final word about the Swedish *ex ante* and *ex post* concepts. It is doubtful that planned savings and investment can best be interpreted [2] as virtual points in the schedule sense; rather, the words usually suggest absolute, and specific, planned magnitudes. If planned investment is 10 billion dollars and planned savings 8 billion,[3] the excess of planned investment over planned savings may be financed in various ways, such as (1) by new money, or (2) by unplanned disinvestment, such as the unexpected sale of inventory stocks. In the first case realized investment will equal planned investment, but realized savings will exceed planned savings by the amount of the new money. In the second case, realized savings will equal planned savings but realized investment will be less than planned investment by the amount of the disinvestment of inventories.

[1] *Ibid.*, p. 123.

[2] See Klein, *op. cit.*, p. 116.

[3] It must be assumed that these plans are actually carried out. Plans that are not carried out can have no significance.

Some authors have used the terms "intended saving" and "intended investment." Assume zero net investment and zero net saving in Period 0. Assume now an increase in investment to 5 billion dollars in Period 1, no part of which is unintended inventory accumulation. The actual investment is thus identical to "intended investment." Let us assume no increase in Robertsonian savings in Period 1, the whole increment of investment being financed from monetary expansion. The *actual* increment of saving (5 billion dollars) is equal to the increment of income, since $S = Y - C$, and consumption has not increased. But this does not represent a *normal* ratio of savings to income, since the *entire* increment of income is saved. Income must rise through an expansion of consumption before the 5 billion dollars of actual savings corresponds to the normal propensity to save.

In Period 1, what is the volume of "intended saving"? Is it zero, in which case "intended saving" is identical to Robertsonian saving, or is it the saving which the society would wish to make if income remained for long at just 5 billion dollars above the initial base period? If the latter concept is accepted, "intended saving," for any given income, can always be read off from the normal savings schedule, and "intended savings" becomes another term for *normal* savings, in the sense in which I have used that term here. Adopting this terminology, "intended saving" would be less than the actual investment in Period 1 in the above illustration, and income would tend to rise until the two were brought into equilibrium. The *actual* saving would stand in a *normal* relation to income only when actual saving equals *intended* or *desired* saving.

Bibliography

ARNDT, H. W.: *The Economic Lessons of the Nineteen Thirties*, Oxford University Press, New York, 1944.

BALOGH, T.: *Studies in Financial Organization.* Cambridge University Press, London, 1947.

Board of Governors of the Federal Reserve System: *Banking and Monetary Statistics*, Washington, 1943.

———: *Banking Studies.* Waverly Printers, Baltimore, 1941.

———: *The Federal Reserve System: Its Purposes and Functions*, Washington, 1947.

———: *Postwar Economic Studies*, 8 vols., Washington, 1945–1947.

CASSEL, GUSTAV: *The Theory of Social Economy*, Harcourt, Brace & Company, Inc., New York, 1924.

CHANDLER, LESTER V.: *The Economics of Money and Banking*, Harper & Brothers, New York and London, 1948.

CLAPHAM, SIR JOHN: *The Bank of England*, 2 vols., Cambridge University Press, London, 1945.

Committee for Economic Development: *Taxes and the Budget*, November, 1947.

COULBORN, W. A. L.: *An Introduction to Money*, Longmans, Green & Company, Inc., New York, 1938.

CURRIE, LAUCHLIN B.: *The Supply and Control of Money in the United States*, 2d ed., Harvard University Press, Cambridge, Mass., 1935.

DE CHAZEAU, HART, and others: *Jobs and Markets*, Committee for Economic Development, McGraw-Hill Book Company, Inc., New York, 1946.

Economic Essays in Honour of Gustav Cassel. George, Allen & Unwin, Ltd., London, 1933.

FELLNER, WILLIAM: *Monetary Policies and Full Employment*, University of California Press, Berkeley, 1946.

FISHER, IRVING: *100 Per Cent Money*, Adelphi Company, New York, 1935 (3d ed., City Printing Company, New Haven, 1945).

———: *The Purchasing Power of Money*, The Macmillan Company, New York, 1922.

HABERLER, GOTTFRIED: *Prosperity and Depression*, 3d ed., League of Nations, Geneva, 1941.

HANSEN, ALVIN H.: *America's Role in the World Economy*, W. W. Norton & Company, New York, 1945.

———: *Business-Cycle Theory*, Ginn & Company, Boston, 1927.

———: *Economic Policy and Full Employment*, McGraw-Hill Book Company, Inc., New York, 1947.

———: *Fiscal Policy and Business Cycles*, W. W. Norton & Company, New York, 1941.

———: *Full Recovery or Stagnation?*, McGraw-Hill Book Company, Inc., New York, 1938.

HARRIS, SEYMOUR E.: *Inflation and the American Economy*, McGraw-Hill Book Company, Inc., New York, 1945.

———: *The New Economics*, Alfred A. Knopf, Inc., New York, 1947.

HART, ALBERT G.: *Money, Debt and Economic Activity*, Prentice-Hall, Inc., New York, 1948.

HAWTREY, R. G.: *The Art of Central Banking*, Longmans, Green & Company, Inc., New York, 1933.

———: *A Century of Bank Rate*, Longmans, Green & Company, Inc., New York, 1938.

———: *The Gold Standard in Theory and Practice*, 5th ed., Longmans, Green & Company, Inc., New York, 1947.

HAYEK, F. A.: *Prices and Production*, George Routledge & Sons, Ltd., and Kegan Paul, Trench, Trubner & Co., Ltd., London, 1935.

HOMAN, P. T., and F. MACHLUP (eds.): *Financing American Prosperity*, The Twentieth Century Fund, Inc., New York, 1945.

HUME, DAVID: *Political Discourses*, R. Fleming for A. Kincaid and A. Donaldson, Edinburgh, 1752.

KEYNES, JOHN MAYNARD: *The General Theory of Employment, Interest and Money*, Harcourt, Brace & Company, New York, 1936.

———: *A Treatise on Money*, 2 vols., Harcourt, Brace & Company, Inc., New York, 1930.

KLEIN, LAWRENCE: *The Keynesian Revolution*, The Macmillan Company, New York, 1947.

League of Nations Secretariat: *International Currency Experience*, Geneva, 1944.

LESTER, R. A.: *Monetary Experiments*, Princeton University Press, Princeton, N. J., 1939.

LINDAHL, ERIK: *Studies in the Theory of Money and Capital*, George Allen & Unwin, Ltd., London, 1939.

Macmillan Report: *Royal Commission on Finance and Industry*. Cmd., 3897, 1931.

MARGET, ARTHUR W.: *The Theory of Prices*, 2 vols., Prentice-Hall, Inc., New York, 1938–1942.

MARSHALL, ALFRED: *Money, Credit and Commerce*, Macmillan & Co., Ltd., London, 1923.

MILLS, FREDERICK C.: *Price-Quantity Interactions in Business Cycles*, National Bureau of Economic Research, New York, 1946.

MINTS, L. W.: *A History of Banking Theory in Great Britain and the United States*, University of Chicago Press, Chicago, 1945.

MORGAN, E. V.: *The Theory and Practice of Central Banking*, The Macmillan Company, New York, 1943.

MYRDAL, GUNNAR: *Monetary Equilibrium*, W. Hodge and Co., Ltd., London, 1939.

PIGOU, A. C.: *Lapses from Full Employment*, Macmillan & Co., Ltd., London, 1945.

POLANYI, M.: *Full Employment and Free Trade*, Cambridge University Press, London, 1945.

ROBERTSON, D. H.: *Essays in Monetary Theory*, P. S. King & Staples, Ltd., London, 1940.

———: *Money*, rev. ed., Harcourt, Brace & Company, Inc., New York, 1929.

SCHUMPETER, JOSEPH A.: *Business Cycles*, McGraw-Hill Book Company, Inc., New York, 1939.

SIMONS, HENRY C.: *Economic Policy for a Free Society*, University of Chicago Press, Chicago, 1947.

THOMAS, BRINLEY: *Monetary Policies and Crises*, George Routledge & Sons, Ltd., and Kegan Paul, Trench, Trubner & Co., Ltd., London, 1937.

TOOKE, THOMAS: *An Inquiry into the Currency Principle*, London, 1844.

────── and NEWMARCH: *A History of Prices*, 6 vols., Adelphi Company, New York.

VINER, JACOB: *Studies in the Theory of International Trade*, Harper & Brothers, New York, 1937.

WERNETTE, J. PHILLIP: *Financing Full Employment*, Harvard University Press, Cambridge, Mass., 1945.

WHITE, HORACE: *Money and Banking*, 6th ed., Ginn & Company, Boston, 1936.

WHITTLESEY, CHARLES R., *Principles and Practices of Money and Banking*, The Macmillan Company, New York, 1948.

WICKSELL, KNUT: *Interest and Prices*, The Macmillan Company, New York, 1936.

──────: *Lectures on Political Economy*, vol. II, "Money," The Macmillan Company, New York, 1935.

WILLIAMS, JOHN H.: *Postwar Monetary Plans*, 3d ed., Alfred A. Knopf, Inc., New York, 1947.

WOOD, ELMER: *English Theories of Central Banking Control, 1819–1858*, Harvard University Press, Cambridge, Mass., 1939.

Index

231

Date Due

HG221 .H27

Hansen, A.H.

Monetary theory and fiscal
policy.

DATE	ISSUED TO
	003279

003279

HG
221
H27

Hansen, Alvin Harvey
    Monetary theory and
fiscal policy

Trent
University

CPSIA information can be obtained
at www.ICGtesting.com
Printed in the USA
BVHW011934060122
625621BV00002B/65

9 781014 385093